THE BALANCING ACT
Settlement vs. Trial

THE BALANCING ACT
Settlement vs. Trial

Steve G. Heikens,
Attorney at Law

Beaver's Pond Press

Minneapolis, Minnesota

ISBN 1-890676-54-3

Library of Congress Catalog Number: 00-100150

Cover Art by Lee Heikens

Printed in the United States of America.

04 03 02 01 00   6 5 4 3 2 1

DEDICATION

This work is dedicated to my mentors, who stood me on their shoulders and let me see a little further:

The late Johnny Powell who demonstrated that thoughtful questions are more powerful than advice and that emotions have their own logic.

The late Loren "Doc" Kline, a Renaissance man, who taught that all social change must be rooted in history and that like-minded individuals will find one another, refine a community of thought and propel change in the larger society.

and

John Preston Ward who repeatedly proved that law is a powerful tool for social change, especially in desegregating relationships between people.

TABLE OF CONTENTS

Life is a series of disconnected happenings;
It does not become experience until you
reflect on it.

Saul Alinsky, *Rules for Radicals*

ACKNOWLEDGEMENTS

Foremost, I want to acknowledge the contribution of Lee Heikens, my spouse. Her artistry provided the book's cover, but her life demonstrates the balance of feelings and genius, the pivotal detail with the big picture and individualism with pragmatic feminism. She was patient during periods of isolation and used wit, humor and love to take the edges off of my abstracting.

I am grateful to RosAnn Bane, my copy editor who enhanced clarity by reordering my short sentences and compressing my longer ones. She simplified cumbersome thoughts and uncluttered my word combinations.

I am intellectually indebted to Neil Mullin for his insightful criticisms of the whole. He identified ideas that were undernourished, overworked or missing. As one of America's premier trial lawyers, his contemplation of my compromise perspectives was lively and priceless.

Proofreaders Michelle Heikens and Mary Coons reduced the number of errors and inconsistencies that would have embarrassed me. Their persistence amidst my preoccupation with content is greatly appreciated. I want to thank Fran Jackson, publisher of the Phoenix, for typing the first draft, filled with unreadable scribbles and organizational disarray. I wish to thank Jim Pawell, President of James Publishing, for coaxing me into writing a book on settlement strategies. We disagreed about the need for multiple annual supplements of this work but I found Milt Adams, owner of Beaver's Pond Press. Milt has provided the inspiration to keep going, extraordinary resources to make it happen and gentle pressure to bring closure to a work that can never be completed. Mori Studio has brought coherence and aesthetics to the design and typesetting of this book and I am grateful.

One organization, or rather its people, has made an enormous contribution. The National Employment Lawyers Association (NELA, previously known as PELA) consists of attorneys who are humans first and lawyers second. Since 1985, NELA's co-founders, Paul Tobias and Naida Axford, have validated my efforts to improve settlement strategies.

Joe Golden, Cliff Palefsky, Nancy Ericka Smith and Michael Leech have been constant sources of delight and ideas, but more importantly they are living reminders that practicing law can be fun and profitable. The contributions of other NELA members are too vast and numerous to identify. Their war stories in the Employee Advocate, at national conventions and informal gatherings provide a backdrop that can never fully be recognized.

My clients provided the raw facts and needs, from which I have tried to abstract, shape and refine for use by others. I hope that future clients of my readers will benefit and appreciate those who went before them. I thank my opponents who have endured my experiments and compensated my clients. I especially thank the new lawyers and clients who were not afraid to ask the "dumb questions."

Finally, to m.d., for inspiring my effort to bring a temporary order to settlement strategies and to this lovely chaos we call life.

Steve Heikens

Introduction

Warriors, peacemakers, crusaders and pragmatists are a few of the roles we play as employment lawyers. We want to believe that law is a search for truth, but we know the metaphor of a sporting contest is more accurate. Trial can be an exciting place for warriors and crusaders: the higher the stakes, the greater the risk. Some trials are highly profitable, but all lawsuits are costly. They impose a high cost on clients, both financially and emotionally. When lawyers factor in the risk of losing a huge investment of hours, we should recognize the need to explore profitable alternatives in playing the role of peacemaker and pragmatist.

Pre-suit settlement is one pragmatic alternative that is often underestimated. Too often we take it for granted that employers are not open to early settlement. Settlement overtures are not made or made haphazardly. Old habits dominate, even if they have seldom succeeded in the past. Too often the approaches are counterproductive and actually prevent pre-suit compromises.

According to one national survey, only seven percent of employment disputes settle before the lawsuit begins. Surprised by this report, I kept a record of my own pre-suit settlement efforts. The results confirmed what I suspected: strategic planning facilitates pre-suit settlement. Since 1986, over 49 percent of my pre-suit efforts resulted in early settlements without litigation. Even when my efforts did not result in pre-suit settlement, they offered opportunities for in-depth learning about the particular conflict or provided insights that enhanced efforts in later cases.

To determine whether this approach can be applied by other lawyers, these techniques have been tested by lawyers, whom I've mentored during the past four years. Their experience confirms that the principles, strategies and tactics you'll find in this book generate success and profit. This book emphasizes practical solutions. This is not a theoretical text, nor is it bound by political correctness. In the old fashioned sense of pragmatism, the focus is on what works. The principles and strategies you'll find here have all been tested and applied in the heat of battle. None of them are hypothetical.

This book addresses two audiences: 1) the new lawyer who feels passionately about justice and needs pragmatic solutions to survive, and 2) the seasoned veteran who recognizes the pragmatism of early settlement and is looking for impassioned alternatives that will move his or her practice from merely surviving to thriving. To meet the needs of these two audiences, this book provides a philosophical perspective designed to reverse the inertia of habit, demonstrate the power of uncertainty, and celebrate the individuality of every lawyer. I am confident that each of you will find a way to apply this perspective in a way that reflects your personality. This philosophical perspective focuses on strategies that are rooted in fundamental principles. Like playing the piano, you can make sounds without knowing the fundamentals, but you'll never make music.

All chess players know the basic rules, but few master the fundamentals. Many chess players learn short-term *tactics* that enable them to immediately capture pawns or avoid capture by an opponent. Some learn *strategies* that involve planning 5-6 moves ahead, deferring short-term successes in favor of the overall goal of checkmate. Only a few masters learn the fundamental *principles* that govern strategies enabling them to play 30 competitors at a time.

Principles, like the concept of due process, are basic, simple and elegant in their flexibility. *Strategies* involve deferring the short-term gain while planning for the end goal: Strategies are large concepts of leverage, covering wide spaces and broad expanses of time. *Tactics* are short-term efforts to gain a slight advantage or avoid a temporary disadvantage: They are small in scope, involving small movements of forces, narrow spaces and short time spans. Principles generate strategies that allow improvisation based on audience response. Strategies shape tactics that consist of moment-by-moment decisions. The consequence of a sloppy tactic is usually small, but the consequence of ignoring a principle is substantial. The failure to follow the principles produces far more serious mistakes than errors in tactics.

Strategy involves mapping the big picture. David Rogers, in *Waging Business Warfare*, notes that "Theoretically, strategy precedes contact; tactics begin with it." He also describes the necessity of a *"feedback loop* swirling between your strategic decisions of today as influenced by the effectiveness of your tactics yesterday."

The negotiation of employment disputes can benefit enormously from applying principles from game theory. As McDonald illustrates in *Strategy in Poker, Business and War* (1950), negotiation and game theory certain elements including:

❖ Both sides are interdependent: One side's moves alone do not dictate the outcome—the opponent's moves are equally important.

❖ No single move has meaning in itself; it makes sense only as part of the whole.

❖ We have to make assumptions about the strategy of the other; their reactions are not mere chance events.

Making demands in negotiation and betting in game theory are both based on the opponent's reactions. Although negotiations cannot be predicted by the probabilities of numbers, like blackjack and poker, they can be predicted by probabilities of human behavior. In playing blackjack, you can bet on the cards without understanding of the fundamentals of probability, but you will seldom win more than you lose. Knowing the basic game rules that define winning and losing or the sequence of moves is not enough. It is necessary to understand the principles of probability that provide a "favorable advantage."

Small advantages matter. The house at Monte Carlo has a built-in advantage in blackjack of only 2.7 percent, but this small difference is enough to allow them to win most of the time, creating enormous profit (when amateurs compete, the advantage mulitplies). The fundamental principles in this book provide you with this kind of "favorable advantage" on liability (who is to blame) and damages.

Taking risks is inherent in being a contingency lawyer. The key to risk-taking is embracing the unanticipated. Instead of fearing surprise, it should be expected as normal. Dynamic risk-taking creates an energy and momentum of its own. To paraphrase Walter Wriston, former chair of Citibank "If wages come from work, rent from real estate and interest from savings, where do profits come from? Profit comes from risk."[1]

As professionals, our objective is to achieve the jointly agreed upon goal of the client, to restore dignity to the client, and to bring closure as rapidly as sensible. This usually involves money, but we should not lose sight of the intangible goals such as ensuring bad actors are punished, changing the policies of a corporation, improving the practices for handling harassment complaints or reforming companies which are overworking employees. These intangible goals are often pivotal in achieving client satisfaction.

Our economic goal is to invest the fewest number of hours to generate the maximum money for the client. As we invest time thoughtfully, higher profits per hour can be generated. Profit is viewed as the amount of fees we recover

---

[1] Daniel Kehrer, *Doing Business Boldly: The Art of Intelligent Risk Taking.*

divided by the number of hours invested in the case. It is my working assumption that $10,000 in fees for 20 hours of lawyer time is better than $70,000 for 200 hours.

In the effort to resolve a dispute, you will put in substantial energy. You can either invest it at the beginning, delay until discovery, or wait until the edge of trial. If you do it early on, you should be able to reap a return that exceeds your usual hourly rate and routinely make $300-500 per hour or more.

INVESTMENT MODEL

Under an investment model, a lawyer invests hours of time in a case hoping to help the client and simultaneously make a profit. Rather than charge by the hour, contingency lawyers usually put their time at risk. They hope to gain a return that matches, exceeds, or substantially exceeds their asserted hourly rate. Otherwise, gambling with their time doesn't make sense. Profit is not the purpose of being an employment lawyer, but it can be the result.

ORGANIZATION OF THIS BOOK

Since pre-suit settlement is the time frame that most often generates the maximum profit for the lawyer and greatest benefit to the client, it is the focus of this book.

FUNDAMENTALS

The first section explains the fundamental principles that apply to all three time frames covered in the rest of the book—early, middle and trial. Don't underestimate the importance of these principles. These principles are essential to your ability to plan a strategy and then improvise tactics during the negotiation. Without a solid foundation in the principles, your improvisation could make you look like a class clown.

Principles provide the big picture. They weave strategies and tactics into a common fabric. The nine principles for employment settlements are:

❖ Settlements are bought and sold.

❖ Settlements can occur at six different stages and each stage has different values and approaches.

❖ Audiences listen to messages that are addressed to their own needs, motives and decision-making methods.

❖ Employers see only their own point of view until inertia is reversed.

- ❖ Momentum magnifies purchase price.
- ❖ Facts have more power than law.
- ❖ Uncertainty leverages a lust for closure.
- ❖ Good lawyering makes a difference.
- ❖ Negotiation cannot begin until the prerequisites have been met.

Pre-suit Settlements

The second section is on pre-suit settlement, but of necessity it begins with strategies for screening out the bad cases. It advocates limiting your *initial* commitment to vigorous settlement efforts, and avoiding a pledge to full-fledged litigation at the outset. Preserve the option of entering an actual lawsuit until after the defendant's perspective and some of their facts has been gathered.

The primary goal of pre-suit efforts is to make the employer thirsty for settlement—to whet their appetite for compromise. Secondly, the section provides strategies and derivative tactics to give power to the negotiation efforts. It clarifies subtle methods for use in the pre-negotiation planning and during negotiations. If this effort succeeds, the dispute is over. If the effort is not successful in achieving the *realistic* goals of the client, then the third section becomes appropriate.

Middle Settlement strategies

The third section identifies the factors that will enhance leverage for settlement at the start of the actual lawsuit and during the discovery phase. It also suggests when to cease settlement efforts and go for broke.

Settlement strategies differ from litigation strategies. Although they sometimes overlap, they usually diverge in goals, methods and timing. Settlement is an effort to achieve a result in the shorter term, while litigation usually concedes that only the long term will produce the result. Litigation requires a winner and a loser. Settlement seeks a win-win scenario. During this middle stage, the strategies must be blended.

This section emphasizes the critical need to educate your client into a new way of thinking for his or her deposition. It helps you scrutinize the defense facts to find the weakest link and attack that weakness with a laser, rather than a shotgun. It provides techniques for upstaging the defendant and getting the jump on the opponent. It also discusses how to use technology to offset the employer's enormous economic advantage. This section maintains a primary focus on using power as leverage for settlement, pragmatic methods to deflect defense attacks and back-door approaches to initiate settlement talks.

TRIAL SETTLEMENT TECHNIQUES

The final section addresses settlement at the point of trial. Since trial is the topic of most books on lawyer skills (M. Belli, L. Nizer, G. Spence, F. Bailey), we do not repeat the wisdom that can be found elsewhere. Rather, this section advocates methods for creating settlement postures late in the game. It highlights techniques to make settlement more attractive and to maximize the employer's thirst for compromise at the point of highest uncertainty.

WARNING

Negotiation requires improvisation. Some readers may feel the urge to skip the section on fundamental principles and jump to the section on actual strategies. Many feel eager to grasp a nugget that will help during a negotiation, already in crises. Haphazard application of strategies may work occasionally, but it undercuts the overall power of the strategy. Unless a strategy has its roots in a fundamental principle, a strategy will often divert your efforts.

If you are already satisfied with your success in early settlement, please pass this book onto a colleague. If you recognize that another perspective may illuminate how you have succeeded and how you have failed, this book may be helpful.

Section One

FUNDAMENTAL PERSPECTIVES

Chapter One

SETTLEMENTS ARE BOUGHT AND SOLD

PRINCIPLE

The settlement amount is the purchase price agreed upon by a willing seller and a willing buyer.

A *Strategy*: Make the product more attractive than the alternative—a verdict—and less costly than the competition—the jury.

A *Tactic*: Delay giving a money demand until the buyer shows appreciation of the need to settle i.e., liability (who is to blame).

As plaintiff's attorneys, we often deal with a righteous cause, and need to be careful that we don't forget the other big picture—the economic mind-set of settlements. In its simplest mode, employers buy settlements and employees sell them. If we set the asking price too high, we can unwittingly inhibit our ability to obtain the highest possible value. Without investing time and effort to determine an attractive, yet fair market price, we will fail to attract the bidder.

When an employee is fired, the employer has usually assigned a value of **zero** dollars to the employee's case. To increase the perceived value, tradition declares that plaintiff's counsel must create certain types of fear—fear of losing, fear of costs, or fear of exposure. This tradition is half true, but only halfway effective. Attempts to create fear are commonly diluted by hyperbole and brazen accusations, exaggerated ploys for sympathy and undernourished thought. Justice rarely motivates settlement; it does, however, create a backdrop. Employers have a reason to fear a jury's versions of justice. It is this context—a jury—that makes the alternative of compromise appear meaningful.

TRADITIONAL POINT OF VIEW

A lawsuit should be about what's right and wrong. Only a verdict will do justice for my client. The jury's award will show the righteousness of the plaintiff's cause—the higher the money, the more society disapproves of the employer's acts. Employers don't want to compromise. Early settlement is for wimps.

ALTERNATIVE POINT OF VIEW

Our legal system uses money to distribute power. Employers buy settlements and employees sell them. The difficulty is agreeing on the purchase price. Early compromise allows early closure. Good money now is often more valuable than more money later. The needs of the buyer and the seller can meet.

The metaphor of settlement as a "product" for sale does not arise from an obsession with money. It is a philosophical perspective. Moreover, sale is intended to reflect the contemporary sense of marketing used by successful businesses who have made the psychological shift from "sales" to "marketing." In sales, you push your product. In marketing, you identify the needs of your audience and connect your product to those needs. The customer is not really buying a product, they are buying the satisfaction of their own needs. For example, a hardware store does not really sell tools per se: the buyers are do-it-yourselfers who want affordable home improvement.

LAWSUITS DIVIDE INTO TWO CATEGORIES: 1) WHO WINS; 2) HOW MUCH.

Winning is only part of the battle. The crucial question is always how much. The fear of who will win influences the employer's incentive to explore settlement. This incentive to settle, however, has little to do with willingness to pay a particular price. In selecting a prospective case, it is not enough to determine if you can win a case: You must also identify a product with value to the buyer. This potential value requires thoughtful evaluation.

In the *rare*, great case, it is enough to let the facts do the screaming. The liability facts will command attention and the damage facts will be largely self-evident. In all other cases, the raw information is not enough. The value of the ordinary case must be built from legally important facts and powerful inferences. This combination, drawn from both hard and soft data, will demonstrate the value for the product of a settlement to the employer.

Competing Buyers

In other types of sales, the price is determined by what competing buyers are willing to pay. In employment disputes, it initially appears that only one buyer, the past employer, has a potential interest in purchasing a way out of the lawsuit. At first glance, there are no competing buyers for a particular employment settlement. Nonetheless, a lawsuit can create competition for the employer's price. The employer's competitor is the jury.

The employer fears that a jury may place a higher price on the product than the employer does. If your estimate of the jury's price tag appears grossly inflated, it reduces the employer's incentive to take your price seriously. On the other hand, if your estimate of the jury's price tag appears realistic to the employer, it will usually raise the sales price of the product closer to your number. It can often be beneficial to subtly remind the employer that when the jury sets the price, it doesn't have to spend its own money. Few things are more fun than being able to buy something with someone else's money. This helps the employer to see your demand as a bargain.

In Rule 68 offers of judgment, the employer essentially admits that it has lost the case, but the employer is betting that its offer is closer to the value a future jury will place on the case than the employee's demand.

Setting Prices in Contingency Situations

Many non-lawyer professionals earn their living by results; e.g., real estate agents sell houses and earn a percent based only on successful transaction and commissioned sales persons earn their income by results. One major difference between these sales and lawsuits is that the asking price of real property or gadgets (the equivalent of our demand) is readily determined in the marketplace. The marketplace sets price and price range for similar products. Agents find comparable properties and project a market value. Moreover, there are usually competing products (houses) for sale in a similar price range. Thus, in the non-lawyer marketplace, the starting point for buyers is an asking price rooted in high degree of objectivity.

Buyers may limit their offer based on their own needs and ability to pay, but they negotiate against the seller's price. The deviation from the asking price is very modest: Discounts typically vary from 1 percent to 10 percent below the asked price. Moreover, the history of prior sales and the existence of a competitor's prices provide an objective valuing.

DETERMINING MARKET VALUE IN LAW

Unlike tangible products or even shares of stocks, it is difficult to determine the market value of an employment settlement because there is little or no reliable market data to set the asking price. Employment disputes are commonly settled for substantially less than the asking price; often 50 percent, 75 percent even 95 percent is knocked off the original asking price. Since many of these cases ultimately settle, the error appears to be in setting the initial asking price.

Employment cases do not have the advantages of personal injury cases. They differ in several respects. Personal injury cases revolve around a single incident, while employment disputes usually involve a series of decisions and the context is a crucial component. Employment cases usually involve disputes about both liability and damages. By contrast, in personal injury cases, the battle is almost exclusively about damages: Liability (who is to blame) is usually a minor issue.

In personal injury cases, the real focus is on the injury. Personal injury lawyers are able to determine the market price by making fairly straightforward comparisons of injuries. There are books and manuals available that provide data for the average case, which can be adjusted upward or downward for the individual case. Thus, the marketplace data is extremely useful and applicable by consensus. This luxury is not yet available to employment lawyers.

Plaintiff employment lawyers have generally been unable to systematically find cases with "comparable" injuries. Using the word "injury" sounds more real than distress. It also minimizes visceral objections. The liability aspects of employment cases are frequently similar, but data for **similar injuries** has not been compiled. There has been no systematic, nationwide or statewide, compilation of results organized around injuries. There are few tables or charts dealing with comparable injuries, and the alternative is relying upon crude rules of thumb. We explore these more fully in the chapter on Determining Value in the Pre-Suit Settlement section.

We need to remember that the database and enormous increase in value of personal injuries did not happen by accident nor by the grace of the establishment. Lawyers, led by Melvin Belli, created the world that resulted in increased value for injuries to a person's body. Belli's 1951 California Law Review article, *The More Adequate Award* was the call to arms that helped unite plaintiff's lawyers into the modern ATLA. ATLA became a force to be reckoned with. As NELA builds a damage database for employees, we carry on this powerful tradition.

Some recent compilations about average verdicts by Jury Verdict Research, Inc. and the Bureau of Justice provide practical data on **average** verdicts.[2] This raw data has not been analyzed to detect any underlying variables. Future variables may allow us to more precisely predict the differences in verdicts and therefore in settlements. The above databases have some general value in awakening us to what's realistic and educating employers about what is likely, especially if you have the elusive "average" case.

We often kid ourselves about the value of the case and ignore a good value in settlement by equating it with trial value. We must rediscover the obvious.

SETTLEMENT VALUE DOES **NOT** EQUAL TRIAL VALUE
Settlement is the point at which
**a buyer is willing to pay and
a seller is willing to let go.**

Trial is going for broke.

To entice an employer to buy a settlement, you must have either 1) *enough* of the *right kind* of facts to fit the legal packages (causes of action); 2) *enough* uncertainty to make cost a major factor; or 3) peripheral facts that the employer prefers to stay out of the public eye. Other facts seldom matter. Unfairness does not count; it is not against the law. Sympathy facts rarely matter on liability. Sympathy may influence the ultimate value assigned for damages, but it seldom motivates a desire to settle. Reaching an agreement on a fair price for the "product," i.e., a settlement, requires more thought and effort. Timing is a crucial variable.

---

[2] 1999 Bureau of Justice Statistics Bulletin "Civil Trial Cases and Verdicts in Large Counties, 1996." The entire report is available through the Lawyers Weekly website. The November 29, 1999 Lawyers Weekly issue provides a useful summary at page 10-13.

Tips to Tackle Wrongful Terminations (LRP Publications 1996). (An array of charts and graphs drawn from 2,000 cases over nine years by type of claim, by type of damages, by win/loss percentages for each type of claim, by the impact of the position of plaintiff and differences by year for compensatory and punitive damages.)

Chapter Two

SETTLEMENTS OCCUR AT DIFFERENT STAGES

"Litigation: A machine which you go into as a pig and come out as a sausage."

Ambrose Bierce, *A Devil's Dictionary*

The concept of litigation as a meat grinder is sadly appropriate, but the idea assumes that lawsuits have to go all the way to the bitter end. Proponents of litigation rarely entertain interim stopping points, but settlements can occur at any stage of litigation. The most common moments for settlements are:

❖ Before the lawsuit starts
❖ After the start of suit
❖ Around summary judgment
❖ The day before trial
❖ After the verdict
❖ After the appeal

Each different stage provides unique opportunities for settlement. As the case progresses through the stages, the settlement value changes, often increasing. This concept was introduced in 1965 by Phillip Herman in *Better Settlements Through Leverage*. He artfully explained that no single value fits at all stages. No amount remains fixed.

TRADITIONAL POINT OF VIEW

If my client's case is worth $200,000 at trial, then she should get $200,000 in settlement. Her harm is clear. There should be no reductions. It is what's rightfully hers.

ALTERNATIVE POINT OF VIEW

Different stages of a lawsuit provide different opportunities: the values and benefits to each side will differ at each stage.

Monetary values change because there are many unknowns at the outset. Six months down the road, both sides have more solid information. Whether it's good news or bad news, it reduces the number of unknowns. Twelve months later, witnesses change jobs, management changes and attitudes change. More solid information has decreased the number of unknowns. These unknowns can be leveraged to facilitate settlement or push toward trial.

To demonstrate the contrast between the time invested by the plaintiff's counsel and time spent by the client at various stages I prepared a four page comparison listing of tasks each performs in a lawsuit. This is the cover page:

CUMULATIVE TIME INVESTED
BY CLIENT AND LAWYER

AGGREGATE OF CLIENT TIME	STAGE	AGGREGATE OF LAWYER TIME
10 hours	Pre-suit, Vigorous settlement efforts	25 hours or more
30 hours	Depositions, Interrogatories, Admissions, Documents Exchange, Medical evaluations, Court battles over discovery, Opposing employer's attempt to dismiss	150 hours or more
35 hours	Briefs and hearing on employer's attempt to prevent trial based on written summaries	200 hours or more
45 hours	Trial preparation	300 hours or more
70 hours	Trial—assuming 3 days in trial	350 hours or more
75 hours	Appeals **NOTE:** Appeals should be negotiated separately	420 hours or more

This chart allows you to foresee your commitment and be conscious of your anticipated investment. Showing this chart to a client may help you explain why you require him or her to demonstrate their commitment by a cash retainer. Often clients assume it is easy and fast for a lawyer to achieve the client's goals. When you quantify the time required, the stakes become more real. It makes you and the client think about the value of this case in relation to the investment required. The chart also helps to educate people who don't understand why you need to see some of the employer's facts before plunging gung-ho into a lawsuit. This chart also illustrates the dramatic growth in time demands as the stages progress, each with its own opportunities and restrictions.

BEFORE THE LAWSUIT STARTS

Many lawyers assume that an employer has no incentive to settle until after a lawsuit has begun. This may be true occasionally, or among certain types of employers, but in my experience over half of the employers can be made thirsty before the sheriff arrives. Employers are educable, if approached intelligently and business-like. The most powerful greeting is a lawsuit-look-alike; i.e., a draft complaint and a cover letter that explicitly declares that they are not *yet* sued. See chapters 10-14 for elaboration of this approach. The actual costs incurred to reach settlement are low compared to defending litigation. Most employers are smart enough to recognize that money paid in many early settlements is cheaper than money paid to lawyers, and it avoids the risks.

Demand letters

A demand letter is a waste of time, unless the case is worth less than $10,000. No matter how detailed or legalistic, demand letters look shallow. They smell like cheap perfume. The meta-message is clear: You did not care enough to make it look real or have enough confidence to start a real lawsuit.

Ghost-Written Letters

There is an exception to lawyer-demand letters that is proving very powerful in selected cases—ghost writing letters for clients who have strong political capital either by their actual performance records, contribution to the bottom line, or the continued respect of high officials. This method is most effective where termination is due to office politics: There can be no issue of misconduct or poor performance. Recently, I had a client with too few facts for a legal challenge, but she had substantial political capital with the decision-makers. The employer had made what they called a final offer of a separation package equal to one year's gross pay. Even though they were terminating her, I decided to try this alternative approach. Following closely the principles of this book, I ghost-wrote a two page letter. It was revised several times, focusing on the point of view of the reader. I also wrote out a script for her final interview. Initially, the employer said no more money. But, two days after the letter was received, they modified the offer. They increased the offer to four years pay, an amount to equal to over $860,000.

Even in smaller suits, a letter ghost-written by a lawyer can be a powerful way to create the backdrop for a retaliation suit. You should, however, confer closely with your client and take care to use the client's language and communication style, without any legalese.

AFTER THE START OF SUIT

Disputes may also settle after a suit has commenced, but before depositions have begun. When the summons and complaint were served, the threat to sue became a reality. Your follow-through demonstrated your seriousness and created a new legal reality. At this stage, the cost investment by both sides remains low, but it has begun to *look* expensive.

Another moment ripe for settlement is after most depositions and document exchanges have occurred, but before summary judgment briefs have been prepared. The out-of-pocket costs have grown, but the defense lawyer's bill still looks modest compared to what will be required for summary judgment, trial preparation and trial. For summary judgment motions alone, employers are given estimates of 60-120 hours of defense lawyer time (a cost of $12-36,000). This may seem modest in the overall scheme, but it has symbolic value. Moreover, defense counsel has to justify the expenditure to in-house counsel or the CEO as against the benefits of a reasonable demand. This results in hedging, caveats and diminished bravado.

AROUND SUMMARY JUDGMENT

By the time a judge is asked to make a decision based on the written summaries, both sides usually have a major investment of time and expense. The age-old phenomena that **only 10 percent of the lawsuits actually go to trial** remains true in employment law.

Historically, the majority of resolutions were by settlement, but in recent years summary judgment has been the sword eliminating trials or narrowing claims for trial. The traditional standard for judgments based on written summaries has been relaxed, in part, due to increased workloads. In some jurisdictions, like Minnesota, federal judges are granting summary judgment on 65 to 92 percent of the employment lawsuits. We often forget that these decisions do not apply to cases that have voluntarily settled. When the buyer and seller agree on a price, the judge has no power to throw a case out of court.

Prior to defendant's summary judgment briefing, the cost factor of preparing the motion gives you a slight advantage, but a bigger advantage is in the uncertainty of which claims will survive. During the interval between oral argument and the judge's decision, the uncertainty of the court's decision usually hurts the plaintiff. The defendant assumes they have already put in the time, so they prefer to wait and see what happens. If all claims are dismissed, the employer's uncertainty is neutralized. [Employers are generally aware that the appeals courts are unfriendly to plaintiff-appellants.] Fortunately, a decision that allows at least one decent claim to survive for trial will shift the advantage back to the plaintiff for the purpose of settlement.

CAUTION

A *few* judges appear to have developed a technique of letting a weak claim survive, but dismissing the stronger ones. The logic appears to be that if you already had a trial on the remaining claims, your appeal will be weakened.

THE DAY BEFORE TRIAL

A significant number of the remaining cases will find a happy breaking point the day before trial. Both sides finally appreciate the enormous uncertainty they are facing. On the eve of trial, lawyers envision the unpredictability of juries or more precisely, the unpredictability of a judge's rulings on key evidence. Since plaintiff has to be prepared first, you will feel the pressure to initiate settlement earlier than your opponent. You can engage in negotiations until approximately two weeks before trial. After that, you should slide negotiations into the background and prepare full-steam ahead. Your commitment to trial will create its own momentum.

AFTER THE VERDICT

Cases that reach the jury still offer an opportunity to settle after the verdict and before any appeal. Any discussion of compromise should begin immediately, while the shock is in place. It is axiomatic that the amount must be somewhat less than the verdict, but every hour that passes enables defense counsel to explain away the adverse verdict and find grounds for appeal. Both sides recognize that post-trial motions are rarely effective in persuading a judge that s/he made a mistake. Nonetheless, the new trial deadline is short and the need to timely identify all errors strong. Thus, the opportunity must be seized before motions are underway. There is precious little time.

Neil Mullin points out an advantage to bifurcation of the entitlement to punitive damages from the verdict on the amount of punitive damages. When a jury during the liability portion of the trial determines that the employer acted with deliberate indifference, you have a great window for settlement. The certainty of achieving some punitive damages is clear. The amount awarded is unknown and the uncertainty provides enormous leverage.

To make a highly favorable compromise at the end of trial, there must be a *mutual* sense that trial was relatively free of "harmful" error. This can happen only if the judge was reasonably fair in evidentiary rulings, jury instructions and jury interrogatories. In other words, if the court patently favored you, discount and settle fast. If liability issues are pretty straightforward and the amount of damages pretty clear, compromise is fairly direct and the discount small. Otherwise, the prospects of appeal weigh much more highly.

ON APPEAL

The nature of issues on appeal affects the prospect of settlement during or after the first level appeal. For example, if the alleged error is sufficiency of the evidence, the argument is so weak that only small concessions by plaintiff are needed. If the alleged error is admissibility of evidence or exclusion, it presents only a small worry for appeal. If the error is a jury instruction, it must command your attention and make you more flexible.

As you move up the appellate ladder, the standard applied is critical. For example, if the first appellate court rules that there was a failure to preserve error, the loser will be more willing to concede liability and damages. The opponent will be far more negotiable. Part of this is due to malpractice exposure and part due to the nature of the error: Errors that fall into an either-or category generate more clear-cut results than fuzzy issues. Defense counsel will still want to save face. S/he will need some discount to justify a compromise without a second-level appeal. The benefits of pragmatic compromise outweigh righteous collection of the entire verdict.

If the first appellate court makes it clear that errors were made, but they were not harmful, compromise is delayed. Harmless error is a fuzzy thinking concept, one that allows defendants to hold onto the illusion that another appellate court may find it prejudicial error. At the same time, a ruling by the first level appeals court is essentially sending a message of "so-what". It will diminish the defense lawyer's confidence in his or her case and should enhance settlement.

PREFERENCE AMONG STAGES FOR SETTLEMENT

I place primary emphasis on early settlement. Based on my experience, it is my firm belief that the client is better served by early closure. Moreover, our profit per hour is invariably higher when the settlement is early. The following comparison of time, effort and energy expended demonstrates this conclusion.

COMPARISON OF SETTLEMENT VS. TRIAL		
	Early Settlement Efforts	*Lawsuits*
How long it takes	3-4 months	12-24 months
Deposition of employee	none	8-32 hours
Deposition of spouse/S.O.	none	4 + hours
Deposition of doctor	none	2-4 hours
Deposition of ex-coworkers	none	4-8 hours
Deposition of family	none	4 + hours
Deposition of friends	none	2 + hours each
Deposition of managers	none	4 + hours
Disclose medical info.	no, or seldom	yes
Disclose financial info.	no, or some	yes
Finding lawyer	easy	very hard
Costs (out-of-pocket)	$1-500	$ 1,000-5,000 +
Upfront payment for fees	2 weeks pay	1 month's pay
Lawyer time	under 30 hours	350 + hours

Few employees can afford to hire a lawyer by the hour: Most want a no-money down arrangement with fees contingent on the result. This type of chart clarifies the various prices an employee will pay for choosing lawsuit over early settlement. It can be shown to a client who is unable to decide. Clients who study the comparison information invariably find a marked interest in exploring the settlement alternative before plunging headlong into a lawsuit.

The audience at each stage is a major influence on the timing of settlement. At the earliest stage, the client is in the foreground. Later, the foreground shifts to the employer then to defense counsel, onto judge, then jury, and finally to appellate court and back to the client. The foreground-background perspective continues to change as we move through the process.

Chapter Three

KNOW YOUR AUDIENCE

> ### PRINCIPLE
> Audiences listen to messages that are addressed to their own needs, motives and decision-making methods.

Every human being sees and hears things differently. Every audience has different needs and different values. Everyone talks differently to their mother than to their child. Everyone talks differently to a best friend than to a neighbor who is known only casually. Yet, we commonly assume that we should communicate to opponents and judges in the same manner. On the other hand, if we shape our communication to address the needs of a particular audience, we increase the probability of success. When we focus on communicating, arguments are secondary. The primary goal is clarity: to ensure each audience understands the information presented.

Historically, salespersons, including lawyers, focused on advocacy and persuasion. Advocacy, at its best, is a thing of beauty. But often it is either clumsy or exaggerated rhetoric. Many lawyers are too "cool" to devote time to preparing both the content and the delivery. Too often, advocacy is a thinly disguised form of manipulation. Advocacy has a role in negotiating settlements, but it is most effective when part of comprehensive audience-centered communication.

As noted earlier, the psychological shift from "sales" to "marketing" is subtle, but powerful. Beginning with the principle that settlements are products that are sold, we emphasize the more effective approach of marketing by identifying and satisfying the needs of each audience involved in the sale. A lawyer cannot be effective or persuasive without grasping the concepts of audience-centered communication.

TRADITIONAL POINT OF VIEW

I talk to everybody in the same way. I make the same arguments to employers, defense counsel, insurance companies, judges and jurors. I talk to appellate judges as if they were jurors. There is only one right way… If you didn't understand me, it's because you weren't listening. It's your fault.

ALTERNATIVE WAY OF THINKING

Each listener has a unique set of values, interests and motives. To treat all listeners as if they are all the same is to invite confusion, misunderstanding and failed communication. The notion that "one speech fits all" contradicts the reality of day-to-day existence. Communication tailored to each reader/listener enhances successful connections.

AUDIENCE-CENTERED COMMUNICATION

Audience-centered communication is the opposite of speaker-centered communication. It is not cause-oriented. It is not idea-centered. It is not feeling-centered communication. It does not focus on the *speaker's* feelings, values and needs. Instead, audience-centered communication focuses on the *listener's* (or reader's) feelings, values and needs. If you pay attention to only your view, you will be distracted from your audience, who has different needs, motives and decision-making criteria.

As Gerry Spence noted in *How to Argue and Win Every Time*, "Listening is the ability to hear what people are saying or *not saying* as distinguished from the words they enunciate."

Considerable research has identified certain fundamental concepts about communication. These fundamentals have been repeatedly verified and prove that audience-centered communication is the most effective form of communication. In *Courtroom Communication Skills* by Smith & Malandro, they identify the following basic premises of audience-centered communication:

- ❖ Communication is based on perception
- ❖ People actively try to make sense out of their environment
- ❖ Perceptions are organized and structured within a brief period of time
- ❖ People use stereotypes to organize their perceptions
- ❖ People tend to see others as similar to themselves
- ❖ People tend to maintain their original perceptions, regardless of contradictory information.

Three decades of in-depth study of communication, in particular small group communication, has demonstrated the errors endemic in one-sided advocacy. It has shown that the ability to focus on the audience when communicating is a better predictor of success in achieving one's goals. Admittedly, communication is both a science and art. But the alternative, the so-called "common sense" approach, is often nothing more than old habits and unthinking stereotypes. Power resides in the audience-centered approach.

THE EVERCHANGING AUDIENCE

In *People in Quandaries*, Wendell Brown points out, "Similarity is when the differences don't matter. Difference is when the similarities don't matter." As you move through the stages in reaching settlement, there will be six audiences whose differences are more significant than their similarities. Each audience has different needs and values. The six audiences you need to consider include:

1. Client
2. Top management
3. Opponent
4. Judge
5. Jury
6. Appellate judges

The person you need to focus on is your primary audience. This person will change as the dispute resolution progresses. At each stage, you should ask, "Who is my primary audience? Who is my secondary audience? and "Who has moved into the background?"

The following chart illustrates that in the first stage, the prospective client is the primary audience. The client's liability facts and damages facts are prominent. In your first communication to the employer, top management becomes the primary audience with opposing counsel as the secondary audience. As you move into discovery, the opposing counsel moves into the foreground as the primary audience. Keep in mind that the opponent will be controlling the flow of information to and from the employer. Later, the primary audience will become the judge who controls the information flow at motions and at trial. During trial, the jury moves to the foreground with the judge becoming a secondary audience, while the employer moves to the background. Down the road, appellate judges may move from the background to become the primary audience.

AUDIENCE	INTAKE	1ST LETTER	DISCOVERY	DEPOSITION	SUMMARY JUDGMENT	TRIAL
Primary	Client	CEO	Opposing Counsel	Deponent	Judge	Jury
Secondary	Employer	Defense lawyer	Employer	Managers	Appeals Court	Judge
Background		Judge	Client	Opposing Counsel	Employer	Appeals Court

You must be sensitive to the changes as your primary, secondary and background audiences shift. Keep in mind that each audience has different needs and values and therefore your audience-centered communications will necessarily change as well.

Whenever you write any non-routine letter, pause...read it from the reader's point of view. Suspend your point of view as the writer and pretend you are the reader. What is the message received? For clients, you should either eliminate the jargon or explain it. For an opponent, you should truly understand your purpose for this letter, anticipate the various reactions and ponder more effective means of expression. For a judge, get to the point. Clarity and brevity are handmaidens of good communication, but attention to the audience is foremost.

Many writers erroneously assume that the reader and writer are equal partners in the transaction and should put in equal amounts of effort to make the relationship work.[3] If the writer asks "what is going on in the mind of the reader?" communication will be more effective. We all recognize the reality of idea overload, yet we continue to overwhelm our reader and blur our thoughts and words. Barry Tarshis offers the concept of staging to make writing more audience-oriented. Staging assumes that there is a difference between the meaning of a thought and the impact of a thought and that there are degrees of clarity. Staging your writing requires you to recognize that thoughts serve different functions: some introduce information but others reinforce. Thoughts that serve the priming function cannot be confused with the important thoughts. You should concentrate on the thoughts you are trying to express more than the words you are using.

---

[3] Barry Tarshis, *How To Write Like A Pro* 18

COMMUNICATING WITH CLIENTS

The most important audience is your client. Clients come with varied personalities, assorted values and widely disparate levels of skill in observation, memory, communication skills and honesty. It is helpful to recognize that your client's personality shapes his or her perspective about the facts, the facts themselves, his or her willingness to compromise and his or her stamina. There are wide variations in employee-plaintiffs including:

- ❖ Simple, honest people who feel wronged
- ❖ People who are righteous about a cause
- ❖ People who say "I don't care about the money"
- ❖ People who are pragmatic and upfront about their self-interest
- ❖ People who see only their own point of view
- ❖ Penny pinchers or cost-conscious people
- ❖ Image-conscious people
- ❖ Aggressive jerks
- ❖ Whiners.

These laymen labels do not provide much predictive information about how a client or prospective client will behave during settlement efforts or give you insight about how they process information when making decisions. A useful model for examining this processing has been outlined by various researchers who have used Carl Jung's theories to articulate four basic personality types. Each personality type approaches decisions in dramatically different ways, values things differently and has differing priorities. The main categories are known by different names, but four useful categories have been provided by juror profilists, like Paul Tieger and Carolyn Koch, which include: the Traditionalists, the Experiencers, the Conceptualizers, and the Idealists. When communicating with clients or prospective clients, you'll find it useful to consider these personality profiles, which are elaborated further in the section on jury as audience.

Like all humans, prospects and clients may have hidden agendas. Each person is unique, and you must be sensitive to similarities and differences. To evaluate the strength and weakness of a potential plaintiff's testimony, it isn't enough to focus on the facts. Your client's value in witnessing the original facts is as important as their ability to be a witness at trial or in deposition. Don't let your loyalty to your client blind you to the needs and values of the other audiences.

21

COMMUNICATING WITH EMPLOYER'S TOP MANAGEMENT

The type of employer and the employer's philosophy toward employees influences settlement strategies. In simplified form, there are five basic employer types:

- ❖ Blind, but educable
- ❖ Cost-conscious
- ❖ Image-conscious
- ❖ Aggressive jerks
- ❖ Unknowns

Since each group has different leverage points, approaches to each group should be planned separately. Strategies for addressing these differences are set forth in later chapters.

BLIND, BUT EDUCABLE—40% OF THE EMPLOYERS I ENCOUNTER.

These employers have a primary need to learn the basic facts. Hard facts will enable this type of employer to accept some responsibility and they will do it faster than other types. This type can be educated as to how it could have "prevented" the harm or inhibited the prohibited actions. It is more willing to pay a fair price upfront for corporate neglect. It is not typically, however, willing to pay much for gross misconduct or deliberate disregard by an individual manager. This entity sees itself as basically good, but it can admit to making occasional mistakes. It has difficulty recognizing institutional problems, but it is willing to acknowledge that "bad apples" may have been employed. Such misconduct is perceived as coincidental and the bad actors as loose cannons, allegedly unknown to management. Education need not be limited to the merits of the case. Sometimes, education about peripheral facts (exposure to lost mangement time, morale, etc.) will motivate this type to explore settlement.

COST-CONSCIOUS—20% OF THE EMPLOYERS I ENCOUNTER.

This group often has an interest in early settlement, but only if it's cheap. They will lowball you and expect a good deal. If you are not careful to promptly present information that educates them about value, they will prematurely calculate a nuisance value and then mentally lock into that amount. They won't budge further until they receive the 2X4 of a big bill. This finally awakens them to the *real* financial costs of resistance and more serious negotiations begin. Neither peripheral facts nor skeletons have much impact on this group.

IMAGE-CONSCIOUS (RARE)—10% OF THE EMPLOYERS I ENCOUNTER.

This rare employer pays for silence and invisibility. One of the ways to recognize this type is by its own initiation of quiet severance talks before any lawyer is involved. Without negotiations, it has put a significant offer on the table, often higher than predicted by local norms or the known facts. It tends, however, to lock into the original amount because it was calculated with its version of "fairness" in mind. This type has a heightened fear, not of wrongdoing, but because it got caught. The fear of being exposed is an influential factor in only a tiny number of cases. [This does *not* refer to what your clients mean when they say "They will want to settle. They won't want my case to be made public." As most readers know, that is nonsense.] Peripheral facts can have a disproportionate force with this group, especially as the publicity of trial becomes imminent.

AGGRESSIVE JERKS—10% OF THE EMPLOYERS I ENCOUNTER.

The slogan for this group is "Millions for defense, not one penny for tribute." This type fights for the sake of fighting. The employer is willing to pay big money, but only for its defense because it believes that protracted warfare will deter other employees from suing. It wants to show who is boss. If you know from reliable sources that the prospect's employer is a jerk, don't waste time discussing settlement. If the case justifies it, just sue it out and go for broke.

CAUTION

Don't prejudge stupid for aggressive. The ignorant may be educated.

One of my employer opponents took the position that it would not offer one penny to settle and that it would fight all the way. We were not sure if the invitation to discuss settlement was "fake", but because of serious legal obstacles, our demand was less than two years pay. Suit began. During the deposition of the CEO, I asked about a comment allegedly made six years ago. "Did you ask the plaintiff if she felt less of a woman after her hysterectomy?" After he denied making the statement, I asked a *stupid* question, "What is a hysterectomy?" He answered, "It's when they cut out the woman's vagina." I was stunned, so I asked the same question again. He repeated the same answer. I asked, "What happens then?" He replied, "They sew her up and she can't have sex anymore." The case settled within days—with a value equal to four years of lost wages.

UNKNOWN—20% OF THE EMPLOYERS I ENCOUNTER.
If you don't have any information about the employer, contact local NELA lawyers or ATLA members. You can find out about other cases, the litigation history and strategies used by the employer. Alternatively, you can run them through LEXIS or use NELANET. Often, the public library has a file of news clippings on local businesses. For national companies, you can also check them out through NEXIS.

EMPLOYER PHILOSOPHIES
Most employers tend to have one of two distinctive philosophies about employees. The philosophy of the employer (or its attitude toward employees in general) will often shape the employer's course of settlement negotiations. If they see employees as essential to the operation of the enterprise, they will usually be more flexible about early settlement. On the other hand, if they see employees as a necessary evil, which must be tolerated and tightly managed, their approach will be more begrudging.

Employer philosophies are distinct from their types, but their philosophy will often shape many of their decisions. It is a useful predictor of their responsiveness to settlement overtures. [Similar competing philosophies that permeate decisions of the judiciary are listed in the audience section on judges.] In simplest terms, one group of employers trusts employees and the other distrusts them. There is also a perverse deviation: Some extremist employers go beyond merely distrusting employees, they actively hate employees.

Once these two basic, polarized philosophies are grasped, they are easily recognized in management attitudes and language. You will find them surreptitiously echoed in written briefs of opponents, in oral arguments and judicial decisions. The way facts are shaded and the spin put onto them is typically an extension of one of these two polarized philosophies. When you see these basic philosophies reflected in the perspective of a particular employer, you will better understand what arguments *not* to use in negotiation. Shift gears and re-focus on arguments that will appeal.

COMMUNICATING WITH OPPOSING COUNSEL

"Oliver W. Holmes divided lawyers into kitchen knives, razors and stings."

Catherine Drinker Brown,
Yankee from Olympus, 1944

As events progress, the defense lawyer soon replaces the employer audience as primary source of information going in both directions. We often blur the defense lawyer with the employer s/he represents. Usually this is erroneous. Defense lawyers fall into categories similar to employers, not because of whom they represent, but because of their own unique orientations. In simplified fashion, the main orientations are:

- ❖ Client-centered and cost-conscious—the true professional
- ❖ Billing-conscious—the insecure, self-centered ones
- ❖ Win-conscious—sports freaks who love competition for its own sake
- ❖ Aggressive jerks—who fight to hurt and malign.

Other labels have been suggested; e.g., Supreme Court Chief Justice Warren Berger once declared that "70% of the trial lawyers were incompetent." In *Imagining the Law*, Cantor recently suggested that lawyers have been hated for centuries because, unlike doctors and priests, we have the power of the state behind us. Lawyers can obtain an order or a judgment that can be enforced by the long arm of the state. The differences in a lawyer's orientation will filter the facts and shape the negotiating positions. Because this orientation influences their strategies, it must be factored into your approach.

CLIENT-CENTERED AND COST-CONSCIOUS

Many plaintiff attorneys assume that this group, the client-centered and cost-conscious professional, is a dinosaur. In my experience they are real. I encounter them in over 30 percent of my cases. This group is eager to settle a lawsuit, unless it appears truly frivolous. This small group of professionals knows that everyone loses in litigation, except the attorney paid by the hour. They genuinely seek the best interest of their client, not out of altruism, but intelligent self-interest. This approach keeps the client happy and returning.

Gerry Spence has noted that sometimes we gain power in argument by vesting our opponent with trust and reasonableness. It has often been my experience that we often mirror what we think we see in others and vice versa. I do not mean to imply that this approach will work with the other types of lawyer, but the client-centered type will often respond favorably to mutual respect.

BILLING-CONSCIOUS

The billing-conscious type does occur, but not as frequently as plaintiff folklore suggests. With rare exception, they do not get repeat clients. Unfortunately, they are, however, attractive to companies whose goal is the deterrence of future suits. To these types, billable time is all that really counts. They are the lawyers who churn a file and then settle the case on the courthouse steps.

WIN-CONSCIOUS

The win-conscious lawyers love competition for its own sake. It is not enough to win the war, they must win every battle. They will continuously fight about every concession. There is no need to take this approach personally or assume it's gender-based. They will participate in the give and take of negotiation, but they must feel successful in pulling you down. Thus, your demand should err on the high side or add an intangible they will hate to give up.

AGGRESSIVE JERKS

The aggressive jerks will always be around. They are motivated by opportunities to hurt, malign and destroy. Be on your guard, but keep in mind that they are essentially insecure little children. You can easily set traps for these idiots and expose them to the judge and the jury. When I have a strong client, I like having a jerk for an opponent at trial. Juries hate them. Sometimes a little background research on the lawyer will enable you to politely remind them of his or her past losses and the parallels with this case. During discovery, you must play hardball with this group and invoke judicial intervention at the second sign of abuse. One method is the costly appointment of a special master. I have also found a cheaper alternative: I bring a videotape machine and aim it at the aggressive defense counsel. This often reduces the nastiness of these deplorable characters.

VARIATIONS IN KNOWLEDGE

On their knowledge of employment law, defense lawyers divide into four groups: well informed, uninformed about the law, uninformed about the facts, knowledgeable about law but not as applied to *these* facts. The worst is uninformed about the facts: You can educate them about the law, but their myopia about the controlling facts is a huge obstacle. Those blind to the changes in the law since 1980 are very resistant and it is seldom worth the effort. They need a paradigm shift and it requires an extraordinary effort.

Defense lawyers often justify their conduct by asserting, "I'm just doing my job." Many times, this may be a fair justification, but only up to a certain point. When it relates to their legal position on the merits, it is fine. But, for tactics like five-day depositions, or dirty tactics like intimidation and ridicule during the depositions or hiding documents or deception to the court, it is totally unacceptable.

VARIATION ON A THEME—LAWYERS HIRED BY THE INSURANCE COMPANY

Insurers are typically cold, hard and cost-conscious. They hire lawyers to seek a way out from coverage, if they have any chance at all. This audience is cost-conscious to the extreme. Fortunately, it applies to money they pay to defend as well as money they pay to settle. The politics of the employer or the cause of the plaintiff does not matter to the insurer, unless it impacts cost.

CAUTION

When the audience is an insurer, remember that intentional torts and punitive damages are seldom covered by insurance.

In such situations, therefore, focus should be shifted away from malicious acts or intentional misconduct. Similarly, punitive damages should not be brought up. If the paying audience is an insurance company, do not emphasize punitive damages. Instead put the big bucks in compensatory damages. Let the willful misconduct be a backdrop for higher compensatory damages. Save the arguments on punitive damages until you have max'ed out the insurance money, then you can argue punitive damages as a reason for the employer to kick in more money. You should concentrate on the negligence of employer in hiring, retaining, supervising, investigating and many creative variations on this theme. If you don't achieve a settlement, you can still go after individuals and punitive damages.[4] Moreover, punitive damages may still be available for negligent supervision.

COMMUNICATING WITH THE JUDGE

New lawyers often express awe for the power of the person in the black robe. Seasoned lawyers are often cynical; e.g., Gerry Spence, in *From Freedom to Slavery*, provides a thoughtful critique of how the judiciary has become a new tyranny of the corporate kingdoms.

New lawyers believe the half-truths about neutrality and governance by rule of law. Impartiality is usually true as to the parties of a particular dispute, but the institution that empowers judges favors the status quo and the entities that breathe money. Seasoned lawyers assume that political values will dictate the

---

[4] See, *Stockett v. Tolin*, 791 F. Supp. 1536 (S.D. Fla. 1992) (a million dollars in punitive damages for individual liability) and the more typical case in *Rosenbloom v. Figare*, 501 N.W. 2d 597, 602 (Minn. 1995) (Jury award of almost two years pay, but reduced to one year).

outcome—either indirectly based on the source of judge's appointment or more directly through the social-political values of the judge.

Both extremes forget that judges are human beings. In *Courts on Trial*, Appellate Judge Jerome Frank noted that a judge makes decisions just like the rest of us. They are influenced by the factors of who I am, how I see myself, how I see others, how I want others to see me, how heavy my workload is, what I ate for dinner, whether my spouse and I had a heated argument and whether my income will provide the economic security I want. These influences are disguised by the articulation of precedent, but they have real impact in the selection of precedent.

The underlying values of the judge are often more important than the concept called precedent. Precedent, by itself, does not dictate outcomes. It is the judge who decides *which* precedent applies and the judge's personal values influence this decision. In addition, a judge's workload influences decisions of which facts and which laws have priority. The workload factor and the use of summary judgment to deflect trial and deter future lawsuits remains a hot issue for employment lawyers.

JUDICIAL HOSTILITY TO EMPLOYEE LAWSUITS

Many plaintiff attorneys believe that judges, in particular federal judges, manifest outward hostility to employee lawsuits. This belief may have some validity, but it often misses the competing causes. As recently as 1980, employment cases made up 2 percent of the federal caseload. In 1998, employment cases were approximately 35 percent of the docket. Thus, employment disputes have now caught up with commercial disputes. Judges often overlook the fact that commercial disputes have consistently dominated the time of federal courts for decades. Either those commercial disputes have taken on an importance akin to constitutional issues or judges simply prefer the sterility of business disputes over the social dynamics of employee disputes.

At the same time, one recent difference is that civil rights cases (primarily employment cases) accounted for 48 percent of the increase in work, according to the 1999 *Report of the Judiciary*. The enormous increase in case filing has greatly increased the number of decisions to read and write. It has dramatically slowed the decision-making rate. Moreover, employment suits are labor intensive for the judge as well as the lawyer. If the measure of caseload is the amount of time spent on cases, rather than the number of case filings, the proportion of employment suits would probably be even higher.

We all know that summary judgment motions are rare in personal injury disputes, but essentially automatic in employment lawsuits and commercial disputes. Case proliferation at trial is also reflected in a huge increase of appellate decisions. These decisions have had a geometric effect on trial court judges who try to be diligent—the number of appellate decisions to read has quadrupled.

Society has decreed that employment lawsuits are important, and employees filing suit are fulfilling this societal value. Thus, judges need to respect employment lawsuits as equally important as commercial cases. However, this respect is unlikely to occur until society puts up more money to keep the workload manageable. As employment lawyers, we need to keep the limited resources in mind and lobby for more judges.

"Precedent" Selection is Not Automatic–Choices are Made

At summary judgment, the judge is the primary audience. Based on written summaries of the evidence, the judge will determine which facts are material and whether the plaintiff has enough of the right kind of facts to create a genuine issue. In theory, precedent will dictate what type of facts are material. In reality, the problem is the multiplicity of competing precedents. Decisions vary widely on the way different elements are measured. In reality, the judge has tremendous discretion in picking precedent and in determining which type of facts are deemed material. Occasionally, both sides offer the same major case as controlling, but more often the precedents are competing. Most commonly, the dispute is on *sub-issues* that then dictate the ultimate outcome.

With the plethora of precedent, the judge's attitude toward precedent will be a major factor in the selection. Many worship precedent as if there is no alternative, but others realize that the selection of precedent is as important as the precedent itself. In deciding which cases are most similar to the case at hand, the judge has huge discretion. Only rarely is there a higher court case directly on point. If the trial court is able to narrow the dispute to a single issue or single element, the court has much greater autonomy in the selection of precedent. Ome judge may see a case as automatically applicable, but another may look for exceptions to distinguish that "precedent."

The judge's past decisions are the best indicator of the attitude toward precedent. LEXIS provides ready access to published decisions by most federal judges. In addition, decisions of many trial court judges can be found indirectly through state appellate court decisions in LEXIS. A search that mentions the last name of the judge in the text will usually yield good results. If not, broaden your search to employment issues generally or check for reversals. Scrutiny of these decisions will reveal the attitude of the trial court.

Study the judge's published opinions and ask yourself, "Does the judge, or the clerks at his direction, take the time to distinguish decisions of higher courts or does s/he treat them as if automatic applications?" Judges who are willing to take the time to analyze the exceptions and address the distinctions of other courts are usually more willing to be educated by you. The opposite type of judge, who simply accepts the major cases as if carte blanche decrees, acts without thought. This judge is a major obstacle.

When looking at a judge's prior decisions, it is necessary to look beneath the surface of which side won. The method of reasoning and the values hidden between the lines are more useful than the outcome. There is no need to obsess about the merits–rather, *pay attention to what's left out* and the method of rationalizing the decision-making. If it's heavy on citations, the judge probably favors easy precedent. If it's light on citations, s/he probably favors concepts of 'felt justice.' [But it may also mean s/he is just lazy.] Arguments should be shaped by these values.

Moreover, precedent is constantly changing. As Dean Hines of the University of Iowa College of Law said in 1980, "Half of what you learned in law school is obsolete. That's the good news. The bad news is we don't know which half."

During briefing and oral argument, it is always an advantage to be up-to-date on the law. Only the foolhardy assumes the law is what it always has been. The law as a whole is stable, but without question, its pieces are dynamic and full of change. Preparation for briefing and oral argument should always include checking for recent decisions. They usually have more appeal to a judge than the older ones.

Some Federal judges, like Mark Bennett of the Northern District of Iowa, do an exceptional job of identifying the factual points of view of both the plaintiff and the defendant.[5] Then, before he applies the law, he explains how and why he reaches his decisions on which facts to believe and accept. If more judges adopted a similar approach, lawyers would have a greater ability to understand the outcomes and law might regain its predictive role. This would help employers and employees to have greater sense of certainty about issues and reduce the number of disputes requiring decisions by judges.

---

[5] Delashmutt v. Wis-Pak, 990 F. Supp. 689 (N.D. IA. 1998)

Deeply-held Values are More Influential than Precedent

The values held by individual judges vary widely, but the institution dictates a particular mind-set. The preservation of the status quo is inherent in their role and shapes their set of values. They are generally pro-establishment because it already has the power to preserve the status quo. The deeply held personal values of individual judges can, however, run counter to the status quo. It is self-destructive to indulge in the presumption that most judges are unfair or biased. Some judges are biased against employees, but more commonly we use this excuse to avoid responsibility for the judgments we ourselves made in selecting, developing and presenting the case.

The benefits of learning about the judge's deeper values are crucial. Begin by letting go of your assumptions about the judge that are based on rumor and folklore. For example, if you believe a judge is conservative, you can either spend time bemoaning his favoritism of employers or you can go deeper and recognize that old-fashioned conservatives often believe in rugged individualism. Don't confuse old-fashioned conservatives with the modern moralistic conservatives who impose their values on others. Read Ayn Rand's novels, *Atlas Shrugged* and *Fountainhead* to explore how this traditional conservative philosophy reflects a value that decisions should be based on merit more than favoritism. These judges respect fairplay over the politics of favoritism. They will resent blatant unfairness in decisions by the employer and disapprove of punishment in the face of good performance, if it is reasonably visible and clear-cut. You cannot build on those underlying values, however, until you recognize them.

To discover a judge's underlying values, consider the following questions:

- ❖ Does this judge focus on details or on the big picture?
- ❖ Does s/he present a conclusion as if it was the only logical outcome?
- ❖ Does s/he present both points of view and demonstrate how s/he reconciled these points of view?
- ❖ Is the judge like the classic "Show me. I'm from Missouri" or the modern "Show me the Money" agent who wants to see only the hard facts, not the conclusions of the lawyer or the empty theories of an advocate?

You should repeatedly ask yourself what *underlying* values appear important to this judge. This issue does not refer to the outcomes nor does it refer to simplistic categories: pro-employer, pro-employee. Rather, you must search deeper; e.g., explore a judge's attitude toward individuals, toward government, bigness, fairness, elitism, and punishing wrongdoers. Hostility to regulations often reflects valuing the freedom to experiment and an unofficial endorsement of the rebel attitude, but it can also be laissez faire. Pro-government attitudes often reflect an emphasis on order and stability and valuing attempts to control autonomy of corporations as well as individuals. Pro-individual often means respect for merit as the factor in decision-making. Conservative commonly means conserving the status quo, but it also has been synonymous with respect for individual freedom.

Style of Decision-making

Judges who focus on the big picture tend to be favorable to plaintiffs and use analysis to do justice. Judges who dance on the head of a needle tend to favor the status quo. They use analysis to resist all challenges to status quo, with the frequent effect of depriving plaintiff of their day in court.

Most judges are hard working. Many lawyers are surprised when a judge is a perfectionist and intolerant of lawyers who are disorganized in their writing or thinking. Many judges are irritated at lawyers who don't proofread their briefs, but others are irked if a corrected copy is submitted. A few judges are easy going with time; others are ultra time-conscious and they despise lawyers who are late for arguments or with submissions. In their world, they are the most important persons—just like us in our world. It is wise to check a judge's general speed of decision making. You can plan motions accordingly without screwing up discovery or wait indefinitely.

Courtroom Arguments

In terms of their courtroom personality, most judges fall within the bell-shaped curve—most are normal, some are better or worse than the norm and a few are deviants. Awareness of this courtroom persona is important as you prepare for oral arguments and trial. Some judges will intimidate or are lazy, but these are a few standard deviations from the norm. Some of the intimidators expect strong lawyers to resist, but it must be done skillfully. They will not respect you if you simply submit.

The personality spectrum ranges from judges who dominate the courtroom to those who are afraid of alienating anyone. Some are exceedingly strong-willed and others passive. A few demonstrate passion, but most display the appearance of calm. They all act as if decisions are deliberative, but many privately admit that an initial decision was made on a visceral basis and later adjusted by the use or influence of precedent.

Reflections of Society

Many judges reflect the times, albeit belatedly. In *Cycles of American History*, Arthur Schlesinger provides an eye-opening description of the cycles influencing decision-makers in politics. He suggests that first we are dominated by decisions protecting the public interest, then the emphasis switches to decisions favoring the private interest. He describes the transitions as 30-year cycles. He also notes different, but overlapping, cycles where experimentation is endorsed contrasted with periods where a manifest destiny is the dominant mindset. These cycles are extensions of the view of our greatest pragmatist judge, Oliver Wendell Holmes Jr., who said "The life of the law has not been logic…it is the 'felt experience' of our times."

EXAMINE A JUDGE'S PHILOSOPHY

The 'felt experience' is interwoven with the philosophy of a judge toward employees. Few of us are conscious of our philosophy, but it permeates our thinking. Philosophy and logic should not be confused. Logic is a method of reasoning, while philosophy is a systematic view of the world or a theory of knowledge. One reason to examine the philosophy of a judge is to grasp his or her world view. When you recognize the philosophies that are reflected in the decisions of a particular judge, you know better what will appeal to this judge and what arguments will be a waste of time. The judge's philosophy becomes an anchor. Your facts, while differentiated from that anchor, are tied to it. If your argument derives from a wholly different philosophy, the judge won't be able to recognize your point of view or even hear what you are really saying. Your success depends on your ability to focus on the types of arguments that appeal to this judge—arguments that make sense according to his values.

Most judges have been employers at some time and have formed a philosophy about employees in general. They may consider their own employees (current hard-working clerks) to be examples of or an exception to the rules that form their philosophy. These philosophies reflect their underlying values. They are often hidden influences that secretly shape many of their interim decisions. For example, it is a crucial interim decision whether facts are framed as a credibility question and therefore a jury issue or whether the materiality of non-materiality of the same facts is the issue. The latter characterization renders the facts amendable to resolution by the judge on summary judgment. The judge resolves this competing characterization by his or her philosophy or the sense shared in common with others.

I examined hundreds of judicial opinions and have identified two distinctive philosophies about employees. They illustrated by the following table:

Employees are hardworking and trustworthy	Employees are lazy and untrustworthy,
Employees are loyal and dedicated	Employees take advantage of employers, with sick leave, breaks...
Fear inhibits productivity	Fear is necessary for productivity
Employees seek meaning in life through work	Employees work to get money
Minimal supervision is necessary	Constant supervision is mandatory
Rewards motivate	Punishment motivates
Performance Appraisals are good measures	Performance Appraisals are not reliable
Reluctance to complain shows understandable concerns about disrupting the team	Reluctance to complain shows consent or welcomeness
Quitting may be the only survival response	Quitting is self-interest, rarely coerced
Employees serve larger interests	Employees serve only their self-interests
Honesty and genuine concern motivates whistleblowing	Whiners, fabricators and exaggerators—creating injuries after the fact, or exaggerate injuries and lie about injuries
Dignity and respect are important	Obedience and compliance are gospel
Reflected in opinions of J. Brennan J. Richey, J. Weinstein, J. Carrigan J. Bennett	Reflected in opinions of J. Rhenquist, J. Scalia, J. Manion, J. Devitt

These basic philosophies are powerful anchors. When you add cumulative experiences with a judge, you will have insight about their values. Remember, judges were all lawyers once. Now they have power, but they often feel isolated and out of the loop. Instead of being disturbed by a judge's rambling stories, listen for their deeper values, noticing what this story reveals about what is important to this judge.

Keeping a Book on Judges

A book on judges is a wonderful tool. Fill it with anecdotes from other lawyer's experience as well as biographical details from the announcements of their appointment. Local law libraries frequently compile background information, but it is invariably one-sided praise. You must gather the war stories on your own, but there is no need to be exhaustive—just enough to be useful.

Attend the Judge's Socials

You can usually get others to introduce you to judges. It humanizes them. You might only talk to two or three at each social, but that gives you a slight benefit of familiarity at the next visit to their courtroom. Even if you do not have a meaningful conversation, it helps to neutralize the opponents who are clustering like hawks. As the years accumulate, you'll know more judges and your confidence will grow.

Personal Attention

Instead of sending a law clerk to file courtesy copies of briefs with the judge, consider doing it yourself. It often gives an opportunity to bump into the judge and maybe chat about things—never the case you have together, but just a little informal bonding. It works best if you know the judge or have already had a trial or at least a motion with him or her. If their decision helped settle a previous case, there is nothing wrong with telling them. They get precious little feedback or encouragement.

> Stereotypes of judges are as misleading as stereotypes of clients. You don't want your clients to be stereotyped. You don't want to be stereotyped. So, why stereotype judges? We are tempted to believe that our point of view reflects reality, but is this any different than defendants who justify their beliefs about race or sex or persons with disabilities? Judges are individuals too.

COMMUNICATING WITH JURIES

"A jury consists of twelve persons chosen to decide who has the better lawyer."

Mark Twain, misquoting Balzac

At trial, the most important audience is the jury. It is not the only audience, because the judge and the appeals court are in the background, but he focus must be on the jury, with the judge as a secondary audience. The jury's presence will dictate most of the issues related to evidence and objections. The jury's need for order and comprehension should dictate the style and length of your opening statement, the order of witnesses and the style of cross-examination. If discovery is planned for the eyes of the jury, you will have wonderful blow-up exhibits; e.g., interrogatories in the words of laymen.

One of the best books ever written about communicating with juries is, *Courtroom Communication Skills* by Smith and Malandro. [Other topics covered by this and other similar books are beyond the scope of this book; e.g., Voir dire as the "first opening statement," embedding arguments within your opening statements, consideration of mock juries and hiring consultants.]

In recent years, one new method of jury selection has found favor with many plaintiff attorneys. This method uses the personality of potential jurors to predict how they will lean at the time of voting. This contrasts with the usual stereotypes based on occupation or lifestyle or political viewpoint or instinct guiding voir dire strikes by response of the hair on the back of the neck. Personality typing based on measures of how individuals process and evaluate information provides far more reliable predictors of juror's values and ultimate voting patterns than the traditional approaches. Personality typing is, therefore, an extraordinarily valuable tool when you are constructing questions for potential jurors.

As mentioned earlier, juror profilists Paul D. Tieger and Carolyn Koch have adapted Jungian theories of personality types to juries. Using a similar system will help you gather solid information to more accurately predict values and therefore, decision patterns. This is not simply happenstance or a variation in intuitive approaches.

This method is extremely useful and has been credited as helpful in several highly successful lawsuits by NELA members. For example, Neil Mullin used personality typing to select jurors and won a $7.0 million dollar verdict for a whistleblower in 1995; *Mehlman v. Mobil Oil*, 707 A. 2d 10000 (N.J. 1998) (affirmed). More recently, Nancy Erika Smith used similar jury selection methods in *Kesler v. WWOR TV* to achieve similar success. It involves a sophisticated method of evaluating personality types based on the answers received to carefully planned questions. Evaluating a juror's personality type helps you predict the type of evidence that will have the greatest impact on that juror. Most lawyers hire someone with substantial experience in assessing the temperament as a way to tap into a juror's values. There are many professional organizations available, and the quality and costs vary widely.

With a system of personality typing, you analyze potential jurors in terms of four decision-making approaches:

- ❖ Traditionalists
- ❖ Experiencers
- ❖ Conceptualizers
- ❖ Idealists.

TRADITIONALISTS

Traditionalists make up about 38 percent of the population in the United States. This group relies on sensory input and uses rules to make decisions. A traditionalist values closure and wants no loose ends. Traditionalists have predispositions to:

- ❖ Believe and trust authority
- ❖ Want to do the right thing and do their duty
- ❖ Value rules; law and order
- ❖ Take things at face value and focus on the present
- ❖ Be thorough, pay close attention to facts and details
- ❖ Be cautious, careful, and conservative
- ❖ Have a strong sense of right and wrong
- ❖ Be responsible and dislike disobedience.

EXPERIENCERS

Experiencers make up about 38 percent of the population in the United States. This group values sensory input to make decisions, but they are comfortable with experimentation and open-ended situations. Closure is not highly valued—they go with the flow. Experiencers have predispositions to:

- ❖ Distrust and be unimpressed by authority
- ❖ Seek excitement and adventure and take risks
- ❖ Be expedient and use an economy of motion
- ❖ Prefer "hands on" learning and are easily bored by sedentary activities
- ❖ Be keen observers, realistic and pragmatic
- ❖ Value spontaneity and freedom to act
- ❖ Be skillful trouble-shooters and handle crisis well
- ❖ Seek to have fun at whatever they're doing.

Conceptualizers

Conceptualizers make up only 12 percent of the population in the United States. This group cherishes thought, independence, the big picture and the "feel" of things as a way to make decisions. They naturally look for the meaning and motives, but they are skeptics who need to be satisfied that the evidence makes sense on a logical level. Conceptualizers have predispositions to:

❖ Think conceptually
❖ Think independently
❖ Set their own standards
❖ Value intelligence, insight, fairness and justice
❖ Read between the lines and see implications and complexities
❖ Be a nonconformist
❖ Look for the meaning and motives
❖ Respect and admire competence above all else
❖ Have a long attention span
❖ Be logical and objective
❖ Be skeptical.

Idealists

Idealists make up the remaining 12 percent of the population in the United States. This group cherishes feelings and cooperation. They tend to be anti-authority and respect uniqueness. They naturally look for motives, but they are idealists who need to be satisfied that the evidence makes appeals on a moral level—whether it favors a mistreated employee or an employer getting rid of a bad employee. Idealists have predispositions to:

❖ Focus on people's feelings and be empathetic
❖ Seek harmony and cooperation
❖ Be idealistic
❖ Admire uniqueness and individuality
❖ Be perceptive about others' motivations
❖ Be non-traditional and possibly anti-establishment
❖ Focus on the future, rather than the present or past
❖ Infer meaning from actions and read between the lines
❖ Decide based upon their feelings and values.

Awareness of how potential jurors make decisions and place value on the types of evidence is useful. Remember the basic principle that when you tailor your communications to a specific audience, your effectiveness is dramatically enhanced.

COMMUNICATING WITH APPELLATE JUDGES

The higher and the highest court of each state (or the federal circuits) are involved in proportionately fewer cases than the trial judge, but as an audience they are ever-present. Appellate judges are more policy oriented than trial judges, partly because they are unavoidably declaring policy through their issue-oriented thinking. A major problem is created by their presentation of facts. They generally fail to explain the competing facts and give the impression that there is only one version. Thus, it makes it look as though the outcome was a foregone conclusion. The underbelly of the conflict driving this case to appeal is thus hidden from the reader's eye. This deprives us of the necessary information to make their decision predictive for other cases.

Many lawyers view a lower appellate court as only "error correcting," but this is only half true. In the process of focusing on sub-issues, appellate courts often make decisions that so strongly favor one point of view that the ruling is effectively a policy decision. More commonly, they decide policy when they identify the adequacy or inadequacy of evidence to satisfy the elements of a cause of actions. When they make simple changes in the burden of proof, articulate new presumptions or resurrect old ones, they are making and endorsing policy.

During litigation, you may not know the panel that will be assigned, but you must know that Big Brother is watching. Trial mistakes can be avoided or minimized if you remain conscious of what the appeals court is doing, especially when similar issues are pending.

One Minneapolis lawyer had a $2 million verdict taken away because he didn't notice, during trial, that the judge had been affirmed in another case on the same evidentiary issue. The issue was whether the judge should decide if a statement was privileged *before* it went to the jury or if it was permissible to wait until *after* verdict. The odd procedure adopted by the trial court could have been neutralized if counsel had emphasized common law malice. The lawyer's failure to notice the appellate decision resulted in his omission of the only solution.

In preparing appellate arguments, the same analysis and LEXIS strategy used with trial judges should be employed to examine the panelists' decisions and discern their underlying values. Their writings reflect their philosophy. Another method is to take the time to imagine that you are one of the appellate judges—stand in their shoes. Imagine you are making this decision. You can *feel* the issues in a different way and you can predict many, if not most, of the questions raised by the appellate panel. Once you appreciate where appellate judges are coming from, you are able to adapt your arguments accordingly.

Chapter Four

REVERSING INERTIA

> ## PRINCIPLE
> People maintain their original point of view until mental inertia is reversed.

D ecisions are almost always made in a context. We do what we have to do in the circumstances. This shapes our original point of view. Gradually, we convince ourselves that the decision was necessary or the best for all concerned. Then we justify our decision as the right thing to do by rationalizing any conflicting information. This process exemplifies the force of inertia—it keeps us moving in the same direction.

This force of inertia is not unique to corporate decision-makers: our clients do it, we do it. We all tend to rewrite history to make it fit with our perception of ourselves. Some do it more than others and a few do it more emphatically.

After a termination, inertia often causes the employee to run-in-place or even stagnate. At the same time, inertia is propelling the employer away from the employee and in the opposite direction. Reversing inertia is a necessary first step in making the employer thirsty to settle. It concentrates attention on issues of liability (who is to blame), while its companion, momentum, centers on damages.

Once the adverse action occurs, the status quo, by its nature, tends to perpetuate itself. Until you reverse the force of inertia, no one will pay attention and nothing will happen. Once you reverse the inertia, you begin creating a reason for exploring settlement—someone may be at fault, the employer may be to blame. This awakening enables the creation of momentum toward damages.

REVERSING INERTIA IS A SHIFT IN VIEWPOINT
Until something starts the re-education, the status quo will persist. Once inertia begins to be reversed, certain cognitive shifts begin to occur in the humans who run a corporation.

Mental Inertia

At the time the initial decision to fire an employee is made, the decision-maker believes that s/he is doing what is appropriate under the circumstances. They tell themselves things like, *"I fired her because she didn't perform. I gave her a chance to improve. I did what I had to do."* They begin to believe that they did what they 'had to do' was really necessary. By the time someone sues them, decision-makers have extended this logic and convinced themselves that they did the right thing. Once his or her mind is locked in, they rationalize all known information to justify their actions. This phenomena is what makes "pretext" a workable method of analysis.

You can't reverse inertia until you create an alternative point of view. The alternative scenario must be more believable than the rationalized position. The alternative scenario should be most directed to a higher level decision-maker whom is not tainted by the individual's rationalization process. These higher ups are affected by the institutional needs and factors like morale of managers may propel them to support the decision-maker, but they do not experience the psychological investment. They have an easier time envisioning your alternative. If the alternative appears more costly to resist than the status quo, your position is enhanced.

You cannot begin the process until you can clearly see the other person's point of view and then its gaps and defects in common sense or logic. Once inertia begins to be reversed, certain cognitive shifts begin to occur in the humans who run a corporation. As the litigation or negotiation moves through time, cognitive shifts evolve as summarized in the pattern of changes set forth below:

"We are certain that we're right" becomes →

"We are confident we can win" which becomes →

"We have a few doubts about minor things" which evolves into →

"We have doubts about important things" which becomes →

"We have uncertainty about who will win."

"We are afraid of losing" (near trial)

The original conviction that "we're right" derives from reactions to being challenged. These reactions include anger, righteousness and denial, all of which may be hiding their fear of getting caught. By the time an employer reduces their conviction to a mere confidence that they will win because they have more money, better witnesses and more aggressive lawyers, they are already starting to reverse their inertia. When they begin admitting some little doubts or minor contradictions, they are either objective, unusually honest or beginning to feel cognitive dissonance. By the time they are discussing issues in terms of fact questions, and facing doubts are on bigger issues, they are conceding the risk and weighing the costs of trial. When documents or witnesses further establish the contradictions, they reach the point of uncertainty about who will win.

At this point, they become eager to negotiate. This eagerness is magnified when they lose a motion; e.g., the denial of summary judgment. At this point, the employer begins to doubt the judgment of its attorney. The attorney was wrong about getting the case tossed out and it was a costly error. The defense lawyer who blames an unpredictable judge or changes in the law does not pacify the employer. At this stage, you are in an excellent negotiating position.

Accelerating these cognitive shifts

Vigorous efforts at early settlement accelerates these cognitive shifts. Your goal is to create uncertainty in the employer. It is not necessary to convince them that you will win big or even that you will win. You need **only** to weaken their sense of certainty that they will win.

STRATEGIES THAT CAUSE COGNITIVE SHIFTS

There are five primary methods for causing cognitive shifts: creating plausible alternative explanations on the same facts, bringing new or unknown facts to the surface, exposing contradictions, hinting at relevant skeletons or shifting the focus from the employee's status to the employer's misconduct.

ALTERNATIVE EXPLANATIONS ON THE SAME FACTS

You can't begin to reverse inertia until something grabs your opponent's attention. You must instill a reason to start the re-examination process that will overcome the very human belief that "our decision was justified." Before employers are interested in paying the plaintiff real money, you must educate them about an alternative that plausibly explains the same facts but legally places enough blame on their shoulders. The CEO probably hasn't seen the big picture nor even had a basic awareness of the sequence of prior events. The person who initiated the decision to fire the employee and obtained approval from HR commonly conceals his or her true motives.

Once you establish that the alternative might be more costly than the status quo, you generate momentum. A carefully worded complaint grabs attention and suggests the costs to come. The effective complaint initiates change in the corporate point of view. As suggested above, finding someone in the hierarchy higher than the original decision-maker is a key factor. A higher-up is more amenable to recognizing someone else's error. If a subordinate can be blamed for a mistake in judgment, your task is simpler.

Initially, the employer assumed they had no real choice. Sooner or later, they start to face the question, "Is there really another explanation of our motive?" At this point, the fear of getting caught becomes real. In fairness, the CEO may not have anticipated the effects when he signed off on the subordinate's decision. S/he may not have known what 'scoundrels' were working for him or her. Psychological guilt rarely exists at the top of the decision-making ranks. You can, however, create *a guilt about getting caught* with their proverbial pants down–the equivalent of a societal arrest for indecent exposure.

BRINGING NEW OR UNKNOWN FACTS TO LIFE

Often it is not bias, but ignorance, that has ratified a subordinate's decision. Investigation that examines a series of decisions often generates evidence of a pattern not previously recognized. Your power often derives from comparisons or contrasts that magnify the exposure of similarities or differences in treatment. You wake up the otherwise passive process that isolates each decision unto itself. If you are able to identify new facts unknown and bring corporate decision-makers to a heightened awareness by providing supporting witness statements or documents, you will often find an audience willing to reconsider its position. Your presentation must be coherently organized. Facts, not sympathy, have power. These unknown facts, if pertinent, can imbue any legal package (i.e., a cause of action) with real clout. The closer the fit, the more life is given. By digging deeply into a wide range of witnesses, you often uncover volumes of memory and documents that expand the fragments of facts provided by your client. These archeological finds help reverse the inertia which has favored the status quo.

EXPOSING CONTRADICTIONS

When you scrutinize their documents, you are bringing a unique point of view to bear on the contents. This will often surface insights that were unnoticed or expressions of unconscious hostility. One client showed me her termination notice. It contained nine reasons for termination. Any one of the reasons would have been sufficient cause to terminate. The question became why so many? The incidents were spread out over time and lent themselves to arguments of condonation. More importantly, the sheer quantity raised the issue of whether they evidenced hostility and an attempt at intimidation. The contradiction became obvious to a higher up, whom was not involved in the original termination.

Other times, the presence of two sets of documents will begin the reversal of inertia. If they can't be plausibly reconciled, the original explanation is suspect and your alternative explanation becomes more reasonable. This approach is the essence of the pretext approach in discrimination, whistleblower, retaliation and even free speech cases.

SHIFT FOCUS FROM MOTIVE TO EMPLOYER BEHAVIOR

In the typical ADA case, the common perception of disability is focused on the "defect" of the employees. The major fight is over protected status, then it progresses to the employer's stereotypes or unthinking behavior. Another method is to shift the focus away from the employee's protected status and place it squarely on the employer's more general conduct. For example, if the underlying problem that aggravated the employee's depression was extreme stress, the focus may be shifted to the employer's habit of understaffing. The common law imposed a duty on employers to provide a sufficient number of employees to perform the work at hand. If understaffing caused employees to be overworked and overwhelmed, there may be a claim in negligent supervision. Be sure that you analyze carefully all the issues and distinguish Workers Compensation claims.

The oddity of this approach forces defense lawyers to appreciate that you may be attempting to create precedent. It causes the employer alarm by your presentation of a "cause" case that may impact its larger workforce. This is a costly proposition to employers. If they believe this is a genuine "cause" case, their fears will magnify the value of settlement.

HINTING AT RELEVANT SKELETONS

Laymen sometimes view a lawyer's role in a distorted fashion. For example, Sol Stein, American publisher and writer, has declared, "A lawyer's job is to manipulate skeletons in other people's closet." While this may be one of the effects of what lawyers sometimes do, it should not be a tactic. It may be viewed as extortion. Unless the skeleton relates to a situation where a whistle was blown or your client engaged in a refusal to participate in an illegal action, using skeletons is a very dangerous tactic. If it relates to whistleblowing or refusals to violate a law, it may be fair game.

Alternatively, if the skeletons plausibly explain a plaintiff's fear of coming forward or going public, they should be recognized as a backdrop for retaliation. Extreme caution must be exercised. Even though the employer created the skeleton, mentioning it may appear as "extortion" and expose you or your client to revenge, Rule 11, or even counterclaims. Even if the employer has a desire to cover it up, you are playing with fire.

TACTIC TO START REVERSAL OF INERTIA

This principle can be implemented by a strategy of initiating communication on liability (who is to blame) in an early settlement overture. The actual tactics are a terse cover letter and draft complaint.

1) Sending a "friendly," business-like overture to the CEO.

   The first communication to the CEO is often pivotal. It is the only time you get to communicate directly to the CEO, without the intervening eye of counsel. If the tone is business-like, it gains credibility. It starts by planting doubt about decisions and the candor of subordinates. No one will admit it to you, but the skepticism starts. If the subordinate manager had handled it properly, no lawyer would be writing letters to the CEO. A detailed elaboration must accompany the letter and explain the reason why a lawsuit may happen and may have clout.

2) A thoughtful complaint should accompany the cover letter.

   The meta-message of an accompanying complaint is that a lawyer cared enough to invest time and effort in this matter. If it is cogently written for this employer-audience, it will have an impact. The document must have 'grab' appeal, but if it has blatant factual errors or obvious gaps, it will be discounted and impede settlement.

CLARITY ACCELERATES REVERSING INERTIA

More than any single fact, clarity is a powerful catalyst. Sometimes, clear concise communication is the equivalent of being hit by a 2 x 4 piece of wood. It wakes people up. It's like the light on the Road to Damascus. Making your point argumentatively is secondary to being clear in explaining the big picture. Your task is to reverse inertia and the audience must understand what you are saying.

Your initial communication anticipates the employer's real weaknesses, but your crispness will cause employer to pause. If you make the hot points visible, it will unsettle them. If you are able to see beyond your client's needs and see clearly the needs of your opponents, the optimum position will be established. Nonetheless, it is pragmatic to pause and sort through various scenarios.

Anticipating the Worst

Breaking inertia is your goal, but there is no certainty about which direction the employer will move. They may be conciliatory or hostile. The employer's prior pattern of responses to this employee as well as responses to other lawsuits can offer guidance, but neither can completely predict the response to the new perspective offered by the draft lawsuit. Once dormant issues have been awakened, the corporate response may be shaped by a corporate mood disorder. Like managers, the legal fiction called a corporation seems to have its own moods, which are typically dormant until some action stirs them up. But, once in motion, the moods tend to keep changing. Often the first reaction to the imminent lawsuit is shock. Then, there are feelings of betrayal. Other folks start with psychological denial. Abruptly, this mood can also turn to anger. If this anger turns to rage, it can manifest as intimidation, retaliation or scorched earth tactics. This possibility makes the skeleton approach a high stakes game and retaliation a major risk. On the other hand, the uncertainty approach can create a state limited to worry about costs, exposure, or losing, which may inhibit the rage stage.

Another possibility to consider is that the corporate repercussions may focus on short-term goals. Strategies and tactics for responding to these goals are provided in the following table:

SHORT-TERM GOALS OF DEFENDANT	COUNTER STRATEGY AND TACTICS
Avoid suit because of costs	Emphasize costs
Kill the messenger who's blowing the whistle	Bolster client for counterattack; use Judo reversals on their aggression. Seek TRO's; go public
Deter suits by other employees	Move Quietly
Avoid uncertainty of winning	Show survival of Summary Judgment.
Avoid embarrassment or exposure	Hint at desire to avoid "adverse" publicity
Fight to show support of management	Divide and conquer. "Assume" CEO didn't know approach/style of manager.
Avoid negative in-house morale	Emphasize many depo's/supporters
Avoid deposition/testimony of CEO	Depose but not too early. CEOs hate to "waste" their precious time but they often contradict testimony of others
Fear of regulatory effects	Hints of publicity
Hide internal investigation which confirmed misconduct	Dig deep. Depose investigators
Crucify s/he who challenges	Batten down the hatches Full steam ahead. Judo tactics

The employer's response is unpredictable, but once you have achieved your goal of reversing inertia, you focus your attention on building momentum that will ultimately determine the purchase price of settlement.

Chapter Five

MOMENTUM MAGNIFIES PURCHASE PRICE

PRINCIPLE
Momentum magnifies purchase price and accelerates settlement.

Inertia relates to the issue of liability, but momentum relates to damages. The opportunity to use momentum is ignited when inertia is reversed. "People buy on emotion and justify it with facts," as Bert Becker declares in *You've Got to Be Believed to Be Heard*. Like the rest of us, employers make decisions based on emotion and then justify it with facts. Momentum drives value. The strategies of momentum include both short-term and longer term approaches to damages.

Employers must unlearn the notion that emotional distress claims are worth less than economic claims. Until you show them the power of emotional facts, they will remain blind. It is our responsibility to portray solid evidence of emotional injury and causation. This allows momentum to enhance value.

MOMENTUM IS A PROCESS

The principles of chaos theory enable lawyers to appreciate the forces at hand. Chaos theory is the science of process, as opposed to product. It assumes things are not fixed, but ever changing. Damages are not like the proverbial light switch which is either on or off. They are more like a dimmer light switch that is dimmer or brighter depending on how it is gauged. Damages occur along a continuum.

Chaos theory is the knowledge of *what is becoming*, not what is. It is not based on what has been or will remain, but on what is unfolding. By participating in the process of assessing damages, you make them something other than they were. If you are too lazy to dig and marshal the damage facts, the claim becomes fragile. If you cavalierly assume the employer *should* know the same facts you know, the value of damages is diminished. Damages will become strong only if you invest the effort to ferret out the damage facts. Then, and only then, can the education begin.

On the one side, the employee is suffering and this creates an urgency to act. You can either build from existing data or acknowledge the momentum created by uncertainty in suffering. You can ignore their damages and let them unfold au natural or you can watch the process and enhance the value by giving them means of expression. On the other side is the employer's eagerness to have a price tag placed on the employee's suffering. This interest does not occur until a state of uncertainty on liability is reached. Then, the changes in momentum occur. They evidence a progression in willingness to consider the impact on the employee. The changes in momentum are summarized in the following chart:

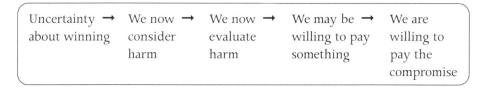

Uncertainty → about winning	We now → consider harm	We now → evaluate harm	We may be → willing to pay something	We are willing to pay the compromise

In hindsight, patterns of cause and effect (i.e., damages) frequently look obvious to clients. He or she believes that the employer caused the injury and often all their injuries then pending. You are skeptical, but optimistic. By the time of negotiation or deposition, the cause and effect connection often feels weaker than at the outset. The way cause and effect is presented in negotiations or deposition is one thing, but more important is the evolution of cause and effect patterns. *The secret is to detect the real patterns early*. It is even more powerful to detect them while they are still in the process of taking shape. For example, you can help your client find a vocabulary for complex feelings and their causal connections with past events. This effort unavoidably influences the descriptions, but in an ethical manner. We are not talking about suborning perjury or fabrication of evidence. We refer to helping employees package emotional facts in persuasive ways. This is useful for you in negotiation. It is critical before deposition when the defense counsel often uses simple-minded questions about damages, but the questions confuse and deceive the plaintiff.

Identifying cause and effect relationships also refers to the discovery of plausible patterns to explain events before an employer coaxes witnesses into misremembering or forgetting. Few people will lie to protect others, but evaporating memories are commonplace. The only means of achieving this goal is to lock in the witnesses with statements handwritten, tape-recorded or typed.

Staging the Momentum

> There is a tide in the affairs of men.
> If caught as the flood begins, you can ride the crest.

On occasion, intrigue can be used to create momentum simultaneous with reversing inertia. Small steps, rapidly followed by bigger steps, builds greater momentum, particularly against an individual in a power position. The following sequence of tactics has been used successfully in sexual harassment cases against executives:

1. Witnesses were interviewed about related facts and statements were obtained. They were asked to keep the request for information confidential.
2. Later, information was consciously leaked to a snitch, who immediately passed on rumors that "lawyer is asking questions about Mr. X."
3. Mr. X checked with employees and found that the lawyer already had been there and been thorough. A small panic ensued.
4. Next, the executive's secretary was called and asked for the executive's home address to mail a confidential letter. Naturally, she refused.
5. The next business day a cover letter and draft complaint was delivered to the executive's office.

The substance of the claim arose from the facts of a sexual assault. The tip offs created an anticipation that magnified the executive's fears of getting caught. The panic generated by staging of the delivery accelerated the appetite for settlement. It resulted in a settlement of 51 years pay, less than six weeks after the client first arrived. This strategy built the momentum to a peak where the executive was ultra eager to end the uncertainty of what was about to happen. This staged information approach to build momentum is not limited to executives; it has also worked in actions against law firms, generating settlements of six to 36 years of pay in sexual harassment cases. It should, however, be limited to cases with strong facts and solid legal claims.

Sometimes, it is wise to build intrigue more slowly. You can set the stage by taking small steps followed by intervals of inactivity (a form of intermittent reinforcement). For example, if the client had requested the personnel file, but had not received a response, another request can be sent on your letterhead. It should not say anything about suing, just state a simple request. Let Human Resources wonder what might be happening and worry about whether to inform higher management. You can then build momentum with a demand letter and complaint.

USE UNCERTAINTY TO BUILD MOMENTUM

Momentum interacts with uncertainty. They build off one another. After the initial overture, it is wise to anticipate an early phone call to discuss a demand. Do not give a monetary demand over the phone.

No demand should be given until both sides share *some* common ground on liability. It is crucial that you **wait until there is a sense that the employer has some respect for your liability position**. Your first demand must look credible. An excessive demand will be counter productive and freeze the employer's positions.

Depending on who calls, it is appropriate to schedule a meeting in person with the CEO or HR manager, at least if they are unrepresented. If the employer is represented, you must meet with defense counsel, but you can invite the caller to attend. Do not discuss the merits once you learn that they have counsel.

At the meeting, you can update them about the strengths of your liability (who is to blame) position, but avoid talking damages. You can express your on-going uncertainty about the severity of your client's injury and the length of treatment, but don't use hyperbole. Uncertainty is far more powerful than inflated demands or exaggerated claims.

When the time is right, usually the second meeting, you can discuss damages. Most economic loss is readily predictable, even if disputed. Thus, the real challenge in damage education is on the intangible pain. When discussing the financial value of damages, it is most believable when you identify the emotional pain in terms of changes in behavior. In one case, I represented an executive whose golden parachute had eliminated almost all wage loss. He was tight-lipped about any emotional suffering or even humiliation. I gradually ferreted information from him. Once able to leverage emotional pain in terms of behaviors, I could show genuine emotional suffering. The damage facts not only reversed the employer's prior opposition to settlement, but also led to a fast $380,000 settlement without any formal discovery.

In another case, Joseph Golden and I created momentum for big dollars where there was no wage loss. Our client was still employed with the company, but we showed that his macho-executive mentality had disguised substantial emotional suffering. His emotional suffering was made visible by changes in his behavior as evidenced by family and neighbors who described the impact on him. We also demonstrated emotional and reputation damage by obtaining statements from co-workers attesting that the suspension changed their attitude about him. The hurtfulness of these suspicions helped sway the employer. This pre-suit settlement of $500,000 was even more profitable because we had done no discovery. It took a few months, but only 35 hours of lawyer effort.

MOMENTUM BUILDS TOWARD ULTIMATE SETTLEMENT

Additional types of information and subsequent events can create enough momentum and induce higher settlements, but they vary from case to case. In general, the following list is influential.

- ❖ Credible data and projections about economic losses, particularly if enhanced by plausible expert opinions.
- ❖ Credible information about the extent of emotional injury, particularly if presented in terms of behaviors that have changed.
- ❖ Credible expert opinions about the duration of emotional injury, projected counseling needs and on causation, particularly the elimination of other causes.
- ❖ Judicial rulings on motions. These are often perceived as microcosms of the case that symbolize the fate to come. When an employer loses a discovery motion or a motion to dismiss, employers often start second-guessing the judgment of their counsel. Many defense lawyers anticipate this demoralization and downplay the importance of the motion. The cost, however, speaks for itself. The loss creates fear because few clients appreciate the subtlety of motion practice, especially a series of losses. Both plaintiff and defendant see it as symbolic of the unfolding picture.

❖ Judicial rulings on summary judgment. This is often perceived as pivotal because it appears as a microcosm of trial. An objective observer has decided that the conflict in facts warrants live testimony. Given the preponderance of cases that are thrown out, the survivors have increased leverage for settlement.

❖ Assumptions about this judge's attitude about punitive damages in this type of case. Once the judge has authorized a claim for punitive damages, the risk becomes known and frightening. The amount, however, looms as a huge unknown.

❖ The jury's so-called "unpredictability." Many employers fear that the jury may believe the plaintiff and not overlook 'minor' mistakes made by management.

❖ The judge's "unpredictability" on motions in limine and pre-trial rulings. Many employers fear that the jury may believe the plaintiff and not overlook 'minor' mistakes made by management.

❖ New court decisions published prominently in the media. It doesn't matter if the case is local or national. They affect the gestalt of the employer and often weaken the arrogance of defense counsel.

RELATIONSHIP BETWEEN LIABILITY AND DAMAGES

Damages are not independent of liability. Liability and damages are usually interwoven and cannot be viewed in isolation. There is often a hidden relationship between liability and damages, particularly at the extremes.

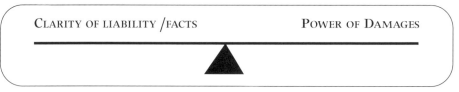

Liability facts can magnify the damage facts. The stronger the liability, the scarier the damages look because their threat becomes more probable. Therefore, when liability is strong, the damage's facts are afforded disproportionately greater value. Momentum is already established. The more compelling the liability, the less crucial the evidence of damages is.

On the other hand, weak liability will diminish otherwise strong damages facts. The weaker the liability, the less threatening the damages. But this means that the damage facts must be a lot stronger to compel interest in compromise.

Reciprocally, if the damages are extremely powerful, otherwise weak liability is slightly enhanced. The damages will still be discounted by the employer's perception of a weak case, but the stakes of losing big loom larger. Strong damages facts will maintain *some* settlement value even with average liability. Extremely low damages, however, diminishes the impact of a strong liability position. It creates an attitude of "Who cares if we lose?"

CAVEAT

Potential momentum can be impacted significantly by a behind-the-scene's presence of third parties such as regulatory agencies, shareholders, and the public. The background presence of a third party audience, not yet involved, can indirectly exert a powerful presence affecting negotiations.

Chapter Six

FACTS HAVE MORE POWER THAN LAW

"Let me find the facts...and I care little who lays down the general principles of law."

U. S. Chief Justice Hughes

PRINCIPLE
Facts determine more outcomes than the Law.

In the beginning, the facts determine which laws apply. Then, the roles are reversed: The law determines which facts are legally important and which are legally trivial. Only certain facts are material. Almost all of the other facts are immaterial to the judge's analysis, but still useful to the jury. It is important to remember that the humans who make corporate decisions in settlement are more like the humans in the jury box than the judge. At summary judgment, the judge is not supposed to decide which facts are believed, but the court's view about whether this type of facts considered material is pivotal. The judge determines which of plaintiff's facts are material and then determines if there are enough to create a genuine dispute.

In litigation, each side puts its faith in one version of material facts. These two versions typically conflict about which facts are legally important. At trial, only one version can be chosen. In settlement, however, the two versions still compete but they can be reconciled or allowed to remain in contrast. It need not be an either-or decision.

The concept of compromise requires the person who decides whether to pay and how much to determine which competing version is more plausible than the other. Typically, this person chooses the set of facts that is closer to their own common sense. Whichever version resonates with the buyer's perceptions, values and point of view about the ways things ordinarily happen and the way people behave, will control the outcome.

SLEEPING FACTS

When the facts arrive at your office, they are, legally speaking, in a deep sleep. If the statute of limitations has run, the facts are dead. Legal meaning does not exist in the facts themselves. You assign meaning to the facts. You initially decide what is legally important and what is legally trivial. Later, the meaning may be reassigned by judges who apply a different set of criteria and different values in deciding which facts have legal meaning (significance) and which do not. In each situation, lawyers and judges bring their backgrounds to bear on the task of assigning meaning.

Good lawyers bring sleeping facts to life by finding a legal package (i.e., a cause of action) that fits these facts. The closer the fit, the more life is given. By digging deeply into the client's memory and documents, you find more fragments of facts. Probing, sorting and judging produces insights into different points of view and generates new inferences. By investigating other witnesses, you add dimension and fortitude to the package. If these witnesses corroborate your client's general perspective and key facts you've discovered, the legal package will embolden you.

The selection and ordering of facts adds color and breathes vitality into these awakened facts. Selection and ordering are not automatic products of a righteous cause, a high intelligence, or even hard work. They require re-thinking the types of facts several ways. As elaborated more fully in the section on gathering leverage, there are six types of facts: basic facts, liability facts, damage facts, linchpin facts, peripheral facts and skeleton facts. Only re-visioning the facts and revising the words will resurrect the sleeping facts.

We must be clear in distinguishing facts from inferences and conclusions. "Discrimination" is not fact; it is a conclusion. "Pretext" is not fact; it is a conclusion. "Defamation" is not fact; it is a conclusion. Inferences arise from connections among facts. They are also extensions of facts rooted in the collective common sense. Conclusions are reached by connecting inferences derived from facts with inferences derived from basic premises.

The secret of powerful argument is to make the gap between fact and inference as small as possible and the number of inferences as few as possible. Nonetheless, we must also recognize that what we commonly call facts are mere guesses.

Facts are Guesses

Appellate Judge Jerome Frank's extraordinary book, *Courts on Trial* (a must read for both trial lawyers and settlement lawyers) explains how facts, not rules, control legal outcomes. To illustrate the traditional point of view about judicial decision-making, Judge Frank provided a crude schemata:

Traditional point of view

R x F = D (where R = the rules, F = the facts and D = decision)

Alternative point of view

Facts are guesses. Decisions are primarily determined by facts, but also by rules, the judge's personal values, frames of reference, institutional priorities and social policies.

Under the old-fashioned theory, if you know the rules and the facts, the outcome is known. Frank emphatically points out the fundamental error in this approach. The rules are not fixed. Rapid changes have made many rules unstable. More importantly, the actual events, actions, or words all happened in the past. As Frank explains, "they [Facts] do not walk into court. The court usually learns about these real, objective, past facts only through the testimony of fallible witness…Thus, the court…must guess at the actual past facts…The facts are the reaction of the judge or jury to the testimony." There can be no assurance that facts and guesses will coincide with those past facts.

Frank points out that if the facts are *not* in dispute, the rule may control, but most commonly the facts are in dispute. Therefore, whenever there is a question about a witness' credibility, believability, reliability, or testimony, the trial judge or jury unavoidably must make a guess about the facts. Furthermore, each side must make a guess about what those guesses will be. The uncertainty of many "legal rights" corresponds to the correctness or incorrectness of such guesses. There is frequently a marked difference between the appearance of facts before trial and in the courtroom. These changes arise from multiple sources, including:

- ❖ Erroneous observation of the past event
- ❖ Faulty, fragmented, or fabricated memory, even when the observation was accurate
- ❖ Misstated narrative at trial, particularly a change in a keyword or phrase, can alter the meaning even if the observation and memory are accurate

❖ Dishonest or, more commonly, biased witnesses even if the remembered observation is accurately narrated.

As noted by Jerome Frank, *"The liar is far less dangerous than the honest but mistaken witness who draws upon his imagination."*

There is a popular notion that the truth will come out and the truth will prevail. According to Frank, the concept of "the truth will come out" is false. It ignores the elements of subjectivity and chance, the possibility of perjury and the probability of bias. It also fails to account for false impressions by honest but nervous or overly scrupulous witnesses, mistaken witnesses, dead or missing witnesses, and the missing or destroyed letter, memo or canceled check.

CREDIBILITY

Many times the guess focuses on credibility. The competing sets of facts (versions) are distilled down to a focal point: Who is believed? Occasionally, credibility is question of which of several pieces of evidence is believed.

This credibility question is overwhelmingly important when the core issue is a variation of "He said, she said."

"He touched me."	vs.	"I never touched her."
"She said I was too old."	vs.	"I never said that."
"I complained about x, y, z."	vs.	"There were no complaints."

When this focal point is a microcosm of the whole case, the entire outcome turns on the decision of who is believed. We are more likely to trust someone we see as similar to us. Reciprocally, we are less likely to trust someone we see as different from us. It's not a wicked conspiracy that propels this search for similarity—it's an ordinary human mind-set. We may find similarity with others in terms of job, career, values, lifestyle, education, prestige, status, geography, politics or other factors. We lack any perfect lie detector, so we rely on the common sense technique of witness demeanor. Clues from the way a person tells a story—intonations, gestures, eye contact, fidgeting or composure, yawning, air of candor or persuasiveness—are useful, but not reliable. Jurors must interpret these nonverbal communications and distinguish the true from the false.

Frank highlights the subjectivity of so-called facts when he writes:

"Judges and jurors are themselves witness of what goes on in the courtroom. They must determine the facts from what they see and hear, from gestures, conduct, and words...As silent witnesses to the witnesses, the judge and juror are not photographic plates. The same errors of observation, lapses of memory or imaged reconstruction of events present defects in the process.... An upper court seldom does anything to correct a trial courts mistaken belief about the facts. Lawsuits depend on rules and facts. One of these is guessable, at best. What the jury or judge will believe are the facts is the major variable, and a guess."

FACTS DICTATE SETTLEMENT MORE THAN THE LAW

When the plaintiff was terminated, the manager had his or her version of why the termination was appropriate or necessary. The corporation may or may not be fully aware of the manager's version.

The plaintiff then submits a different version of the important facts. It might be a detailed elaboration, a hyperbolic set of conclusions, or a terse explanation. The executive who decides whether to entertain settlement must evaluate which version makes more sense. This evaluation is not made in a vacuum. There are completing influences; e.g., backing up the manager, deterring others from suing, avoiding costs, avoiding manager time in deposition, and avoiding the longer term risks of losing as well as losing itself.

More often than not, the initial decision to explore compromise is guided by how closely the plaintiff's version tracks with the common sense of the executive. This decision does not relate to the amount of settlement; it only relates to whether to respond to the overture. The law does not dictate the outcome. Justice does not dictate the outcome. Simple facts do not dictate the outcome. The "perceived facts" control the outcome.

The facts perceived by a potential plaintiff lead them to an attorney. You select from those perceived facts and submit the ones you believe to be material to your goal. The defense lawyer selects from the facts perceived by the manager and submits a competing set of material facts to the executive. This decision-maker reviews both versions and decides which makes the most sense. If the manager's version makes more sense, the decision-maker will back the manager and refuse settlement or talk small numbers. If, however, your version makes more sense, the executive will authorize serious negotiations.

When the competing sets of material facts are presented to a judge for summary judgment, the judge selects those facts he or she finds most credible and deems most legally important. The judge sorts through the paper summaries and perceives certain facts. Inherently, the judge is selective. These perceived facts will determine which presumption is applied as well as which laws and cases are applied. If the outcome still makes sense, a decision is made. If it doesn't quite fit, the judge may look at certain presumptions that may tip the scale. If the versions of material facts are essentially the same, the only issue remaining is whether any legal consequences attach to these facts. After the decision on facts is made, cases will be selectively cited as precedent to support the decision. It may be revised if the precedents deemed controlling are totally contrary, but this is rare.

At trial, the version of facts is measured by the Jury's common sense and inferences are measured against the legal principles; i.e., jury instructions.

FUZZY THINKING REPLACES EITHER-OR THINKING

Our adversarial system is premised on win-lose. This generates a great deal of confusion between the decision-making process and the ultimate outcome. It leads to the *erroneous* assumption that all decisions leading up to the ultimate outcome are based on either-or thinking.

In earlier times, judicial reasoning fit the either-or model. In recent years, however, we have progressed to a type analysis referred to as "fuzzy thinking". This mode of analysis recognizes that data should be weighed and balanced, not simply pigeonholed as all or none or one or the other. "Fuzzy thinking" is not a negative phrase: it is a descriptive one. This development is concurrent with changes in the logic of science—instead of two-valued decisions (binary), we see an emphasis on multi-valued decisions (multi-valence). Stated differently, either-or thinking is like a light switch–it's on or it's off. Real life is more like a dimmer switch—a light is off…partly on…mostly on…on. There are few sharp lines that demarcate these points. It is a continuum. Legal analysis should reflect real life: Fuzzy thinking is more honest and useful than either-or analysis.

This quiet revolution in thinking has profound consequences for evaluating evidence. When the judge or jury weighs the evidence, they need not determine all-or-none. It is enough to determine which outcome is 'more likely' based on the competing facts presented.

For example, conclusions about discrimination were historically viewed as either-or: Either there was discrimination or there was not. Now courts ask whether discrimination *more likely than not* motivated the decision. [See *Burdine*; *Ellerth* and *Farragher*]. This same phenomena is present in other phrases such as "Were defendant's decisions *more likely to disfavor* blacks than whites?" It is also recurring in other types of cases, such as tort decisions that ask, "Was negligence more probably the cause of the injury?"

In 1974, the Supreme Court had opened the door to statistical evidence as a method of proof in discrimination cases (*Griggs v. Duke Power*). This approach belatedly paralleled scientific thought based on probabilities. Previously, proof was required to be all-or-none, but since probability theory enabled flight to the moon and back, its validity ultimately satisfied legal standards of proof.

The effect of this mental shift is even more pronounced on summary judgment. The judge is *not* deciding should plaintiff win. Instead, the judge asks, "Does plaintiff have enough of the right kind of facts that there is a genuine issue whether plaintiff's version is more likely than defendant's version?" This effect is decidedly favorable to plaintiffs.

This difference also affects presumptions and affirmative defenses. The fuzzy thinking approach magnifies your ability to find the loopholes in the defendant's approach. The managers and supervisors who have rationalized the decision-making process as "logical" are the most vulnerable. Uncertainty is a force that drives people to see the world as either-or. Most people, including too many lawyers, see the world as win-lose or all-or-none. Ironically, according to DSM-IV, this is also the dominant mind-set of persons who suffer from depression. This mind-set is dangerous, unless the speaker knows that win-lose is only a tool, not a reality.

> *"Things look simple to the stupid.*
> *The intelligent see the complications, but try to simplify*
> *them."*

> George Bernard Shaw

FACTS ARE OFTEN UNSTABLE

Facts often sound good, but they rest on shifting sands. Applying a "think backward" approach, which is discussed in greater detail in Chapter 12, will invariably show you the weakest link in the process. When the decision-making process is traced backwards to its real origin, the weakest link surfaces. The weakest link is invariably a human—even though it is disguised as a policy, practice, custom, or rule. For example, the reason given for termination might be too many absences. Under either-or thinking, the assumption is that you either satisfy the attendance criteria or you violate it. But fuzzy thinking analysis uncovers a real source of "discretion." Someone has discretion to determine if a violation really occurred or should have been excused.

This approach can be used in advance to identify the defendant's weak points to highlight in the complaint and negotiations. Frequently, it is most powerful in the deposition questions. See detailed example in the section on deposition preparation. Once the weak link is found, the sequence can be reconstructed going backwards and forwards up the chain of decision-making. This illustrates the benefits of focusing on facts and their origin.

At outset, all employers have some concern about the facts, but more concern about the costs. As you reverse inertia, you have the power of material facts to add concerns about winning to the original concerns. A new momentum is underway. You are ready to leverage uncertainty into a lust for closure.

Chapter Seven

POWER OF UNCERTAINTY

> **PRINCIPLE**
>
> Uncertainty drives people to find closure.
>
> A *Strategy*: Make a demand that tempts the opponent to keep negotiating.
>
> A *Tactic*: Remind them of the unknowns.

The essence of a military situation is uncertainty. Uncertainty about the strength of the enemy, but in addition, rumor which exaggerates his size…

Clausewitz, *Principles of War*

Uncertainty has two primary dimensions:

❖ It is a lever that can either propel a buyer (defendant) to pay more to avoid the risk of a worse verdict or propel a seller (plaintiff) to accept less for the same reasons.

❖ It is the result of a series of unknowns, which gradually become more knowable.

Uncertainty is a state of mind. It is not real. Uncertainty, like darkness, often unnerves us because it clouds what we can't see. Instead of clear shapes, we see shadowy appearances. Fears are enlarged by our own projections. Humans resort to many tactics to reduce uncertainty; turn on a light, close our eyes, seek solace in the opinions of others or make decisions rapidly based on "the devil you do know." When we can finally recognize shapes that look vaguely familiar, we find some comfort.

The familiarity of shapes allows us to identify which possibilities are within the range of probability and which are outside the range. In *Patterns in the Mind*, Ray Jackendoff suggests that meaning comes with inherent uncertainty around the edges, but that the uncertainty is around the edges only. In these gray areas, context is crucial to a sense of meaning. Language and shapes have the illusion of precise meaning, but this is only in the center: Elsewhere, they are inherently imprecise. It is natural to have fuzzy around the edges.

UNCERTAINTY AS A LEVER

When an employer communicates an offer of very little or nothing, it is easy for the plaintiff to decide to go to trial. There is nothing to lose. There is no reason to fear the uncertainty of a jury verdict—it can't be any worse. The employer has removed the plaintiff from any threat of uncertainty.

The same is true in reverse. When a plaintiff communicates an excessive settlement demand, it is easy for the employer to go to trial. There is nothing to lose. There is no reason to fear the uncertainty of an unlikely jury verdict—it is very unlikely to be any worse than the amount demanded. The plaintiff has thus removed the employer from the threat of uncertainty.

The secret to settlement is determining what is an appropriate range for settlement. If your settlement demands are within the range, even at the high end, it tempts your opponents to consider your offer or at least make a counteroffer. They have incentive to keep the ball rolling. If defense settlement offers are within the range that tempts you to counter with a reduced demand, the ball keeps rolling. The process will continue so long as each side perceives the other is within the range of reasonableness.

The realistic range of settlement can usually be identified objectively. *Initially* assume full liability and compute the high end of the range as well as the low end. [Later, we apply appropriate discounts or premiums based on risk factors.] Verdicts above the high end are extremely unlikely, so it is almost a certainty that higher verdicts are not a meaningful risk to your opponent. Similarly, verdicts below the low end of the range are highly unlikely. Thus, it is almost certain that a verdict beneath the low end is not a meaningful risk for your client.

> Uncertainty resides within the range of realistic highs and lows. Demands below the high end will be tempting to the buyer (defendant) because the amount allows the buyer to avoid the uncertainty of a higher verdict. Offers above the low end will tempt the seller (plaintiff) to avoid the uncertainty of an even lower verdict.

To make starting demands above the high end is counter-productive. They remove your opponent's uncertainty and make it easier for the buyer to reject negotiations. It justifies entering into an aggressive litigation defense. Reciprocally, starting offers below the low end are also counter-productive. They remove your uncertainty and make it easier for the seller to stop negotiations. It justifies recommending aggressive litigation.

If you initially assumed 100 percent liability, you need to either take a discount for risk or to add a premium for unusual strengths. Normally, it is useful to assume 50:50 is the norm. Thus, a good settlement assumes approximately 50 percent of a realistic trial value. The dollar amount is increased or decreased according to your estimates of success on liability. This is relatively straightforward to compute if your perception of liability is acute and you take the time to be objective in estimating the real trial value.

Unknowns Made Knowable

The second dimension of uncertainty is the number and significance of the facts that are unknowns. When the first negotiation begins, there are many, many unknowns. As time passes, some of these unknowns become knowable and the consequences become more predictable. As they become more knowable and more predictable, they feel more manageable, measurable and easier to incorporate into the value.

At the beginning, only some of the suffering described by plaintiff's counsel is real to the employer; a good deal of it is hypothetical. Later, the hypothetical becomes real. The condition may stabilize or change via improvement or deterioration. At the outset, the primary unknowns related to the plaintiff include:

1. We don't know how long s/he will be unemployed.
2. We don't know if a new job will be comparable in terms of salary, benefits, or career advancement opportunities.
3. We don't know if depression will respond to treatment or how quickly it will become manageable. Symptoms may get better, or they may get worse. The symptoms are usually real at the start, but the duration is hypothetical and the severity undetermined.
4. We don't know if there will be side effects from losing the job— delinquencies on mortgage, rent in arrears, eviction, late car payments, loss of insurance coverage, loss of a good credit rating.
5. We don't know if ugly, harmful statements have, in fact, prevented a new job or injured the employee's reputation among prospective employers, former co-workers, or the more general public audience.

6. We don't know the amount of future fees and costs, but we know they are modest at the beginning.

As time passes, we have more solid information. Either good news or bad news reduces the number of unknowns and shrinks the amount of uncertainty.

The unemployment status remains unknown until the client gets another job offer. The offer may be a lot better, comparable, or worse, but either way it makes the losses more predictable and precise. If your client makes a career change, it may reduce the unknown status, but it will add a layer of uncertainty that may alter damages.

These unknowns tend to cluster into three types:

❖ Unknowns made knowable by time
❖ Unknowns made knowable by investigation
❖ Unknowns made knowable only by later events

Each of these types is slightly different. The first is outside anyone's direct control and requires patience. The second can clearly be influenced by your efforts. The third type simply requires patience.

UNKNOWNS MADE KNOWABLE BY TIME

Several unknowns are addressed by the passage of time. They are less subject to influence by the parties, but serendipity to other people may alter the unknown; e.g., prospective employers or therapists may affect the outcome. These unknowns include:

❖ Duration of emotional injury
❖ Duration of embarrassment and humiliation
❖ Whether reputation damage will diminish or increase
❖ Motivation and stamina to fight (anger may subside or grow)
❖ The likelihood of future economic losses.

There is very little plaintiff's counsel can do to influence these unknowns. They must work their course.

UNKNOWNS MADE KNOWABLE BY INVESTIGATION

The second type of unknowns include:

❖ Witnesses and documents supporting or negating liability
❖ Witnesses and documents supporting or negating damages

- ❖ Amount of therapy likely to be necessary
- ❖ Depth or severity of current emotional pain
- ❖ Extent of reputation damages
- ❖ Current state of the law.

These unknowns can be directly affected by your efforts. Investigation will make a powerful difference on these issues. Some of these unknowns can be meaningfully addressed by expert evaluations.

UNKNOWNS MADE KNOWABLE, BUT ONLY BY LATER EVENTS

The resolution of these last type of unknowns are probably the clearest and most likely, but they involve actions by others over whom you have little influence:

- ❖ A job offer to plaintiff
- ❖ A reinstatement offer by defendant
- ❖ The comparability of the new job with the old
- ❖ The costs of plaintiff's case and ability to pay or be subsidized by you
- ❖ The costs of defendant's case and their willingness to pay
- ❖ Insolvency or bankruptcy
- ❖ Employer witnesses who stay or leave
- ❖ Judge assignment
- ❖ Rulings by judge on motions, summary judgment, evidence, jury instructions
- ❖ Jury
- ❖ Changes in related court decisions.

All of the above unknowns should be scrutinized. They are not a mere laundry list. Leverage will be greatest when certain unknowns remain uncertain. These will enhance settlement value, but the type of audience will impact their relative meaning. If you emphasize the unknowns that are most applicable to a particular audience, greater leverage will be achieved.

The severity and duration of emotional pain remains unknown until some event occurs. The event may be simply time that heals the problem (an infrequent event), hiring a health professional who diagnoses and successfully treats the injury, or self-help and the support of friends and family. The wronged employee may become adjusted to the situation. Diagnosis and treatments frequently make the duration somewhat more predictable. It also allows the costs of treatment to be forecasted and sometimes the extent of injury. This usually enhances the overall value of the injury.

Therapy, however, may increase the nature of the unknowns and alter the client's willingness to pursue litigation. If therapy changes the client's view of the ugly treatment s/he has suffered, the client may choose to forego litigation. For example, Naida Axford and I once represented a university professor who wanted to challenge the denial of tenure. He offered a $50,000 retainer. A few weeks later he changed his mind. He had encountered Norman Mailer who helped him recognize that lawsuits keep you looking backwards and that it is more healthy to look forward. He dropped his case and the retainer was returned. If therapy makes the client aware of other hurts and angers that have been successfully suppressed, the client may be unnerved by the experience.

Therapy may illuminate causes for the employee's pain, but it may also surface causes *other* than the alleged job-related event. It may create uncertainty about whether these other causes are more likely the root of the client's current distress than the job-related behavior. Alternatively, if the employer knew about the pre-existing conditions, the employer's conduct may have aggravated them and created thin-skull liability. See *Jensen v. Eveleth Mining*, 130 F. 3d 1287 (8th 1997) where the Eighth Circuit reversed both the special master and trial judge because they used the wrong burdens of proof where there was a pre-existing condition. The court also ruled that amounts of $2,500 to $25,000 for emotional distress were inadequate.

The employer's responsibility can become more dramatic and made to have direct legal consequences if other stressors are present. If the employer knew only about a certain atypical stressor that does not rise to the level of pre-existing condition criteria, the employer may still be held impliedly accountable for injury caused by conduct that disregarded these known facts.

Humiliation and embarrassment should be viewed differently than emotional distress. By their nature, humiliation and embarrassment are more predictable at the outset. The duration of humiliation and embarrassment also tends to be more knowable than that of emotional distress. Unless there are recurring events that aggravate the original injury, humiliation and embarrassment tend to subside with time. Recurrent incidents will, however, provoke a downward spiral.

At the outset, no one can be certain which employees will remain employed by the corporation. Witnesses who leave the employer often acquire better memories or even become more honest. Over time, the employer's view of the facts may change or the corporation itself may be restructured. Uncertainty will set the stage, and if you are thoughtful, you can maneuver this uncertainty as a means of reversing the inertia and building momentum toward settlement.

UNCERTAINTY IN LAW

The uncertainty of multiple precedents is disturbing to many lawyers. Many lawyers try to dodge this bullet of uncertainty and seek security in the 'tried and true' approaches. They accept established case law as sacred. They forget that some lawyer, somewhere, created that legal precedent. See the recommended readings for several books by Gerry Spence and biographical works like Melvin Belli, *My Life on Trial*; Louis Nizer, *My Life in Court*; or Rosenblatt, *Trial Lawyer*. Some lawyer built a new theory of law by standing on the shoulders of his or her ancestors.

As plaintiff's lawyers, we create precedent. The beauty of the common law is its adaptability and flexibility—it is designed to evolve to meet the 'felt necessities' of our time. In the 1970s, only discrimination and overtime statutes protected some employees. White middle class males pushed for equity and now we have adapted new contract theories, good faith and fair dealing, and misrepresentation. In the 1980s, discrimination cases were not tried to a jury. Plaintiff's lawyers pioneered negligence theories and intentional torts in the employment setting to create the right to a jury trial. This evolution is not unique to law. A popular theme in contemporary business circles is what Peter Drucker calls the "systematic sloughing off yesterday." This theme necessitates not merely a willingness to abandon, but a systematic commitment to let go of what we already know for the sake of what we discover or create.

The uncertainty of new precedent is frightening to many employers. They don't want to incur the cost of fighting a crusading lawyer willing to push a principle to the highest court. At least five of my settlements over $300,000 have come in cases where there was no precedent in Minnesota, but potential causes of action were imported from Arizona, California, Montana or New Jersey. The injustice of the facts screamed so loudly that the particular employer did not want to risk paying to create new law. However, the threat of "changing the law" is only meaningful if meticulous effort is manifest—a haphazard or sloppily analyzed complaint is a waste of time. You must show that you really care.

Many lawyers are cautious in the face of the powerful force of uncertainty. We can either accept inevitable change or we can create it. In these times, there may be more security in new methods, new ideas and new precedent.

KNOWLEDGE OF OPPONENT'S SENSE OF UNCERTAINTY

The ability to use uncertainty as a lever on the opposition is enhanced by knowing your opponent. If the opponent has a high volume of cases, but seldom goes to trial, it is fair to assume that s/he is heavily influenced by uncertainty. Reciprocally, if they frequently take cases to trial, uncertainty is probably less threatening to them.

Your opponent's past settlements provide signals. If defense counsel has a reputation for agreeing to liberal settlements, you may infer that uncertainty is a big force. Reciprocally, if you have a reputation of being "unusually" reasonable, there is reason for your opponent to suspect a history of smaller settlements. These may show that uncertainty has an unusually strong impact on you.

In poker games, player B looks for obvious clues given by player C. But if player C is poker faced, B must probe. To probe, B pays closer attention to the way C handles the betting. Often, plaintiff's counsel probes by making a demand at the high end of the reasonableness range or even exceeding it. If it fails, the demand is reduced the next time, **IF** there is a next time. More often, a high demand destroys negotiations and weakens your credibility.

A poker player can win with a minimum number of good hands because s/he observes how the betting, the cards dealt, and the uncertainty affect his or her opponent. Observing your opponent's response during the give and take of negotiations will give you more information about their tolerance for uncertainty.

TACTICS TO MAGNIFY UNCERTAINTY

If you can refer to two or three cases that are very similar to the one at hand, a benefit is readily apparent. Even collateral cases will influence your opponent's thought processes if they share a related measure of damages. The impact is more profound where the cases involve not only similar liability, but also similar injuries.

Defense lawyers often use humor to disguise their concerns for an adverse verdict; e.g., a $1,500,000 loss is referred to as "we got nicked." This opponent is likely willing to pay a substantial premium to avoid another loss. To magnify this mind-set, you may choose to play hardball. For example, you can express sympathy for another local defense lawyer who lost a big client after a bad verdict. Vague generalities, however, rarely have impact. The most effective remark is regarding someone your opponent knows. Subtle remarks referring to real people and specific examples will strike to the core of anxiety.

Prolonged litigation can affect the pocketbook of both you and the client. Even though we do not want to believe this financial dilemma applies to us, it can become a consideration. Vigilance about its influence is crucial.

UNCERTAINTY AND INSURANCE ADJUSTERS

Insurance adjusters and their bosses are under enormous pressure to hold down the amount of claims paid. Subordinates seeking to rise to better positions want to be right, and above all, to avoid criticism. When litigation becomes sizable, the expenses become a major source of irritation within the insurance company. When a verdict exceeds the final demand, apprehension will build, especially when there is a rash of verdicts in the local community. To the adjuster, large amounts of litigation and related expenses lead to criticism from bosses and risks demotions. Thus, knowledge of adverse verdicts can be used, subtly, to enhance the value of the claim.

References to mega-verdict can occasionally be effective to magnify the amount set aside in reserve for this claim. *Money placed in reserves cannot be invested by the insurance company*. Thus, cases with high reserves tend to receive faster attention. You must, however, retain credibility. Mega-verdict must be used selectively and even then, you should explicitly declare that you know they are rare and you do not intend a comparison to this case. Often a back-handed reference is a more useful reminder. For example, a P.S. in your demand letter: "We are not suggesting that this case is like the $4 million verdict where the jury determined that the reason given for termination, sexual harassment, was used as an excuse to fire an older employee." Alternatively, a similar footnote in your chart of damages often suffices to jolt adjusters into contemplating the worst case scenario.

CAUTION
References to mega-verdicts often backfire. You may diminish your overall credibility by elaborate comparisons that don't fit your case.

The Mind-Set of Adjusters
In cases where a verdict comes in lower than the final demand of plaintiff, we would logically expect an insurer to celebrate. This lower verdict, however, creates suspicion that the same adjuster may have overpaid previously settled claims. Thus, it still enhances uncertainty. Both extremes are sources of irritation and the fear of these irritations heightens the effect of uncertainty.

Relevant verdicts exceeding final demands can be used to educate an agent. Insurance agents usually want to keep their client (the employer) happy because this preserves his or her commission payments. The agent may put pressure on the adjuster to put more money on the table to end the dispute and this may magnify the adjuster's uncertainty.

The enormous changes in employment law since the 1970-80s have largely bene-fited employees, while many of the changes in the 90s have advantaged employ-ers. Uncertainty in either the law or the facts tends to favor the plaintiff more in the early stages than during the discovery phase. Uncertainty at trial favors the plaintiff more than during the discovery phase. As we learn to make uncer-tainty our friend, our power is magnified.

Chapter Eight

GOOD LAWYERING MAKES A DIFFERENCE

The difference between the right word and the almost right word is the difference between lightening and the lightening bug.

Mark Twain

PRINCIPLE

Lawyers can't create facts, but good lawyers create powerful inferences.

Lawyers are not fungible: You cannot substitute one for another and expect the same results. Lawyers may not be necessary for cases with great facts—they find their own sales price. Sadly, such cases are rare. Bad facts don't get better, even in hands of a great lawyer. Ordinary facts can, however, be improved by good lawyering. Diligent, thoughtful lawyers usually contribute more value to cases than brilliant, lazy ones or shouters without substance. Like an archeologist, a lawyer digs to find fragments of facts. Then he or she weaves the fragments into a good story and fits the story within a legal package.

The personality to pursue trial is often seen as different from the personality to pursue compromise. It can be, but need not. Most people who graduate from law school possess the raw intelligence necessary to perform the job. The difference is how they apply their intelligence and how they utilize their personality to further their client's goals. At trial you can *choose* to become a gung-ho advocate and demonstrate unequivocal belief in your case. This same conviction and strategy, however, rarely enhances compromise. More often it is counterproductive during settlement efforts. There may be an exception when you are creating precedent—but then, your passion is about the concept of fairness, not a blind belief in your facts.

Plaintiff attorneys share many basic needs, but one requirement stands out: stamina. This ability to endure has four primary dimensions:

* ❖ Mental stamina
* ❖ Emotional stamina
* ❖ Physical stamina
* ❖ Financial stamina.

> *Reading makes a full man;*
> *conference a ready one;*
> *and writing a precise one.*

> Francis Bacon (gender not adjusted)

MENTAL STAMINA

Plaintiff's lawyers must be mentally alert for facts that are legally important and inferences that create cognitive dissonance. Dissonance arises from new contexts, comparison and contrast, and opposition thinking. You must be able to suspend judgment and ask, "What if?" In preparing for negotiations, it is often more valuable to stop pursuing pure advocacy and see the inferences from neutral or opposing point of view (like the ultimate viewer—the jury).

Creativity is critical

A lawyer's mind is most productive when it telescopes facts into universal images, but also microscopes a tiny, yet powerful detail that tips the scale. If you keep probing until you find that lynchpin fact and express it with clarity, you can strike terror in your opponent. Moreover, you will be emboldened.

The organizing principle of any cluster of facts is not the automatic result of a righteous cause, a high intelligence, nor even hard work. It requires thinking and re-thinking the basic facts several times. Re-visioning the facts will allow you to dimly recognize a working theory. Then as you flesh it out and compare it to known facts, the theory will become clearer. It will sharpen the persuasiveness of your pleadings. My personal style for complaints averages about eight revisions. In one case, I revised the complaint 27 times, largely because the client had no claims under existing Minnesota law and the best cause of action, good faith and fair dealing, had been rejected by Minnesota courts. The 21 page complaint, combined with two handwritten pages of witness affidavits, generated a $400,000 settlement, involved no discovery and only one hour of negotiation.

Judgment is critical

You must reduce hundreds of miscellaneous facts to the core elements of each potential claim. Then, you must refine the elements into the issues that are conceded versus those that are truly in dispute. Finally, you must identify which facts will persuade others that an element is or is not met. These persuasive facts then become the focus for favorably resolving the remaining dispute. The key difference between trial and settlement is that in compromise we also focus on the needs of the opponent.

Intellectually, we need the stamina to read a decision that opposes our point of view and tear it apart. Even better, we adopt a judo tactic to convert the bad opinion into affirmative support for our own position. If we learn to think backwards, we stand in the shoes of others and see the world more clearly.

Writing stamina is critical

When we are lazy, we write off-the-top-of-our-head, vent our anger or hurriedly express ourselves. If you want to make an impact in a brief, answering discovery or simply a letter, you must begin with asking what do you hope to accomplish. Ask yourself:

> What do I want my reader to think or do as a result of reading this communication?[6]

This simple question has transformed many communications from futile, impulsive gestures into writing with real power.

Playing with rhythm

Consultant Stephen Wilburs makes a strong case for using punctuation to convey the music of your words: Use colons like a three quarter note rest to create anticipation and a semicolon like a full stop to suggest a connection. Periods are like whole note rests or pauses, they should be plentiful enough for emphasis and important words should be placed immediately before the pause. Commas are only slight pauses—the fewer the pauses, the faster paced and more direct your writing. Dashes creates an abrupt interruption. It gives the most emphasis.

EMOTIONAL STAMINA

Patience and calm are crucial, but they are not inconsistent with passion and intensity. Patience and passion can co-exist and actually nurture one another. Indifference is the one quality that will destroy a plaintiff's attorney.

---

[6] Mary Munter, *Guide to Managerial Communication*

Emotional stamina includes a sensitivity to feelings and needs of the other—whether the client, the opponent, the judge or the jury. This sensitivity can enable you to recognize the real needs of your audience in a particular situation. Money is often only a symbolic measure of other needs that crave to be satisfied. Abraham Maslow provided a flexible hierarchy of needs that is useful in looking at clients, opponents and yourself. His hierarchy includes: 1) physiological needs; 2) safety and security needs; 3) love and belonging needs; 4) esteem and respect needs; 5) needs for self-actualization; 6) need to know and to understand; 7) esthetic needs[7]. In general, we progress up the hierarchy of needs as the lower ones are satisfied according to our own needs, at least partially. We must realize that movement from one need to another does not require complete satisfaction of the lower need. Partial satisfaction is sufficient. If you can look to the deeper needs, you can more creatively address them.

Family and friends are crucial to your emotional stamina. Hopefully, you work to live, not live to work. You subject yourself every day to the advocacy culture and you need real people to counterbalance the effects of this submersion. Take at least one or two 24-hour vacations from the law every week. This release brightens your mental health and broadens your horizons. Input from people outside of your family is also valuable. A network of non-lawyer friends is also a wonderful opportunity for bouncing ideas and escaping the myopia of lawyers. You will often be enlightened by their common sense perspectives.

Laugh at yourself. We all make stupid mistakes. Laugh with your peers and opponents. If you look for humor in things, you will find it. Sharing these moments with opponents will humanize the process. Last year, tensions were heating up in a case. My opponent had been arguing with me about setting a motion date. He later left a huffy voice mail—"Let's just do it." My fax reply was terse:

"I'm not sure if you refer to

   a. doing the motion; or
   b. doing a settlement;" or
   c. some unspeakable act between the two of us.
     But in any event, I have no personal interest in you."

He laughed for days, as did my client. It removed the edge off the burgeoning tensions.

---

[7] Gerald Niremberg, *Fundamentals of Negotiation*, p. 82-89 citing from Maslow, *Motivation and Personality* (New York: Harper & Row, 1954)

Physical Stamina

It is commonly recognized that trial demands endurance coupled with the ability to remain alert for long periods. Strategizing for settlement involves a different set of physical skills—a type of quiet calm mixed with alertness and patience. A lawyer can hurry her or his way into settlement, but the success rate is increased if you can enter a relaxed state of mind to explore the possibilities. This mind-set will allow you to see the big picture, unencumbered by the details. It allows you to see the various options and assess the competing strategies; e.g., when to emphasize the intangibles or the cause and let the money be secondary.

Often, a relaxed state of mind is nurtured by getting away from the office. Sit with an empty pad of paper in a coffee shop or café. This will enable you to *feel* your way through to the bigger picture. It will allow you to ask what seems right in this situation from the plaintiff's point of view. But it is important not to stop there—examine settlement from society's point of view (a jury at trial) and the employer's point of view. This struggle with the larger felt-experience will generate empathy with other points of view and enlarge your objectivity. It provides a framework for putting simplicity and clarity into your argument. Then, back in the office you can prepare a letter using selected details from liability and mitigation facts.

Technological Stamina

Technology is a tool. It can be leveraged to save enormous amounts of effort and thus extend your stamina. Computers allow you to store enormous amounts of data in a tiny space, to check your spelling and grammar and if used thoughtfully, to minimize re-inventing the wheel. I strongly discourage the use of standardized forms—they replace thinking and tailoring your work to the audience at issue. Nevertheless, the computer can allow you to ensure that you haven't overlooked any elements, procedural or statutory references or made errors in citations. Scanners can eliminate the need for re-typing the interrogatories and document requests of the defendants. Zip discs can create storage for massive volumes of documents. Moreover, it you do daily back-up, you can eliminate much of the worthless paper and move toward a paperless office. Deposition should be obtained on disc to be used with your computer for cross-referencing. Real time deposition can be great timesavers.

Fax machines can send letters faster than a speeding mailman. This is especially applicable if you use an internal modem in your computer; I have often faxed confirming letters to my opponents before we ended a phone conversation. Most simple letters are sufficient by fax.

There are other methods to enhance your physical stamina; e.g., reduce your distractions by accepting phone calls or interruptions only during certain hours like 11:00 to noon or 3:00 to 5:00 p.m. These intervals can also be used to return calls. To avoid excessive absorption in a task, your computer can be set to go off every hour on the hour as a reminder to get up, stretch, take a walk and give your psyche' a break. Computers can be set to play music at preset intervals. The short gap frees your mind from the details and invariably generates a fresh perspective on the situation. Technology expands your stamina.

FINANCIAL STAMINA

There are both short-term and long-term dimensions to the financial position. Many plaintiffs' lawyers start without any reserves or clients. They seldom obtain hourly clients other than friends, until they have procured some degree of visible success. Thus, they usually begin on a contingency basis, earning their keep by results. It is not effort that counts, nor your union card; i.e., your lawyer license. You make money only if you win a settlement or a judgment.

Most plaintiffs' lawyers are in solo practice or in small firms. They have no one to rely upon. A primary purpose of this book is to show how to use early settlements to build a base. Then, you can be ready to jump on the good or the *occasional* great case that comes along. This method generates wonderful cash flow, a good income, and reserves energy for the worthwhile fights.

MAXIMS ABOUT GOOD LAWYERING

❖ A lawyer can't invent facts, but a good lawyer digs up new ones and fattens up the skinny ones by creating contexts, comparisons and contrasts.

❖ A good lawyer applies a microscope to the central incident, magnifying tiny details that tip the scales on credibility.

❖ A good lawyer applies a telescope to the details, enabling the bigger picture.

❖ A good lawyer shuffles time dimensions, looking backwards in time exposing thoughts and beliefs that preceded decisions and forwards in time to the consequences of decisions.

❖ You got to know when to hold 'em: You got to know when to fold 'em.[8]

---

[8] Kenny Rogers song, *The Gambler*

Gunther Max, a sociologist, studied people in several different fields who were perceived as having more 'luck' than most. He identified certain elements of the "luck factor," including networking, the willingness to follow hunches, the pessimism paradox (never assume luck), the ratchet effect (anticipating failure and locking in your position) and "boldness." Successful lawyers make use of these factors in trial and in settlement. We help cause our luck to happen. Go for it.

Chapter Nine

MEET THE PREREQUISITES

Certain core strategies are crucial to maximizing settlement and generating a higher profit. Each strategy derives from one or more fundamental principles. Strategies and related tactics are woven into the fabric of this text, but they are concentrated here for clarity. In many respects, these strategies illustrate the continuing benefit of rediscovering the obvious.

- ❖ **Buy/Sell**: Start with an asking price that tempts the employer to continue bidding. Increase the sales price by GRADUALLY converting the jury from a shadow to a competing bidder.
- ❖ **Stages**: Narrow disputes to those issues most applicable to the needs of a particular stage. Emphasize the unknown nature of damage facts.
- ❖ **Audience:** Defer asking the client's *bottom line* until you and the client are adequately educated about the trial value and your opponent's views.

> Objectivity is not enough: Look through the eyes of the opponent. See their point of view, anticipate their hiding places and understand their needs.

- ❖ **Inertia**: To reverse inertia, illustrate an alternative point of view on the same facts, provide new facts or furnish peripheral facts that involve third parties.
- ❖ **Momentum**: Enhance value by accelerating with a series of small steps or staging the delivery of damage facts.

> Never make a money *demand* **until** your adversary has shown some respect for your liability position. This strategy is crucial.

- ❖ **Uncertainty**: Do not fear unknowns, build from them. Create uncertainty about losing the opportunity to settle.
- ❖ **Facts**: Focus on fact development: Law is only a method of organizing facts around the elements and the relationships.
- ❖ **Lawyering**: Care about your client and balance a good outcome against speedy closure. Suspend disbelief and see the world through the eyes of the employer.
- ❖ Guidelines are not rules—they require improvisation.

Ratios between the trial value, bottom line and demand must be reasoned.

Trial value is a predictable but fungible figure. If the demand is less than 50 percent of the trial value, too much liability is probably conceded. If the demand is more than 80 percent of the trial value, reality is being ignored.

If the demand is more than triple the bottom line, you risk losing the opportunity to settle. If the demand is less than 150 percent of the bottom line, you deny yourself room to move and let the employer save face.

COUNTERBALANCES TO RATIOS

Employers are rarely willing to pay, in settlement, more than triple the hard losses at that moment. The exceptions include: "smoking gun" evidence, retaliation facts, direct evidence or objective evidence that the employer caused emotional or reputational damage. These exceptions have a huge multiplying effect on the employer's willingness to pay more.

SMALL THINGS ARE IMPORTANT

Often we focus only on the big factors, but small things often accumulate advantages. In blackjack, the house has the advantage, but less than 3 percent. This difference is enough to allow them to win the majority of the time. In baseball, a hitter who succeeds more than three out of ten tries is outstanding, but one who succeeds two out of ten tries is mediocre. In trials, little things like the burden of proof or presumptions are often the difference between winning by a preponderance of the evidence or losing. Based on my experience, I offer the following rough rules of thumb:

Facts contribute 40% of the influence

> (Client versions, investigation, witnesses, documents, employer versions, discovery, luck)

Law contributes 20% of the influence

> (Substantive law—jury instructions, changing precedent, motion practice)

People collectively contribute 40% of the influence

> (Plaintiff, plaintiff's attorney, the defendant, the defense witnesses, the defense lawyer, the witnesses, the judge, the jury and the appellate judges)

Each of the individual persons contributes a small portion to the whole, approximately 4 percent toward the outcome (40 percent/10). Although we feel a tendency to give credit or to blame one individual for success or failure, each influences the outcome by only a small amount. The plaintiff, the plaintiff's attorney, the witnesses, the defendant, the defense witnesses, the defense lawyer, the judge, the jury and the appellate judges will each affect the ultimate outcome but only by a few percentage points. Some will exercise more influence, others less. By trial, most witnesses will counterbalance one another. This narrows the leverage points to a few issues to be decided by the jury. Still, we need judges. Judges, like baseball umpires, are not needed for obvious balls or strikes. They are needed for the close calls.

Small things, properly leveraged, can lift enormous weights. Little things matter. The quality of your effort can magnify small differences into momentous effects. Tactics based on well thought out strategies derived from fundamental principles will empower you to maximize settlements.

Section Two

PRE-SUIT SETTLEMENT EFFORTS

Chapter Ten

SCREENING POTENTIAL CLIENTS

The most profit is made on the cases where you say no.

Abe Lincoln

Before you can explore a settlement opportunity, you must separate the worthwhile from the possible. Our existence as caring persons does not require us to help every prospect who wants or needs help. Our role as lawyers does not require us to take every dispute into litigation. Some of us have consciously experimented with accepting *only* those cases that he or she is willing to take all the way to trial; i.e., making no effort at settlement. It's great bravado, but the risks are so high that the venture is ultra high stakes. Moreover, reasoned efforts can avoid the mistakes inherent in the unknowns that are pervasive at the outset. Most lawyers forego serious settlement efforts purely out of habit. There is an alternative: Select certain cases as settlement cases only or delay the decision on litigation until you have exhausted settlement efforts.

SCREENING IS ESSENTIAL TO SANITY

For every 100 prospects who call a lawyer, there are probably 20-40 who are worth interviewing, either because their cause is just or their case has value in settlement or trial.

From the approximately 30 prospects worth interviewing, probably only 15 will have enough good facts/inferences to generate value in early settlement; the rest will not. Among the 15 good settlement prospects, there may be five cases worth litigating. If you limit[9] your initial commitment to vigorous settlement efforts, you will be far wiser in selecting prospects whose cases are viable for a full-fledged lawsuit. By the time you have exhausted vigorous settlement efforts, you will have a pretty fair idea of the employer's defenses, both factual and legal. You will also have more insight into the negotiating positions and flexibility of your opponent and your client.

---

[9] See ABA Model Rules of Professional Conduct, Rule 1.2(c) and your local equivalent rules. *Lawyers Weekly* 12-13-99 B5 has an article outlining the boundaries of this type of approach.

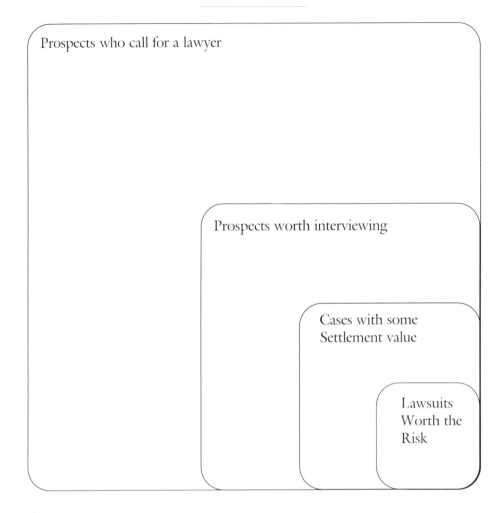

Prospects who call for a lawyer

Prospects worth interviewing

Cases with some Settlement value

Lawsuits Worth the Risk

AVOID PHONE SCREENING

It seldom makes sense to let someone tell you the details of their suffering over the phone. Minutes, even hours, of time will present rambling narratives, unorganized tirades against their employer and requests for hasty opinions. At the same time, a prospect's morale often requires some human interaction. Many good prospects may be hurt or insulted if the lawyer fails to show respect by taking a *short* phone call. If the lawyer tries to screen them all by phone, a huge amount of time and energy will be consumed by weak or non-existent legal cases. S/he will be attending to facts that may be interesting, but are legally unimportant. Thus, a three-minute phone conversation is desirable, but alternative methods for detailed screening are more useful.

If your workload is already overwhelming you, tell the prospect immediately and refer them to another NELA lawyer or a good PI lawyer, who belongs to state or national trial lawyers association. If you have time to listen, you should focus their inquiry by asking "What happened most recently to lead you to call a lawyer?" Soon, you will get enough information to decide whether to send a questionnaire to them, agree to review a written narrative, or reject the prospect. If they are in the wrong jurisdiction, refer them to NELA lawyers in the state where the dispute originated. If it appears that they are close to a deadline, you should take steps to ensure that they appreciate the rigidity of statutes of limitation. Failure to advise a prospect of its imminence is likely malpractice, even for a prospective client. You must be crystal clear about what you are doing or not doing on their behalf. In the phone call, do not leave uncertainty or ambiguity. Immediately send them a letter.

If it appears that all the various statutes of limitation are *clearly* blown, there is little benefit in wasting your time or theirs. Some lawyers debate whether to tell or to remain silent, because either option may risk malpractice. Personally, I err on the side of communication and choose to take that risk—I run through the checklist of all the potential limitations' intervals, then I say that "you waited too long and now I can do nothing for you." I still suggest second opinions.

SCREENING PROSPECTS BY A WRITTEN QUESTIONNAIRE OR NARRATIVE

It is important to obtain the prospect's version of facts in their own handwriting or typed notes. This is important, legally and psychologically. It shows their commitment to the process of resolving the dispute. Written information also demonstrates a fragment of their communication skills, memory, perception and *may* provide insights into their sincerity. It also protects you from initial misunderstandings of facts and later ethics charges if there were omissions or deceptions.[10]

Narratives

Most narratives come unsolicited. They are typically rambling and disoriented. The prospect doesn't know what is legally important—that's why they are calling a lawyer. For quality control, I usually insist that the narrative portion be limited to three pages and in simple, chronological order.[11] If they already have a 20 page narrative, I direct them to summarize it in three pages. There is little rea-

---

[10] One client filled out a questionnaire stating that she did not belong to a union. When the employer moved to dismiss on grounds of pre-emption, by a collective bargaining agreement, I had basis to withdraw and avoid sanctions.

[11] The ideal is reverse chronological, because analyzing facts in a backwards direction enables one to see different patterns. The approach, however, seems to confuse many prospects.

son to encourage an interview, until you have seen whether the narrative displays some potentially viable legal claims or side issues with leverage potential.

Questionnaire

The written questionnaire is much more effective. It organizes information in a comprehensive fashion. Its familiarity facilitates your quick review. Joseph Posner of Los Angeles' NELA originated a model questionnaire that remains a marvelous invention. The sample on the CD/disc is simply my variation. The questionnaire allows a lawyer to quickly discern whether an interview is warranted.

REASONS TO REJECT PROSPECTS

There are many reasons to reject prospects. The reasons include:

1) No liability facts
2) Poor liability facts
3) Weak or no damages
4) Prospect wants free ride
5) Prospect has offensive personality
6) The presence of contradictions on core issues
7) Prospect wants to vent, not really serious about dispute.

As plaintiffs' attorneys, we frequently want to help and often have the extreme confidence that we can do something for everyone. This altruistic[12] attitude usually results in big mistakes. We all make errors in judgment, but the most common mistakes can be devastating to a sane, successful practice. The most common blunders are:

❖ Saying "yes" too quickly
❖ Saying "yes" too often
❖ Saying "yes" to litigation without exhausting the options like vigorous settlement efforts and learning the opponent's positions
❖ Failing to educate the prospect about the probability of settlement
❖ Failing to educate the prospect about *realistic value* for settlement and the differences between settlement value and trial value
❖ Depriving yourself of the leisure time to brainstorm, anticipate developments, and actually plan strategies—usually a result of taking too many cases into litigation

---

[12] "Generosity is an inborn trait: altruism a learned perversity. No Resemblance." Robert Heinlein, *Time Enough for Love.*

❖ Making a dollar demand before they respect your liability

❖ Failure to ascertain the client's real needs and genuine willingness to settle, if the price is right.

Rejecting Interviewed Prospects

Most prospects appreciate honesty and bluntness. To avoid risking malpractice by giving legal advice, many lawyers use euphemisms; e.g., "I'm too busy," or "I only take cases like this on an hourly basis," or "Try Jane Doe. She handles your type of case." These convenient excuses do a disservice. Many folks are not really seeking a fight, but they want an honest opinion. Often they want some closure on this conflict. You are knowledgeable and they deserve your honest opinion.

A candid opinion helps bring closure. When a lawyer takes the time to explain that the law does not require fairness, the client begins to understand their difficulty in finding a lawyer. For example, if you state: "The law is not justice. It sets a series of obstacle courses and I don't think you can jump over them. [The legal (or factual) strengths of your cases are overwhelmed by the legal weaknesses.] I cannot justify investing 300 hours into a case with a small chance of winning. Even if you win, the jury awards for these types of injuries are so low, that it doesn't make economic sense to do the battle. You could pay me by the hour, but it's not smart for you and you are probably not able to invest over $50,000." Personally, I take the time to explain in detail the legal obstacles and specify the real reason I am unwilling to take their case. Sometimes, the real reason is, "I'm too busy." But more often, workload has been used a convenient pretext for avoiding bluntness about a mediocre case.

Know Thyself

We all fluctuate in our receptivity to the sympathy factor. I'm a sucker late on Friday afternoon, but I'm solid Monday-Wednesday.[13] Armed with my self-knowledge, I leave early on Friday.

SUMMARY OF SELECTION CRITERIA

When I look at a prospective client, one criteria overrides all others:

> 1. Do I like this person? Do I want to commit to 300 hours for this person's case? Or should I start with a sample of 30 hours?

---

[13] If you like the prospect, that's a strong plus. But, be cautious. I used to have a caseload consisting of 70 percent sexual harassment cases. When I realized I was into "rescuing damsels in distress," I reoriented my practice to insure I was making decisions on the basis of good business.

The other criteria go to the merits. It is useful, especially in evaluating the prospect for initial settlement efforts, to ask:

2. *Do the facts fit within accepted causes of action (statutory or common law)?*

   If yes, go to #3. If no, consider the viability of importing new causes of action, examining peripheral facts, or rejecting the prospect.

3. *Is the "fit" sufficient to leverage an employer to:*
   a) *pay money to avoid the dispute; or*
   b) *avoid paying substantial costs to defend itself?*

   If yes, go to #4. If not, consider gathering related facts and go back to #2, or reject the prospect.

4. *Is the alleged harm verifiable?*
   a) *economic harm? (Or the side effects)*
   b) *emotional harm? or*
   c) *reputation harm?*

   If one category is yes, go to #5 and #6.

5. *Can the harm likely be connected to the employer's decision?*

6. *Can the harm be translated into sufficient dollars to justify 30 hours of time?*

7. *Is there a clause requiring arbitration or prior grievances?*

   Arbitration is not a reason to reject a case, but it enables you to appreciate the forum that is your competition for settlement. The changes in mandatory arbitration in recent years prove that one person can make a difference. For several years, Cliff Palefsky spearheaded efforts to stop mandatory arbitration. He led NELA's lobby that has successfully pushed many companies and institutions to stop validating mandatory arbitration by their participation in employment disputes. Mandatory arbitration is less of a threat because of this effort.

If the plaintiff is very likeable and his or her case feels like a good "cause" case, the criteria are less important. In all other cases, you must also look closely at the potential dollar value of damages and reciprocally, fees. The numbers must be large enough to take the risk, but pre-suit efforts involve far less risk. Thus, damage expectation should be lower and fee expectation should be lower. I charge a retainer for fees (not costs) equal to two weeks gross pay at their job and a 20 percent contingency for pre-suit settlement. At this reduced rate, the settlement minimum to ensure profit is predicted by five times your hourly rate multiplied by the expected number of hours. The multiple of five is derived by dividing 100 % by your contingency percentage (20%). If you expend the typical 30 hours, you will need $6,000 in fees to achieve your hourly rate ($200 per hour x 30 hours = $6,000 for fees). Thus, this $6,000 in fees is multiplied by 5 and demonstrates that the case must have settlement value of at least $30,000 to justify your effort if profit at your hourly rate is the goal—as opposed to a cause case. Remember, it is a minimum threshold.

(Hourly rate) X (expected hours) X (100%/20%) =   Early Settlement
                                                   minimum to make a
                                                   fair profit

e.g. $300 per hour X 30 hours X 5 = $45,000 minimum (at 20% for fees)

e.g. $150 per hour X 30 hours X 4 = $18,000 minimum (at 25% for fees)

This crude formula is not cast in stone. It's a method of calculating backwards from what you need to justify the efforts. Most decisions are made on gut level. The formula may merely provide a rationale for feeling good about the choice to accept a case and limiting your commitment to vigorous settlement efforts.

Chapter Eleven

GATHERING LEVERAGE

The creative process is a complex gathering of influences.

Shawn McNiff, *Trust the Process*

Once you decide to interview a prospect, you must gather the important facts. The facts are fundamental to the whole process. They are the building blocks for the inferences that win cases and settlements. Fact gathering requires you to be sensitive, yet probing. You must be systematic, yet open to impromptu disclosures. It is essential to maintain a dual focus: See the big picture but also identify micro details. There are seven steps that are essential to get reliable data and create a healthy mind-set. Without these steps, days of your life may be wasted:

1. Finding facts
2. Extracting details and subtle facts
3. Identifying the damages facts and external impact
4. Explaining the limits of your initial commitment—bifurcation
5. Controlling expectations of prospective clients
6. Giving the client/prospect a homework assignment
7. Obtaining signed releases

FINDING FACTS

LOCK IN CLIENT'S VERSION ON PAPER

If you haven't obtained the prospect's version in a questionnaire or in his or her own handwritten or typed notes, it should be obtained before the interview. As mentioned in Chapter 10, a client's willingness to complete a detailed questionnaire shows commitment and demonstrates his or her communication skills. It can also protect you from initial misunderstandings, omissions or deceptions that may result in blaming you for not knowing something important. A written questionnaire is more effective than narratives because it organizes information in a comprehensive fashion and in a way that is familiar and easy to read.

Interviews

In the oral interviews, the lawyer can either let the prospect do the talking, control the interview from the outset, or do a combination. I have found it is often wise to let the prospect begin discussing what seems most important to him or her. Then, I gradually assert control by directing the questions.

Tape recorders may free your hands from taking notes, but they can also cause suspicion and inhibit the client's sense of confidentiality. Some lawyers use a paralegal as a note-taker during the interview. While there is benefit in another's perspective and questions, the presence of a third person inevitably alters the dynamics of candid disclosure that is essential to good evaluations.

Many lawyers have a paralegal conduct the initial interview. This may be an efficient use of lawyer time, but it has other consequences. Unless paralegals are exceptionally well trained or intuitive, their empathy may outweigh their "crap detector." They may not know how to bring the depth of information needed for a thoughtful evaluation to the surface. Liability facts are not enough. You need to devote special energy to eliciting the other types of facts and judging this plaintiff as a potential witness.

YOUR MIND-SET DURING INITIAL INTERVIEW

Skillful interviewers learn to listen with their brain and eyes as well as their ears. Many folks listen to the words, but not the meaning behind the words. Others hear the words, but fail to listen to the intonations, the silences and the pauses. Many fail to listen with their eyes and miss the clues offered by gestures and positioning. At the first interview, the most important clue to listening is often "what is not said." It is critical to recognize what is left out.

During these interviews, it is crucial that your "crap detector" is working. Beware of blatent dishonesty, but more importantly watch for hasty conclusions, inaccuracies, misperceptions, faulty memories, and hidden agendas. Your "crap detector" is your latent common sense—a feeling that tells you when things just don't jive, that something doesn't feel right or make sense. If your personal common sense derives from actual experience, it will be strong and reliable. If it's rooted in unconscious stereotypes, such as automatically believing plaintiffs, you may easily be blinded. Pay attention to what is NOT said. This is especially true for information that feels like it should be there.

SEEING PATTERNS

Looking at a chaotic array of facts is analogous to listening to music. The more diverse your experience, the more you will be able to recognize and appreciate the patterns that provide meaning.

> Sounds become Music when we see a Pattern.

In *Patterns of Mind*, Ray Jackendorf points out that if we hear a sequence of notes that conform to a pattern we are familiar with; e.g., "Happy birthday," we recognize a melody. If, however, the notes are played backwards; e.g., "Yadhtrib yppay" the rhythm feels irregular and it doesn't make sense. It has no melody. It is still sound, but it doesn't make sense as music. Our ability to make sense of music comes from having a collection of musical patterns in our heads. We use these patterns to organize the sounds we hear.

Music communicates emotional states and is sometimes symbolic, but music does not have feelings. It is nothing but sound waves. The feelings are emotional responses we have individually learned to associate with the sound waves.

Similarly, the facts we observe take shape according to the patterns we are able to see. If our mental database is large enough and varied enough, we are able to see many possibilities. If the facts are blurred and confused, there is no pleasure in their connection. Until the facts make sense and take shape in some coherent pattern, they do not produce a melody, much less any music.

Feelings do not reside in the facts. They are emotional responses we have learned to associate with certain fact patterns. Experience is a powerful source for generating patterns to measure a particular set of facts against. It is much like reading the same book ten years later. The book became more intelligent in the intervening years. The meaning we get from a book comes largely from within us, from what we bring to bear on the book's contents. The price of this book is adjusted by experience levels of its reader. My premise is that it will have increased value for the experienced lawyer, because of what s/he brings to bear on the concepts. The same is true of court decisions we read. Ultimately, the meanings we get from the morass of facts presented by a client are derived from our own experience.

Your ability to see clearly is largely shaped by knowing what to look for. Part of this skill is your legal training and experience, but if you appreciate differences in types of facts, your progress is accelerated.

DIFFERENT TYPES OF FACTS

The very act of *looking* for different types of facts enables the lawyer to find them and do it earlier. Facts serve different purposes. Some persuade opponents that the legal threat is realistic—they give special incentive. Others help establish value. Certain facts become anchors for dissolving or sidestepping arguments of the defense during negotiations.

The basic types of facts include:

- ❖ Basic facts
- ❖ Liability facts
- ❖ Linchpin facts
- ❖ Damage facts (including impact facts)
- ❖ Peripheral facts.

Basic facts include identities and locations of the employee and employer, the dates of employment, job title, job description, supervisors, and position changes. They include the events that bring the client to a lawyer; e.g., termination, promotion, harassment and failure to hire.

Liability facts are the material facts; i.e., the elements of each cause of action. They are generally consistent from one jurisdiction to the next, but with slight variations.

Linchpin facts are not basic facts, nor even liability facts. Rather, they are certain pivotal facts that make one side's version more believable than the other. They go to credibility of persons or documents. When we are confronted with a situation of his word vs. her word, we should identify one fact which can tip the scale, even a tiny fact. This is the linchpin fact. For example, in one sexual harassment case back in 1986, I had the classic her word vs. his word dispute with no witnesses to the main events. After he won the unemployment hearing, I obtained a reversal based on the internal consistency of her story. Thus, both sides felt stalemated by a third parties' assessment. Before commencing suit, I kept searching and found one witness who saw him standing very close to her, his crotch near her shoulder. The witness also confirmed that one day she had seen my client exit the defendant's office angry and very flushed. Those two facts were sufficient lynchpins to tip the scale and result in a good settlement.

Damages facts are those that evidence the injury. They may be emotional facts, diagnosis facts, harm to reputation or economic losses. Impact facts refer to other consequences suffered by the plaintiff (eviction, bankruptcy, etc.) These are elaborated more in Chapter 13.

Peripheral facts are background facts, prior employment successes/failures, family issues, quirky details that make someone special and may invoke a sympathy factor. They help flesh out the big picture to the jury, but have little value in settlement. One other form of peripheral facts is commonly referred to as skeletons or dirt. These facts are details that someone else does not want brought into the light of day. It may be illegal conduct, currently hidden from public view or embarrassing conduct like a sexual affair. At most, these types of facts should remain as a quiet backdrop. To emphasize them is to risk claims of extortion. No case is worth the risk of jail time. On the other hand, if they arise in the context of whistle-blowing, refusing to participate in illegal acts or fear of retribution, they may come front and center.

EXTRACTING DETAILS & SUBTLE FACTS

The initial probing should be gentle, but then you must get to the hard questions. As you grasp a sense of the potential legal claims, you will know where to dig deeper. The exhuming of facts is absolutely essential. The case is superficial without the artful probing.

Typically, you will be flooded with soft facts and conclusory statements. You must dig deeper. You should initially give them the benefit of the doubt about their conclusions, but keep looking for that something that triggered their superficial beliefs. While probing the strength of data underlying their conclusions, you should remind them that beliefs usually come from somewhere. You are eliciting the clues that led them to their conclusions. Often, it is useful to ask them what led them to suspect that discrimination was the motive. Most of the time, the facts are soft and inferences are coincidental, but sometimes you hear hard facts that they took for granted.

FACTS TAKEN FOR GRANTED

When you listen to prospects, you must take notice of what the prospect is assuming. What is the prospect taking for granted that you know? There is always considerable miscommunication during this first interview. The prospect has lived through a reality first hand for several months or years; you are just touching the surface.

The act of trying to condense years of employment or days of harassment into a few hours is very difficult. It is inherently unfair, but summarization is necessary to grasp the big picture. Other details will surface later, but their importance cannot be fully appreciated at the beginning. You need a big picture to first anchor the details. As more details gradually emerge, this vision will change. A sense of facts being overlooked will allow more pointed questions and better information gathering.

Clients prefer to focus on the effects; they assume or avoid the issues of causation. These causation issues are, however, critical to you. You can refine their focus on the effects or external consequences, but you must equally focus on motive or causation.

IDENTIFY THE DAMAGE FACTS

In addition to gathering liability facts, it is necessary to acquire a general sense of the injury and the impact of events on the client both internally and externally. To do this, you should inquire about the following:

- ❖ *Loss of income*
- ❖ *Job search*
- ❖ *Negative references*
- ❖ *Emotional injury.*

Loss of Income

Has the prospect been able to replace his or her former income? Fully, partially or not at all? This is not simply an income issue—look at the effects of losing income. How has the prospect survived to date? Unemployment compensation, savings, loans from family or friends, exhausting credit lines, part-time wages? Was he or she forced to relocate or pushed into foreclosures or evictions, obligated to move into a smaller place, take on more roommates? Was he or she forced into bankruptcy?

You should get a feel for the prospect as a person. Will he or she be able to survive during a lawsuit? Will the prospect have the stamina to go forward, to contribute to the out-of-pocket costs or keep up the struggle? These impact facts may have little importance as legal facts, but they will bear on the ability to endure and may enhance the "empathy" factor.

Job Searches

Has the prospect been active in job searches? Did he or she get any interviews? Any offers? Poor offers? Did he or she turn any jobs down? Why? How does this job search compare to prior search experiences? It is helpful to explain that only 10 percent of the jobs are found in newspaper want ads. It is appropriate to encourage networking and using employment agencies (for employer pay only) for both a paper trail as well as success in finding a job.

Negative References

Many prospects suspect they are being "bad-mouthed" around the industry. Does the prospect have any plausible basis to suspect that the former employer has actually given a negative reference or "put the word out?" Is that hypothetical reference the real cause of rejection or is it the employee, work history or the termination itself without reference to the reason? You should discuss ways that these word-of-mouth comments or rumors that be traced to the former employers; e.g., fake reference checks. Has the employee self-published the false and ugly reasons for termination? What was the response of the prospective employer?

Emotional Injury

When trying to gather emotional facts, it is not wise or necessary to grill the prospect right away. Similarly, do not start with open-ended questions. They are too hard to answer. Start with some simple, straightforward inquiries. Then move to open-ended ones. Open-ended inquiries elicit more honest answers. They also provide a sense of the prospect's ability to communicate as well as his or her other priorities in the information they select to reveal.

To ferret out additional details and damage facts, direct questioning must be resumed. People often speak in shorthand. They take for granted that the listener knows their experience, is familiar with their employer, and that the listener understands what they mean. They lived through the experience; it's second-nature to them. Often prospects assume the workplace and the effects should be equally obvious to the lawyer. Keep in mind that emotional pain is often invisible, but your job is to make it visible by translating into behavior. Try to elicit the emotional impact in terms of changes in behavior. Changes in behavior have more persuasive value than conclusory words. One valuable technique is to ask the prospect to compare his or her behaviors *before* the incident to behaviors *after* the incident. (See Symptoms Questionnaire on CD/disc.) This is especially important in relation to coping skills. An invaluable supplement is to ask friends and family to provide a similar comparison of *before* and *after* behavior.

When you initially probe for intimate detail, you can explain your invasion privacy by educating the client about the judicial attitude toward emotional distress. Courts often criticize characterizing emotional distress as easily fabricated and untrustworthy. The courts suggest that emotional distress is not easily verified in any objective way. [You must recognize that these arguments have some legitimacy, but there is no need to fight this issue head on. It's better to come at it sideways or from behind. For example, we also know that the defendant's story is easily fabricated, yet we give them the benefit of the presumption of honesty. Plaintiff's description of emotional pain should be afforded the same presumption of honesty.] Your reminder of this attitude will be even more crucial later if depositions are necessary.

LIMIT YOUR COMMITMENT

Most employees are unsure if they want to be in a lawsuit. There is no law or rule that requires you to agree to represent a person to the ends of time, to go all the way through an appeal, nor even all the way through trial. But once you have agreed to do so, you are essentially bound to pursue it. Attorney-client relationships are terminable at-will, but only the will of the client matters. Termination is the luxury of the client, not the lawyer. The lawyer must have cause. Some federal magistrates have even required lawyers to reveal their cause on the record in front of the opponents.

You can, however, ethically limit your initial commitment and base further obligations on what information is acquired from the employer. One method is to use two retainers—a bifurcated approach. In this approach, the first retainer involves your commitment to vigorous settlement efforts only (e.g., investigation, a draft lawsuit, and negotiation). The second retainer then involves traditional terms for full litigation. I actually use a bifurcated document—one page for use in vigorous settlement effort and a separate page for suit. (See sample retainer on disc.)

Be sure a section of your lawsuit-retainer contract cuts off your obligation to handle appeals. At a minimum, identify appeals as something to be separately negotiated. You may want to handle the appeal, but give yourself the choice. This choice should not be made until after you have acquired more information and can decide more intelligently.

CONTROLLING CLIENT EXPECTATIONS

EXPLAINING IMPORTANCE OF FACTS TO PLAINTIFF

People are intelligent, but they usually assume that law and justice are the same thing. It is very important to explain that law is not justice. Law consists of pigeonholes which lawyers call causes of action or legal theories. These pigeonholes have built in obstacle courses called elements. I make sure my clients understand the following key point.

> Unless you have the *right kind of facts*, all the other facts don't matter.

This insight is followed by: "Your personal facts showing success or pain will not motivate a settlement. They don't require a judge to allow you to have a trial. These type of facts are side issues. They may have an effect later, on a jury, if the judge let's you get to a jury. But, you must have enough of the right kind of facts to get past the judge."

It is not necessary to demoralize prospects, but it is necessary to give them a dose of legal reality. Many want to dump their conflict in your lap. You must be upfront about the obstacle course and strive to create a relationship as partners in this major project. You must be rooted in a realistic perception of what you can and cannot achieve.

Assumptions about the legal system are commonly mistaken, but deeply ingrained. Erroneous assumptions will control the client's point of view until you achieve clarity on this topic. Clarity requires both lucid explanations and considerable repetition. Be sure to ask yourself, "Does this prospect understand my jargon and limitations well enough that I want to go forward with their case?"

Controlling Expectations of Value

Client expectations of the value of a lawsuit have been enormously shaped by media distortion of other lawsuits. Only the big verdicts are reported: The press seldom reports when the verdict is low or when the employer wins. The media almost never follows up on a big verdict to reveal that post trial motions (or the appellate courts) drastically reduced the jury's verdict.

It is crucial to immediately start helping the prospective client **unlearn** these media distorted expectations. It may feel uncomfortable to disembowel a prospect's hopes, but you must bring some balance to the expectations of a future client. One method is to mention some recent cases that the press did not report. Discussing a case where the employer won or when the verdict was low will often zap prospects with a new reality. Alternately, the lawyer can illustrate a few "famous" local cases where big verdicts were later taken away on appeal.

> *Do Not Reduce Complex Facts To A Simple Dollar Amount*

Invariably, clients want you to reduce their complex facts to a simple number. My advice is strong: **don't**. At the onset, do not give them a single value for their case. You should educate them about the three different values of every suit—the trial value, the bottom-line value, and the demand value. It is also beneficial to explain how values change over time. Later, you can give them ranges for their case, but even then, proceed very cautiously.

Many times, morale is an important issue in deciding whether to sue. If the case has a low value and you candidly disclose this opinion, morale will be lowered. Blind confirmation of a high value is, however, stupid. You can reassure the client about the strengths of their case, but only if you simultaneously discuss the weaknesses. It may be prudent to confirm that they are doing the right thing, but you must maintain the prospect's intelligent **uncertainty** about value.

Another method is to mail them copies of factually similar cases with modest verdicts or large ones that were later taken away. It's often useful to discuss the differences between their case and other highly publicized similar cases. If you identify the facts that justified big dollars in those cases—the hospitalizations, bankruptcies, medications, extensive therapy, lengthy unemployment—the clients will begin to recognize the differences with their own case.

Often, a handout summarizing the results of a study of settlement will enlighten clients. For example, the Rand study reported that the median verdict in employment cases in California from 1985 to 1992 was $225,000. [Median means 1/2 the verdicts were higher and 1/2 were lower.] The appellate courts, however, reduced the median to $150,000. After deductions were taken for attorneys fees and costs, the median amount finally received by the plaintiff was $30,000. (See sample handout on CD/disc.)

Some prospective clients may feel uncertain whether a lawsuit makes sense and insist on an estimated value. To put the uncertainty into a new perspective, the following "If" grid can be presented orally or in writing.

If key documents support your claims,
　　　and if witnesses support your version,
　　　　　and if management witnesses falter or move away,
　　　　　　and if the judge allows it to go to trial,
　　　　　　and if the jury believes you got shafted,
　　　　　　　THEN, the verdict range is $ _____ to _____
　　　　　　　　(it may be higher if punitive damages are allowed)

Many clients believe their case is also good for punitive damages. Before answering, ask yourself if punitive damages are a good reason to accept a prospect's case. Rarely is this the case. More typically, you should explain how the courts usually refuse to allow punitives. Historically only a small percent of cases were likely candidates for punitive damages—perhaps 5 percent against corporations and 10 percent against individual tortfeasors. This is changing significantly based on the ripple effect of the Civil Rights Act of 1991. Even though the judges are ten years behind, as they were with CRA 1964, 19% of discrimination cases received punitive damage by Jurys according to the 1996 survey by Department of Justice, infra.

If you have one of those few cases, where *both* the liability claim and the claim for punitive damages are **clear-cut**, you can delight in it, but hesitate to hurriedly declare its potentiality to the client. You don't know enough, yet. If you chance upon one of those *rare* cases, don't waste time trying to settle. There is more leverage if you just sue it out rather than merely threaten to sue. Once you ensure that your judgment is objective, wait for them to come to you.

Calculate Actual Losses as of Today

Inflated expectations can be made more realistic by helping the client calculate actual losses to date. What is their actual wage loss, as of this moment? For example, in a case of defamation during the termination, you can say,

> "If trial was held today, your *actual* losses are two month's pay. The embarrassment of being fired hurts a lot, but it is similar to what everyone experiences at being fired. When the injury is the same as everyone who is fired, it has a low value—probably under $10,000. If things happened that make your firing unique and more painful, there could be more value."

Or if the reason was not per se, but required context, you can explain,

> "We suspect your reputation has been hurt, but we need evidence that your reputation was actually damaged—who believed the words. Right now the value, based on the proof we have, is very small. The reasons they gave for firing you are insulting, but they are vague and sound more like an opinion. The statement doesn't sound like a fact we can prove is false. In this type of case, damages are not automatic. We must find people who heard the false and ugly statement and changed their view of you as a result of the statements."

At the same time, you should conclude by pointing out, "As time progresses, your injury may grow worse or get better. For your sake, I hope it gets better. But if it doesn't, the lawsuit's value may be higher. Right now it is very uncertain."

Giving the Client a Homework Assignment

Clients need to be engaged in the process. They need to feel involved in this major undertaking. Besides, they are the best source of information. I recommend giving a homework assignment consisting of:

- ❖ A timeline of key events that includes a one page list of key events and an expanded list which layers all significant events.
- ❖ A list of witnesses that should specifically state what they are likely to know (i.e., what they saw or heard, what they likely know of relevant procedures, policies, past discipline, promotions...). This is *not* a listing of character references. Be explicit.
- ❖ The client's personnel records. It is usually best to help the prospect to obtain his or her *own* personnel file since it's less of a tip-off that a lawyer is involved. If the employer suspects that a lawyer may be involved, it can change the dynamics. The request initiates a low-level form of anxiety and a timing momentum.

Obtain signed releases

Before the prospect leaves, he or she should sign a release for medical records that may have corroborating information for either liability or damages. In addition, he or she should sign a release for personnel records. If the employer fails to respond to the employee's requests, this will allow you to follow up.

After a two-hour interview, if you feel ready to accept the case (on limited commitment or full-fledged lawsuit), tell the prospect. If you are not sure, let him or her know you need to study the documents, think about the big picture, and do some computerized research. This implants an awareness of your high-tech capabilities, the cost factor, and your willingness to invest effort into a thorough evaluation.

Chapter Twelve

Magnifying Strengths & Diluting Weaknesses

Your real analysis begins once the initial facts are identified. The morass of facts tossed at you, orally and in that box of papers, must be sifted and weighed. In *Waging Business Warfare*, David Rogers identifies three useful dimensions for seeing through the clutter of facts confronting the battlefield:

❖ grasping the situation as it really is, perceiving the information, the data, with as little prejudice as possible;

❖ rejecting the non-essentials—the junk, the garbage, the information that doesn't bear on the issues at hand—holding in mind only the essentials and the connections between them;

❖ seeing with what [military genius] Clausewitz called the "mental eye." Now you stop being objective. You are the only actor in the drama going on inside your head. You are distilling a decision from all your synthesized knowledge, experience, instincts and mental courage.

You cannot begin to appreciate the essence of a case until you are saturated in the facts. The act of scrutinizing facts from multiple points of view will allow the right decision to come to you, often in a flash of intuitive insight. The details will be fleshed out later…but you've got the answer and know what has to be done. Once this flash of insight has occurred, it is invariably accompanied by a powerful sense of confidence.

Your next task is to sort out what is legally important. To do that you will:

❖ Sort out MATERIAL facts

❖ Outline the first draft of the complaint

❖ Polish the complaint by filling the gaps and re-visioning the facts.

One half hour spent thinking about the big picture is worth several hours of impulsive scribbling or chasing a quick solution. Foresight is more powerful than hindsight, because it allows you to anticipate problems and prevent mistakes.

SORT THE MATERIAL FACTS

Your general sense of things should readily identify the most probable areas to focus on. But before identifying the precise legal claims, it is helpful to think in terms of the nature of the dispute. Ask yourself which of the following frames of reference apply:

❖ Broken promises

❖ Lies

❖ Decisions rooted in stereotypes

❖ Deliberate injuries

❖ Unintended, but preventable injuries

❖ Violations of statutes.

Once you have clarified your feel of the underlying conflict, these frames of reference can be readily converted to specific causes of action.

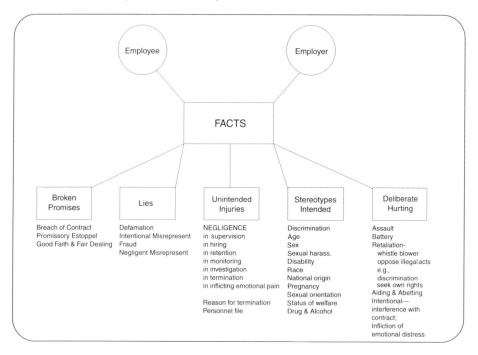

GUESSTIMATE THE CAUSES OF ACTION

You can trust your instincts, but recognize that your habits may neglect some worthwhile potential claims. To enlarge the possibilities, brainstorm all the possible causes of action that appear promising in your jurisdiction. Then shift to the left brain and evaluate the fact patterns against a checklist. (See sample checklists in the disc/CD that identifies 35 potential causes of action.) When you take the time to compare your brainstorm to a systematic listing, you become more comprehensive and exhaustive. You should have one checklist organized by legal causes of action, another by statutes of limitation, and if possible, a third by fact concepts. By classifying the claims in different ways, it's easier to see the possibilities and remember the deadlines.

IDENTIFY THE ELEMENTS OF EACH CAUSE OF ACTION

Once you have identified the causes of action, you must identify the **minimum** elements of each cause of action. This is critical: its importance cannot be understated. Too often, a lawyer's view of the elements is the product of reflex thinking and old habits. For example, we often assume that damages are an element of every claim, as it is for defamation. But the legal reality is that damages are not an element of Title VII. It is necessary to show an offensive environment, but you are not required to show legally-cognizable damages as you are in defamation or wrongful interference with contract.

The analysis of the elements will enable you to sift out the facts you have and the ones you don't have, yet. The analysis of elements will also enable you to identify where to look to obtain helpful information; e.g., from people other than plaintiff's witnesses, personnel records or from documents outside the personnel file.

Personnel records often contain valuable timeline information and statements unfiltered by the employer's lawyer. Generally it's best to obtain them indirectly through the employee. If you request them, they may be reviewed by a company lawyer. Most small employers try to save money and rely on their Human Resources personnel to be "correct" in response to all requests. You may wait to obtain the personnel records, but be sensitive to the risk of errors that could be prevented.

Medical records will have information that corroborates either liability facts or damage facts. Request them immediately. These records usually provide a more accurate timeline of events than your client. If the doctor recorded some of the employer misconduct that triggered the consultation or appears related to the consultation, the document may also provide legitimacy to the sequence of events and may help negate defenses of recent fabrication. Best of all, they may also contain evidence of causation. Some lawyers rely on clients to get their own medical records. This approach save pennies, but it is risky as some clients may withhold embarrassing documents.

Update Your research with LEXIS, WESTLAW or NELANET

*"Some books are to be tasted, others to be swallowed,
but only a few to be chewed and digested."*

Francis Bacon, 1605

Francis Bacon's thought on books applies equally to court decisions. Only a few are worthy of study, but those keep changing. Case law and statutes are constantly growing and updating your research is essential. Research can illuminate the policies underlying holdings and provide variations on the elements of the causes of action. These variations often provide opportunities to exercise creativity in evidentiary inferences. Computer research is an extraordinary tool not only for finding cases, but also as a valuable method of enhancing strategic thinking. It will generate cases that help you recognize subtleties that will allow you to better frame the issues. It will enable you to grasp new variations on a theme or types of facts that may be linchpin issues. Our NELA colleagues are creative in building inferences. This extraordinary asset should not be wasted.

Computer research can also identify *evolving* trends. For example, in 1997 I found 102 cases on depression, but 97 were tossed out as failing to meet the definition of a disability. At first, I made the easy assumption that hostile judges were hurriedly clearing their calendar. But as I wrestled with the data, I had to cope with the fact that many good judges had thrown out these same cases. I reread the cases and re-assessed my analysis. I realized that almost every lawyer, including myself, had handled ADA claims by assuming "working" was *the* major life activity. This turned out to be the fatal error. It created a "Catch 22". If your physical or mental condition prevented you from working, then courts held you were not qualified to work and you failed the second element.

A very few courts had adopted the EEOC regulations that working as the major life activity should be the *last* major life activity considered.[14] Under the regulations, you should have first checked if depression limited *other* major life activities; e.g., concentration, learning, reading and speaking, or the other seven originally listed. Only if none of these applied, should you check working.

This revision of case law has enabled dozens of cases to survive summary judgment for the author and other colleagues. The series of disability cases decided by the United States Supreme Court in 1999 reflects this analysis.[15] The Court

---

[14] *Merry v. A. Sulka.* 953 F. Supple. 922. *925 n8 (N.D. Ill. 1997). See regulations and Interpretative Guidance @ 1630.2(j).

[15] *Sutton v. United Airlines, Inc.* 119 S. Ct. 2139, 144 Led. 2d 450 (6-22-99) and three other disability cases decided that same day.

expressed doubt that working should be viewed as a major life activity. Although the *Sutton* line of decisions narrowed the application of the ADA by requiring consideration of mitigating measures where there was a "cure", it broadened the application to encompass the side effects of mitigation. Recent case law also reveals the benefits of updating research: The concept of working has finally been expanded to something more reasonable.[16]

The power of LEXIS and other computer research tools to help generate great settlements should not be underestimated. It can highlight variations on a theory. For example, in 1994, I had a sexual harassment, but the bad conduct was by a third party. There was very little Title VII law holding an employer liable for the acts of third parties. Through carefully selected search words, I broadened my search and "accidentally" discovered a wonderful theory of premise liability.[17] This approach did not require notice, only foreseeability. It also clarified my forgotten knowledge that notice is narrower form of foreseeability.

Similarly, in lure-away cases, I like many lawyers had applied only contract theories like breaches of contract and promissory estoppel, but no tort theories. LEXIS broadened my thinking. It enabled me to find uncommon causes of action including fraud-in-inducement and negligent misrepresentation. These added enormous leverage for settlement value to contract claims which had only minor consequences.

Computer research can also provide new spins on underlying theories: Often, I use LEXIS to cull opinions on particular issues by Judge Richard Posner of the Seventh Circuit Court of Appeals. Then, I do the opposite. I shepardize the cases that Posner distinguishes or mocks. This leads to other cases and invariably produces a more thoughtful analytical approach from another court that explains theories supporting employees.

LEXIS is a great tool for focusing on unique fact situations. For example, a search for "Section 1983" by itself will generate 7,000 cases *per year*, but if you add "Section 1983 and verdict," it will reveal approximately 300 cases that made it to trial. If you narrow the search again to "Section 1983 and verdict and police w/1 reserve," the result will be 16 cases—a readable number.

It is often valuable to run a prospective defendant through LEXIS. Usually, there is nothing. But other times you acquire little nuggets about their losses/wins, related evidence and sometimes insights into their litigation strategies.

---

[16] See *Fjelstead v. Pizza Hut*, 188 F.3d 944, (8th Cir. 1999) 1999 U.S. App. LEXIS 20138.
[17] See, *Maguire v. Hilton Hotels Corporation*, 899 P. 2d 393 (HA. 1995).

SEPARATE HARD FACTS FROM ALL OTHERS

Another method to improve the fact analysis is to write down the hard facts, but only the hard facts. Then, separately identify the soft facts that exist or are assumed to exist. Can your soft facts reasonably fit with the hard facts? If they do, go forward. If the facts don't fit, you don't have to acquit, but you must scrutinize the gaps. Apply common sense to see why something doesn't fit, what's missing or what is wrong with this picture. Unless your soft facts are consistent with hard facts, you have a problem.

Second, you should examine the legal conclusions you need for each count and contrast the hard facts with the inferences needed to reach the conclusion. The inferences can help fill the gap between soft and hard facts and connect both to the conclusions. To weigh the strengths of the claim, ask how many inferences are required. The more inferences required, the less believable the conclusion.

The following types of facts count as hard facts:

- ❖ Dates, if documented or the client's memory if specific and certain
    - ❖ dates of starting with company, job, position, assignment
    - ❖ dates of ending job, position, or assignment
    - ❖ dates of changes in the job
    - ❖ dates of performance reviews
    - ❖ dates of notice or complaints
- ❖ The incidents themselves
    - ❖ termination decisions
    - ❖ promotion/demotion decisions
    - ❖ hiring decisions
    - ❖ harassment—each specific occurrence
- ❖ Sequences of incidents—what happened 1st-2nd-3rd
- ❖ Who was present for incidents'
- ❖ Job title
    - ❖ Usual job duties
    - ❖ Changes in job, recent, and over the last 12 months
    - ❖ New duties added
    - ❖ Duties removed
- ❖ Facts very likely to be agreed to by both sides, if related to elements
- ❖ Key documents that are undisputed or likely to be accepted by both sides.

Most other facts are soft facts. They are not readily verified nor corroborated. They are typically single-person perceptions that do not meet the test of consensus reality. These include statements, attitudes, beliefs, mental anxiety, emotional pain, and subjective performance reviews.

Inferences are even more elusive. They are not clear-cut, but they act as links between known facts and conclusions. The inferences must be reasonable. Reasonableness is tested against ordinary perceptions of how things happen, against the conventional wisdom of the audience and occasionally, by common sense. Both the soft facts and the inferences must be reconciled with the hard facts. All three are necessary to create a theory that fits. The theory should be woven between the hard facts and the soft facts. At a minimum, it must also be consistent with the hard facts of the defendant. Hopefully, it explains away the defendant's soft facts. A theory that makes your inferences more probable than the employer's theory will be more powerful.

SCRUTINIZE THE FACTS IN COMPETITION

Certain facts are in competition not only at trial, but also in settlement negotiations. At trial, the judge or jury will be asked to select from competing facts. In settlement, the decision maker often acts as a fact finder by assessing credibility. One way to prepare for that fact-finding decision is simply by suspending your advocacy. Bluntly ask yourself, "If I was the judge, *how* would I decide who to believe? *How* would I make the credibility decision?"

As noted earlier, we trust others who are the most like us. Each of us benefits by looking at how we have made similar decisions in the past. For example, assume your children are fighting. One is accusing the other of some "horrible" conduct. How would you decide whom to believe? Would you consider their non-verbals, their eyes, the contradiction between tone of voice and words, the gaps between words and gestures? Would you defer the decision or look for some other solution; e.g., ignoring the credibility decision and simply punishing them both or appealing to some larger interest such as your need for *their* bedtime. A judge deciding not to decide may be acting in parallel. You must be like the judge and apply both gut instinct and analysis to decide credibility. Whether you call it left brain/right brain or the difference between science and art, analysis differentiates the facts, while gut instinct integrates the big picture.

IDENTIFY KEY FACTS

Few defendants will dispute all your key facts. It is important to identify specifically which key facts are likely to be disputed and which are not. Then focus your attention on the key facts that are likely to be disputed. This makes efficient use of your time in settlement preparation and maximizes your leverage during settlement talks. When you hear the employer's case, the nature of key facts may change, so it is necessary to be flexible.

You can use a key fact as an anticipatory strike. For example, a young sex harassment client claimed her boss had put her in a drunken stupor and had sex with her. We saw evidence of unwelcomeness, but then she reluctantly revealed that she had written a letter expressing her adoration for him. She didn't have a copy, but the letter sounded lurid and explicit. It weakened her argument of unwelcomeness. She claimed the letter was done at his request. We were skeptical, but we chose to believe her because her explanation made sense: She said he had asked her to write the letter to enable him to masturbate when he was traveling and she was not around. Her acquiescence, though naive, was plausible. We assumed that he intended to use the letter to show the sex was consensual and welcome. We adopted a judo tactic. Rather than hiding from this dangerous document, our draft complaint blatantly referred to it as a "coerced" document. It was a letter obtained by deception, tricking the clerk by bolstering her adolescent ego; i.e., he needed her. It appeared as if we had a copy of the letter and we used it to show his knowledge of his wrongful acts and a demonstration of his attempt to cover them up. His cleverness had backfired and magnified his fear of punitive damages. The result was a settlement of 51 years of pay.

OUTLINE THE FIRST DRAFT OF THE COMPLAINT

Once you have identified and sorted the material facts, you are ready to begin drafting the complaint. There are numerous issues to decide that can influence later settlement including:

- ❖ The number of defendants and which to include
- ❖ The number of counts to use
- ❖ The number for forums and which to use in the "draft" caption
- ❖ Whether to file charge with EEOC or State Human Rights
- ❖ Whether to request an immediate right to sue or wait for the natural course of EEOC to run.

These options are discussed in more detail in the entitled Mid-Stream Settlement section, referring to the moment after you have exhausted settlement efforts and are actually starting a lawsuit. For now, the considerations are briefly described.

Caption

The caption is important because commencing suit is "declaring war." Even though we are using a draft complaint, the forum selected will send different messages. The employer may be intimidated by federal court, but the defendant's lawyer may welcome it. Defense counsel appreciates the higher rate of dismissal in federal court, but clients rarely see past the aura of the U.S. Government or worry about a challenge to their lucrative government contracts.

Federal court is actually more attractive for cases with strong liability facts, but it should be avoided where the liability is a close call, and must be avoided when you are trying to create common law precedent. The pros and cons tend to be court-specific and as Tip O'Neil said, "All politics are local."

The forum on the draft complaint need **not** be controlled by the plans for a later lawsuit. The choice is, however, symbolic—if you are viewed as an experienced lawyer and you choose a federal caption, defense counsel may appreciate your expression of confidence.

Individual or corporate only

There are pros and cons to "suing" the individuals in the draft complaint. Often, suing individuals interferes with settlement because office politics mandates supporting managers. Other times, it enhances settlement by allowing the bad guy to become the fall guy.

CAUTION

"Divide and conquer" is a useful strategy, but it can impair a claim that the employer is vicariously liable for the conduct of the individual.

Number of counts

There is no right answer on whether to have three or six or ten counts. Multiple counts may generate more legal hooks and give more flexibility, but you risk dilution of the strong ones. Fewer counts will provide more focus and clarity, but may neglect other legal hooks that have grab appeal. It is crucial that you weigh the benefits of the clarity and power of a few versus the opportunities of the many.

In the first draft of the complaint, it is essential to list all the elements needed for each count, but **only** the elements. This preserves what you need without clutter and confines you to what is truly important. See Chapter 17 on Starting Suit. It is frequently beneficial to leave large blank spots to remind yourself where the gaps are. These gaps also help the client recognize what type of evidence is currently missing.

CHARGES WITH EEOC

Usually, it is advisable to make an overture to the employer *before* filing an EEOC charge. By delaying the filing of the charge, you can use it later to break a stalemate in negotiations or show renewed vigor.

IMMEDIATE RIGHT TO SUE OR WAIT

For years, I filed a charge and simultaneously requested an immediate right to sue. Historically, the EEOC was so overworked, understaffed and underfunded that delays of 6-18 months were the norm. Thus, an immediate right to sue avoided delay. Under the new EEOC regime, that, however, may be changing. They are committed to prioritizing and have new ground rules for weeding out time-consuming unlikely claims.

CAUTION
Immediate right to sue letters may now be dangerous in light of decision by the D.C. Circuit that the right-to-sue letter is **not** valid until 180 days after the charge was filed.[18] The window between 90 days to commence the suit and 180 after filing is thus a minefield.

The strategy of an immediate request of right to sue was also based on the fact that EEOC rules for the employer 92 percent of the time, on average. Most state human rights organizations generate similar data. The result demoralizes both prospects and clients. No matter what the explanation, the effect is the same. It is wise to forewarn your clients that both EEOC and most state human rights organizations rule against the employee over 90 percent of the time. Worse, a no-probable cause ruling emboldens employers into believing that a liberal government agency has approved their behavior and rejected the employee's claim. This inhibits negotiations. A timely, but not premature, withdrawal and right to sue avoids the no-probable cause demoralization.

Occasionally, there is significant benefit in waiting for the employer's written response because it can narrow the issues. It can lock in the factual justification

[18] *Martini v. Fanny Mae*, 178 F.3d 1336 (D.C. Cir. 1999).

and the articulated reasons for termination. Thus, waiting until the employer's response can simplify the issues on pretext.

Once in a great while, the subpoena power of EEOC will also generate more documents for inspection. Where there is some evidence of witness intimidation or retaliation, EEOC can and will obtain a court order to stop the intimidation or even the destruction of oral and written evidence. NELA lawyer Dee Rowe has developed this technique to an art form. She has identified leverage points to invoke EEOC's authority and uses them very effectively. Even the threat of EEOC intervention will often generate a stipulation to stop intimidation. This agreement can later be used to justify punitive damages, a civil penalty, or to explain an employer's "missing" evidence.

As a general rule, experienced lawyers defer to EEOC for investigation only in those cases that appear exceedingly weak, where they want to delay their own decision pending better information or they don't like the prospect and want to deflect them.

POLISH THE COMPLAINT

To polish the draft into a complaint that will have an impact on your opponent, you should:

- ❖ Re-vision the facts
- ❖ Show gaps to client
- ❖ Incorporate additional facts
- ❖ Adopt the point of view of the defendant
- ❖ Revise and revise again

RE-VISION THE FACTS

As you flesh out the outline of the draft complaint, juxtapose the client's timeline of key events with the medical and personnel records. This often reveals blurring of events and dates that need clarifying. If you let this blurring slip through, your opponents may seize on even a tiny error and derive an extraordinary sense of cockiness from it. Take the time to be precise with your sequences and hard facts. Constantly step back and ask yourself if all the facts fit together.

The act of re-visioning the facts opens doors to creative thinking. Persuasiveness comes from putting your facts into powerful packages. The Power of Opposites is a marvelous technique for expansion. It contrasts what happened with what should have happened. It makes use of factual contrasts to illuminate other ways of seeing the same event. It often generates a creative tension that sandpapers the brain, smoothing crude assumptions and clarifying elusive and subtle issues.

SHOW GAPS TO CLIENT

When you meet with your client again, use the obvious gaps in the draft to explain the problem areas. Highlight the contrast between problems that perpetually exist compared to the unique ones in this case. To help the client recognize the impact of these gaps, you can point out that the jury may not find the facts believable if the gaps are not filled; i.e., some of these gaps may be fatal.

This education provides a fertile opportunity to ferret evidence that is partially missing. You must maintain morale and identify the strengths of the client's case, but cannot neglect putting it in the context of weaknesses or obstacles apparent to you, the lawyer. Remind your client again and again of the importance of realistic expectations (e.g., refer to the handout on median verdicts mentioned in Chapter 11.)

You have limited time to investigate, so discuss witnesses with your client. Decide together who will be really helpful on liability facts. Remind the client that you are not looking for witnesses who will confirm a vague sense that termination was unfair or who provide character references, but rather people who can provide hard facts, specific statements or similar experiences. For strategy reasons, it is also important to identify who should be saved for last, perhaps because they might leak information to the employer.

EXPANDING THE FACT BASE

When you've identified the gaps, you know where to look to gather additional information. One prime source is the witness list you develop jointly with your client. Often lawyers drag third party witnesses down to their fancy offices for an interview. This is unwise because it is a foreign place that puts witnesses ill at ease. Go to their turf. This is especially true when they have important evidence. I have developed one technique that is user-friendly and successful. We meet at a café or coffee shop. After the social amenities and a brief discussion, I ask if it is okay to take notes. Then midstream, I discretely prepare a handwritten statement from the witness' point of view summarizing material facts. I record only solid facts and avoid conclusory statements. Then I ask the witness to read it for accuracy. After he or she confirms it or makes changes, I ask the witness to sign it. It is already written out, so it's easier and the witness has already agreed it's accurate. As he or she signs, I ask, "Do you swear this is true?" Once signed, the notary seal can be slapped on and voila, you have an affidavit. There is no need for fancy word processing. Handwritten statements have their own authenticity.

Good private investigators can be the source of great facts. Cultivate a relationship with a single investigator who may give you a discount or better and faster service because you work only with him or her. An investigator who is skilled at getting people to open up is worth his or her weight in silver. It's not necessary to worry about incidental details or cross-examination, which comes later. Some private investigators can find witnesses who disappeared years ago, even tracing them through several unlisted telephone numbers. They can also do asset searches on employers and executives.

Private investigators can make a tape or written record. In Minnesota, it is an ethical violation if a tape recording is made by an attorney or his agent without the consent of the witness. When I hire a private investigator, I give explicit instructions that they are to use their own professional judgment on whether or not to tape. This has been deemed to distance them as my agent.

THINKING BACKWARDS

When you feel frustrated by missing facts or missing elements, you must explore the alternatives. It often helps to think backwards. Generate reverse chronologies. This approach creates new connections that leap out as the facts are seen from a new point of view. New theories often emerge almost spontaneously.

When you are frustrated or sense something is wrong, a powerful way to dig deeper is to apply the Rule of Probabilities. Articulated by Louis Nizer in *My Life in Court*, this Rule relies on the probabilities of human behavior to consider what events likely happened before the liability event. I've expanded Nizer's approach into the art of thinking backwards. First, identify the event or incident (termination) that is known and the decision which caused this event. Then ask,

❖ What behaviors would have logically preceded this decision?

❖ What thought processes would have logically preceded the decision?

❖ What emotional reactions would have logically preceded the decision?

❖ If the decision-maker had been neutral and not pre-judged the outcome, what planning steps should have logically preceded the decision?

❖ What information would this person have to have to take this action?

❖ What beliefs would an ordinary person have to have in order to justify the way this decision was executed?

This strategy generates hypothetical information. After you generate possibilities by thinking backwards, apply what you know of likely human behavior (Rules of Probabilities) to the events, incidents to predict what thoughts, beliefs, assumptions, information probably preceded this crucial decision. This approach is invaluable in preparing the complaint, for depositions or cross-examination. It helps you see not only what probably happened, but also to anticipate what should have happened.

ADOPT THE POINT OF VIEW OF THE DEFENDANT

Plaintiff's lawyers often blind themselves to the point of view of the defendant. If we put on the hat of the opponent and diligently wear it for an hour, we usually gain a valuable insight or two. Because we are advocates, it takes extra effort. This process almost always generates a new way of seeing. Consider these questions in a sexual harassment case:

❖ How will I prove that she welcomed his overtures?
❖ How can I overcome plaintiff's evidence of pretext?
❖ How can I knock it out on motion to dismiss?
❖ How can I show the fact questions are not material?
❖ How can I show there is no genuine dispute?

Don't be trapped by legal frameworks. Think bigger. This will allow you to find both legal defects and factual defects and to see contradictions, incongruities or omissions. It will allow you to balance sequences and events against common sense. Once the gaps are identified, they can be filled and alternative explanations pursued. This approach greatly reduces the surprise factor during your first negotiation. Consider using LEXIS from the defense point of view.

Decide what to withdraw

While you are in the defendant's point of view, consider what facts you want to hold back for staging a later delivery in negotiations. Remember, evidence is more highly valued when they think you don't have it and you do. Alternatively, if they hinge a factual defense on something they don't know you have, you blast their defense away by producing it. Similarly, ask what facts do you want to preserve for litigation?

REVISE AND REVISE AGAIN

The complaint and thus, the potential for negotiation is now at a "C⁺" level. To bring it to the "A" level work requires a significant investment of time and effort, but the rewards are almost always worth it. Expand the details, then revise to make the facts tighter. Restructure for persuasive impact. Excessive detail detracts from the power of your weapon, but excessive compactness can cause the reader to skip over important details or sequences.

On important facts, the complaint should be specific, nitty-gritty specific, but you must keep some flexibility. [You can change to notice pleading at the time of suit.] Focus your communication on clarity, not argument. When the facts are clear, the argument speaks for itself. Words are our weapons. Therefore, we must use Power Verbs. Cut out the adjectives. Novel expressions are helpful, but only if they enhance clarity.

It is essential to remember that you are *not* trying to convince the employer that your side is 100 percent correct. You need only awaken them to an alternative point of view that raises uncertainty about their position. It is enough to raise doubts. Since the managers had previously convinced themselves that they did the right thing, you are only trying to show an alternative explanation for the facts—an explanation that *may* be seen as illegal or tortious.

You are unlikely to reverse inertia unless the alternative (a lawsuit) realistically appears to be more costly than settlement. At the early stages, losing is seldom real to employers. Disruption of management time is not yet real. Cost is speculative until the lawyer's first bill comes. General embarrassment usually has zero value, but the exposure of specific wrongdoing often provides incentive. This is especially true if it involves sexual harassment at high levels, obvious falsity or contradictory documents. Sometimes blatant and clear-cut unfairness will motivate, but only if your point of view on unfairness is truly objective. Alternatively, if dirt is involved, the complaint should hint at its presence, but only hint at it. Dirt should not be used unless it is relevant to some key issue.

Decision-makers tend to rigidly defend their position. Thus, it is important to come at the facts from a "business" perspective instead of a victim point of view. It is also preferable to provide a perspective that they have not likely considered.

Employers rarely act without consulting a lawyer. At the same time employers are not stupid; they usually recognize the vested interest of defense counsel in hourly litigation. Thus, they often do not routinely defer to the advocate's point of view. They seek objective input from the lawyer on the likelihood of their success and costs of defense. Thus, you should keep in mind that the defense lawyer is part of the audience who will read the complaint.

Now, the draft complaint should be ready and as perfect as you want it to be. This sets the stage for your next big picture: determining the value of this case. Stated another way, how much will an informal buyer be willing to pay to buy this settlement? What is a good sales price?

Chapter Thirteen

Determining Value

Every lawsuit has three distinct values. The differences between these three values cannot be overestimated. These values are interrelated, but each is distinct. It is hazardous to your legal health to blur them or to confuse them. The three distinct values are:

- ❖ **Trial Value**
- ❖ **Bottom Line**
- ❖ **Demand Value.**

The initial negotiation is with your own client. Before this negotiation, it is crucial that you compute the trial values and generate some estimates about demands. The bottom line comes from the client, but she or he should not be asked for a bottom line until you have thoroughly educated him or her about the weaknesses and strengths of the case. It should not be solicited until you have discussed a range of settlement amounts that are likely to be acceptable to the employer.

These value calculations cannot be made in a vacuum. Instead, you must compare your facts with verdicts for similar cases and ideally with the facts of other known settlements. Rather than seeking cases with similar liability evidence, you should look for similarity in the damages' evidence. The type of damages sought and received is important for finding persuasive parallels to your case.

You must make a vigorous effort to educate clients about the differences of these three values. When clients are walked through the process, they more fully appreciate the numbers, understand the different purposes for their uses and your strategies. Before your client can be educated, you must compute your own best approximations and you must "get real" with yourself.

TRIAL VALUE

Trial value is a baseline to use for other computations. It is necessary input for the client's intelligent assessment of a bottom line, but it can be dangerously misleading. The trial value should never be given out of the context of the weaknesses and obstacles of this case. Both the trial value and the client's bottom line are used to create the demand value. To compute the trial value baseline, you must address the value of each component:

❖ Economic
❖ Emotional injury
❖ Reputation damage
❖ Retaliation evidence
❖ Punitive damages.

Lawyers often treat economic losses as hard damages and emotional losses as soft damages. This emphasis on economic losses is misleading and usually distorts the big picture, but it is part of the reality of the audience and so must be addressed. The logic for this conventional wisdom is threefold: a) economic losses are easier to compute because they are essentially simple mathematical calculations; b) the loss is readily established by being unemployed or underemployed; and c) it is easily corroborated. In the last several years, we have seen a paradigm shift toward accepting emotional distress and bigger awards. NELA lawyers are largely responsible for causing this paradigm shift.

ECONOMIC LOSSES

Economic losses should be subdivided in three primary categories:

❖ Back pay
❖ Front pay
❖ Lost earning capacity.

You should make your basic calculations for each one separately.

Backpay = Income Lost Between Termination and Trial

Back pay income is salary plus all benefits that would have been earned if the client had remained employed, minus income from actual mitigation (the next job). The time frame is from trial backwards to termination. It is pragmatic to assume one year from the time of computation but this should be adjusted for actual data. As a rule of thumb, benefits are 30 percent of salary when viewed from the point of view of the employee. Later we discuss when to look at the *cost* of benefits to the employer that is sometimes closer to 70 percent of salary.

A plaintiff must try to reduce or mitigate his or her injury by looking for other work. If you inform clients that their settlement leverage is increased by their job search efforts, and explain that one or two applications per week is the bare minimum and four or five applications per week is the ideal, it usually increases their efforts.

CAUTION

If the client's efforts to find new income have been meager or undocumented, you must modify your calculations for jobs that a reasonably diligent person could have found.

Front Pay = Income Lost Two to Three Years Into the Future

Front pay is salary or wages plus all benefits that the employee would have earned with the employer in the years ahead minus mitigation that has happened or is reasonably likely to happen. The time frame is from trial to a time when the new income catches up with the old income, at least theoretically. You can add in pay increases that were likely had the client remained employed. Historically, there was a major difference between partial replacement of future income and total replacement. When there is only a small pay differential between former and current job, ten years has been accepted.[19] When the replacement income was zero, three or four years was the maximum, unless the employee was close to retirement. With the advent of lost earning capacity, there has been a shift that narrows front pay, but elongates lost earnings through this new use of an old theory. Although Title VII cases have caps on compensatory damages, back pay and front pay are **not** included in the caps.[20]

CAUTION

To be eligible for front pay, the complaint must request reinstatement.

You should avoid routine extensions of front pay to age 70; they look bogus. The exception is if the employee is close to retirement; i.e., five years. If the measure of lost earning capacity applies, it is pragmatic to limit your claim to two to three years of front pay.

Lost Earning Capacity = Income Lost Over Lifetime

Lost earning capacity is different from front pay. It is a tort concept aptly illustrated by one case more clearly than any other.[21] In *Williams*, the employee had a salary of $44,000 per year, but the Seventh Circuit affirmed the award of compensatory damages of $500,000 and lost earning capacity of $250,000 in addi-

---

[19] *Hukkannen v. Int'l Union of Operating Engineers, et al*, 3 F. 3d 281, 285 (8th Cir. 1993).
[20] *Martini v. Fanny Mae*, 178 F.3d 1336 (D.C. Cir. 1999).
[21] *Williams v. Pharmacia, Inc.*, 137 F. 2d 944 (7th Cir. 1998).

tion to backpay of $180,000 and front pay of $115,000. The court beautifully explained the differences between lost earning capacity and front pay:

> Reinstatement (and therefore front pay)...does not and cannot erase that the victim of discrimination has been terminated by an employer, has sued that employer for discrimination, and the subsequent decrease in the employee's attractiveness to other employers into the future, leading to further loss in time or level of experience. Reinstatement does not revise an employee's resume or erase all forward-looking aspects of the injury caused by the discriminatory conduct. ...On occasion, courts have awarded damages under the rubric of front pay that may be better described as lost future earnings. ...Damages for lost future earnings, in contrast, are not limited in duration in the same way. The reputation or other injury that causes the diminution in expected earnings can stay with the employee indefinitely. Thus, the calculation of front pay differs significantly from the calculation of lost future earnings. Whereas front pay compensates the plaintiff for the lost earnings from her old job for as long as she may have been expected to hold it, a lost future earnings award compensates the plaintiff for the diminution in expected earnings in all of her future jobs for as long as the reputational or other injury may be expected to affect her prospects. Id.

CAUTION

You should anticipate evidentiary needs and show harm to reputation. The *Williams* decision included this caveat: "To recover for lost earning capacity, a plaintiff must produce id competent evidence suggesting that his injuries have narrowed the range of economic opportunities available to him.... [A] plaintiff must show that his injury has caused a diminution in his ability to earn a living."

Sometimes an economist is necessary to calculate lost earning capacity. Other times, an employee at a vocational rehabilitation center can generate the number at a lower cost. Whomever you choose, you should discuss with the expert, whether retained or merely consulted, the *plausible* assumptions to be made on plaintiff's facts. If this projection is left to chance, a revised opinion may be costly.

Evidence of harmful impact on career is not new. In the late 1970s, NELA's Bill Holloway was very creative and successful in an early variation on lost earning capacity.[22] The award was mid-seven figures, and it was 18 years ago.

---

[22] *McGrath v. Zenith*, 651 F.2d 458 (7th Cir. 1981).

Another example was when a lawyer was terminated from a big law firm.[23] An economist showed it would take 20 plus years to earn income at a small firm or in solo practice comparable to what he would have earned at the big firm. In *Brooks*, supra, the big dollars were offered as economic loss, but the jury applied them as a measure of reputation damages for the defamation claim.

Other Losses—Specials

Some courts have allowed employees to recover for job search expenses, including career counseling, travel to jobs and parking.[24] A few courts have added other specials, including aggravation of marital difficulties, aggravation of general anxiety, and depression separate from mental anguish. These were prior to the availability of compensatory damages under Title VII, but they may still be useful under state law claims. Keep in mind that Title VII has significantly expanded compensatory damages and eventually we will persuade the trial and appellate judges that they reflect community values and should not be reversed as excessive. Prejudgment interest is also presumed.[25] This is often a significant value and becoming increasingly common.

Increasing the Basic Calculations

Straightforward back pay computations are often conservative and do not reflect the true picture. Be sure you:

- ❖ Add in growth factors
- ❖ Compute with and without benefits, stock options
- ❖ Make the time factor and amount look reasonable
- ❖ Check for true career damages.

Add in growth factors

If there has been a history of income growth, it is appropriate to factor in the history of raises and project them forward into the back pay calculations. This adjustment extrapolates even further into the future with front pay and lost earning capacity.

For example, if the employee earned $50,000 in the last calendar year, one year of back pay and two years of front pay equals $150,000. If the employee's earning history had shown an average rate of growth equal to 10 percent, the ripple effect increases growth curving the value considerably to $182,500. This $30,000 increase is easy to justify. The increase compounds upon itself.

---

[23] *Brooks v. Doherty, Rumble & Butler.* 481 N.W.2d 120 (Minn. App. 1992).
[24] See *Valdez v. Church's Fried Chicken*, 683 F. Supp. 596 (W.D. Tex. 1988).
[25] *McKnight v. General Motors Corp.*, 973 F.2d 1366 citing *Morales*, 825 F.2d 1095 (7th Cir. 1987).

A further illustration projects the amount of growth where the employee had an average history of 15 percent increases and could justify a front pay of five years. The easy method showed a loss of $250,000, but when the pay increases were added in, the loss is $336,600. Both figures must be offset by mitigation income.

					$87,000
				$76,000	
			$66,100		
		$57,500			
	$50,000				
$43,500					
1997	**1998**	1999	2000	2001	2002

Year of termination

Calculate growth curve of salary with and without benefits

The growth curve should first be computed including benefits in the income history. But it should also be computed without including benefits. The inclusive approach often dilutes the percentage of growth because the value of benefits is more stable than salary. It is better to experiment before deciding which is most favorable and salable. Stock options usually have a dramatic increase on the percentage of growth and they should be computed separately.

Make the time factor and amount look reasonable

When you calculate future earnings with the salary history, the amount of change is dramatic. You must be careful not to inflate the length of time or amount. To maintain credibility, the number cannot be artificially transparent. Adjust the numbers to look systematic and reasonable.

Check for true career damages

Career loss can be a measure of lost income **or** injury to reputation. Some economic evidence may also be used either to show direct income loss or indirectly to evaluate reputation damage. In *Brooks v. Doherty, Rumble & Butler,* supra, the jury received career loss data offered as evidence of income loss, but then used the same data to put a dollar value on the damage to the reputation. The expert, a law firm consultant, testified to the income differences between big law firm employers and smaller law firm employers—an amount estimated at

$2.1 million. He gave an expert opinion on the impact of how long it would take to catch up if a lawyer was blackballed from big firms. The employee had a two-year contract at $55,000 per year, but was fired after only six months. The verdict on defamation was almost exactly $2 million—36 years of pay based on his contract income. Although the defamation claim was taken away on privilege grounds, the impact on the jury was clear. Reputation loss was equated with income loss.

EMOTIONAL INJURY

You cannot evaluate the emotional injury until the emotional facts are gathered. The phrase "emotional distress" often creates mental blocks. If you refer to it as emotional injury or emotional pain there are fewer built-in prejudices and more flexibility. Either way you refer to it, a comprehensive way to evaluate your client's emotional pain is essential.

One method of obtaining basic emotional facts is to ask the client to complete a detailed listing of his or her suffering. Over the years I have developed and expanded a Symptoms Checklist. It uses laymen's language for clarity (see exhibit on disc/CD). The checklist helps clients find ways to talk about the often "unwordable" feelings. Simultaneously, it organizes the necessary information in an easy-to-read fashion. It is not a substitute for medical records or expert analysis, but it provides a useful, low cost starting point.

Another method is to ask clients or prospects to write a narrative about their emotional pain. The result is, however, often inadequate. Frequently, it is cluttered with anecdotal details that require exhaustive sorting. The checklist seems to make it easier to identify the effects.

At best, medical and psychological records can provide *direct* evidence of emotional suffering. More often, it is only by inference. At worst, they reveal the absence of corroboration. You need medical records for at least two years preceding the incidents at issue. They provide a bigger picture that may corroborate, contradict, or enhance the initial evaluation. Often, it is necessary to read between the lines, but looking for prior symptoms and the evolution of symptoms is exceedingly useful. Medical records are not enough; therapist and psychological records are also required.

When you listen to the prospect or client discuss his or her emotional pain, you must listen with your brain, your eyes, and your common sense. This will help you decide whether to merely consult or actually retain an expert for evaluation. A series of questions to consider include the following:

Does the Pain Sound Genuine?

Does it have a ring of truth? Does it resonate with the non-verbal communication? Ultimately, you must trust your gut on this one. If the client's words jive with their body language, it's more likely to be reliable. If the verbal communications is not consistent with the nonverbal or if something feels strange, it is wise to worry about suppressed pain or be skeptical about hidden agendas. You must probe and improvise when to be gentle and when to be blunt.

Is the Pain Clearly Communicated?

Can the client articulate the different aspects of how she or he feels, how the incident has affected them? Is the deterioration of condition clear and coherent? Why does client suspect that it is connected *only* to only events in the employment setting?

Is the Pain Documented?

Is it available or can it be reconstructed honestly from written sources such as memos, e-mails, letters to managers or Human Resources, diaries, journals or letters to friends/family?

Is the Pain Corroborated by Others?

Is the pain corroborated by others, such as the treating doctor, psychiatrist, psychologist, MSW or religious counselor? Can family members or roommates attest to changes in personality or behavior? Can objective testing; e.g., CPI or MMPI support the client's claims?

Is there a Diagnosis?

It is very important to verify whether the injury has manifested severe enough symptoms to be a diagnosed condition. If there is no diagnosis, perhaps the information was not conveyed sufficiently to the health care professional. Sometimes, a diagnosis seems obvious, but is utterly lacking. Perhaps the health care provider had blinders on. The DSM-IV is gospel in the psychiatric and psychology professions. It is important to familiarize yourself with the diagnoses reflecting the most common extremes; e.g., depression, anxiety, disorders, PTSD.[26] Progress on a formal diagnosis of "workplace trauma" is still ongoing, but confirmation through traditional channels remains slow.

---

[26] For cases on PTSD, See *Webb*, 861 F. Supp. 1094. If you anticipate opposition, see 688 F. Supp. 1072 and *Perkins v. Spivey*, 705 F. Supp. 1487. Another good case explaining PTSD is *Hutton*, 663 A.2d 1289 (40 page discussion in context of child sexual abuse and discusses civil vs. criminal uses). See also *Belcher* 621 A.2d 872 (Md. 1992) on the evolution of court's acceptance of emotion vs. physical harm (ignore work comp backdrop of case, but read the ebb and flow of separating vs. integrating physical with mental. See also *Wheeler*, 829 P.2d 196 (Wa. 1994) on causes and non-separation of causes. See *Byrd*, 552 So.2d 1099, 7 IER 1782 (Fla. 1989) for policy reasons separating work comp from sexual harassment claims.).

> ## Symptoms do NOT establish Causation
> ## Diagnosis does NOT establish Causation

A diagnosis focuses on the effects that someone is experiencing; it does not say anything about the cause of that suffering. Similarly, the client's identification of pain or symptoms does **not** say anything about causation. It is easy to assume the two phenomena are connected, but this is often incorrect. Even if the symptoms are clear and seem uniquely related to the incidents at issue (an uncommon event), you will need to consider an expert evaluation if serious injuries are to be blamed on the employer during settlement negotiations.

Health professionals who provide treatment are trying to help the patient heal. They must not be confused with experts for evaluation. The decision to hire an expert should be determined by the extent of injury and a likelihood of causation. If there appears to be a significant injury and a cause-effect relationship appears obvious (a rarity), an expert's evaluation is strongly recommended. The threshold is the dramatic impact in the person's life.

If the client can't afford an expert, you should consider investing your own money. This opportunity is like an investment in penny stock—it is relatively low cost and can reap enormous dividends and prevent disastrous results. Many lawyers prefer to wait on an expert until it becomes necessary; e.g., the disclosure-of-expert deadline midway through discovery. But anticipation is often the key to success. Whether this is a potential big bucks case at trial or in settlement, the investment in an early expert evaluation is very worthwhile. In most cases, it will at least pay for itself.

Obtain Expert evaluation

Like lawyers, experts are not interchangeable. They have specific talents and specific ways of viewing problems. Most psychologists focus on verbal treatment, not on causation. Psychiatrists focus on medication as treatment, not on causation. The expert witness can be, and usually should be, distinct from the treating physician. The expert is specifically looking for causation. Moreover, the expert is making a snapshot evaluation. It must not be confused with treating physicians who provide an image more akin to an ongoing video presentation.

Whether to Consult or Retain Expert?

A tactical advantage is gained by consulting with the expert before retaining her or him. This may prevent disclosure of an uncomfortable opinion. It is critical to find a potential expert who is skilled and willing to look at causation as part of his or her analysis. It is cost effective to develop a primary relationship with one expert. This can also enable the consulted expert to trust you and provide oral summaries on both the extent of injury and an opinion on the probabilities of causation. If the oral summary enhances the value of your claim, then you can obtain a written report. If not, you can delay. Ideally, it will be brief and to the point. Conclusions, however, are not enough; they must be supported by poignant details and thoughtful analysis.

At minimum, any expert should conduct a four-hour examination with two hours of objective testing and two hours of interview. Seek an oral opinion first. This will provide the option of additional input by the client and/or a refocus on the facts or on causation. It may also prevent a written report that otherwise creates a paper trail. In cases of severe injury, an expert evaluation is strongly recommended before your first settlement talks. The estimated cost is $1,000-$2,500. It's usually a good investment.

If neither the client nor counsel choose to invest in an expert's evaluation, you must make inquiries to test your gut reactions or visceral conclusions. Causation facts must be sorted out.

A COMMON SENSE TEST OF CAUSAL CONNECTION

The threshold question is "How clearly do the symptoms seem connected to the incidents?" It is related to the legal framework of how likely is it that you can prove the incidents caused the symptoms. Some step-by-step questions include:

Did the Symptoms First Arrive After the Incident in Time and Sequence?

If there were no prior symptoms, this is positive. But, it is still necessary to eliminate alternative triggers that occurred parallel in time to the workplace incidents (divorce, abuse, death of a close relative, alcoholism, drug abuse, financial hardships, car accidents, illnesses, surgery, traumas). If there were no prior symptoms and no parallel triggers, you probably stand on strong ground.

If there were alternative triggers parallel to the workplace incidents (divorce, abuse, death...), it is necessary to determine if these alternate causes can be negated or if they were side effects of the workplace conduct. Once again, you must study the sequence of events. If the side effects were parallel in time, you should evaluate proof that the employer's misconduct caused the side effects (divorce, alcoholism, home shifting, family discord, counseling, and hardships). This is extremely difficult and rarely possible.

If similar symptoms occurred *before* the incident, you must probe further:

- ❖ If some of the symptoms preceded the incidents, how do the levels of severity compare? Did they get worse?
- ❖ Does the client have a period of reliable functioning between prior incidents and current events? Was a gap where there were no symptoms?
- ❖ Can the emotional pain of the prior problems plausibly be portrayed as resolved earlier and independent of the emotional pain suffered now?
- ❖ Was there prior counseling? Was it sufficiently successful to render the symptoms substantially independent of the recent similar symptoms?
- ❖ If counseling was stopped, was it because the problem was resolved, s/he ran out of money, insurance coverage ended or was counseling seen as futile or worthless?

Once insights are gathered, the rules of probability should be applied to reach a plausible conclusion.

Can you Negate these Other Alternate Causes?

You must step back and look at the big picture. The rule of probabilities asks "Is the current emotional pain **more likely** to be seen as the result of the employment decision or the non-employment stressors (financial, stability of home setting, children, abuse of chemicals or alcohol)? What is the more plausible explanation?"

JUDO TACTIC

If prior causes cannot be negated, you should determine if employer had notice of the condition. Until recently, a defense of pre-existing condition created a nightmare for plaintiffs. The Eighth Circuit recently reversed that problem.[27] It reallocated responsibility to the employer to carry the burden of proof on a crucial issue. Simply stated, the employer must now show that it is possible to distinguish between the prior pain and the subsequent pain. The employer must also carry the burden of proof on how much of the pain is attributable to the prior causes. If they fail, all pain is presumed to be recoverable for the plaintiff.

---

[27] *Jensen v. Eveleth Mining*, 130 F. 3d 1287 (8th 1997) reversed special master and trial judge, in part, because the amount of the award for emotional distress was inadequate and the court used the wrong burdens of proof where there was a pre-existing condition.

SOURCES FOR TRANSLATING EMOTIONAL INJURY INTO DOLLARS

The assignment of value to an emotional distress component is always awkward and frequently fuzzy. Partly this is true because emotional distress does not readily lend itself to quantification, and part of it is due to its subjective nature. Until recent years, we had no data for inferring the value a jury would determine. Now, with groups like the Jury Research Project, we are beginning to see data that allows us to generate averages and means. Similarly, the quarterly reports of the *Employee Advocate* provide us with enormous amounts of raw data. However, the databases only give averages and have not been organized in a manner that predicts variables in future cases. Moreover, these are trials, not settlement values.

Until we have reliable compilations of data, the most useful source is to regularly exchange data with NELA/ATLA colleagues. We all need a reality check. Confidentiality is seldom inherent at the outset of the negotiations. There is nothing to prevent you from brainstorming with colleagues or discussing your anticipated demands in forthcoming negotiations. This can be done openly before the confidentiality issue is raised or its good faith equivalent kicks in. Once confidentiality is raised or agreed upon, the facts can still be discussed, as long as the parties are kept anonymous.

A log of local settlements related to emotional distress can provide abstracts of the facts and the amounts asked, offered and ultimately agreed upon. There are substantial benefits in keeping records of local verdicts, particularly those on emotional distress. Plaintiff's counsel who won will eagerly share the pivotal evidentiary facts and a whole lot more. In a later negotiation with your opponent, these emotion facts can often be compared and contrasted with your case. Your awareness of the details of the recent verdict will also enhance your credibility.

SEPARATE EMOTIONAL DISTRESS FROM

HUMILIATION AND EMBARRASSMENT.

Humiliation and embarrassment are almost a form of per se damages and they should routinely be pled. The jury doesn't need expert testimony to understand embarrassment and/or humiliation. Neither does defense counsel. It speaks for itself. Even if the defense lawyer is reluctant to admit this consequence, it is felt. Humiliation and embarrassment are common experiences, they have a different meaning and an inherent value. They are tied to the ugliness of the behavior itself and connected to the effects on the average person, more than the actual suffering of the individual. On the other hand, emotional distress is the unique experience of the individual—a response to a particular situation.

One Gauge of the Value of Emotional Distress

The following summary is based on published cases and settlements in the Midwest. The amounts may be higher or lower in your jurisdiction.

Values Achieved in Early Settlement	
Self-help	$10-$30,000
Discussions with social worker, pastor	$20-$50,000
Limited counseling	$30-$100,000
Substantial counseling after the event	$45-$125,000
Taking medications (varies frequency & duration)	$50-$150,000
Short hospitalization for trauma	$100-$300,000
Long hospitalization for trauma	$150-$500,000+

Remember, these are settlement values. Jury verdicts may be substantially higher.

Recently, NELA member JoAnn Mullen and colleagues at Reinhart & Anderson, broke the sound barrier in Minnesotas' emotional distress verdicts.[28] They achieved a $650,000 verdict for a male who had **no wage loss**—he was still employed by the defendant. The jury reacted to his emotional suffering in a retaliatory, hostile work environment. On a statutory claim where the judge was the fact finder, the trial judge later added one million dollars. This verdict is already impacting local settlement values. We can use such verdicts to help employers unlearn the belief that emotional distress claims are worth less than

---

[28] *Jones vs Yellow Freight* (Dakota County, Minn. 19-C7-98-7880 1999)

economic claims. The education process will not begin until you show them the verdicts and remind them that the "times they are a changing." In every settlement conference, I try to figure out a way to mention this verdict and identify the similarities with my case. To show my objectivity, I also candidly disclose the differences, but discreetly.

There are many factors that dramatically increase or decrease the values. Occasionally, mega-verdicts are rendered, but they rarely survive appeal intact. Thus it is essential to discount them when analyzing the data for settlement purposes.

Factors that Increase Value

Major facts that may enhance the value of emotional facts include:

- ❖ Multiple incidents
- ❖ Corroboration
- ❖ Ripple effect of projected treatments
- ❖ Client communication skills
- ❖ Thin skull applications.

If plaintiff has endured multiple incidents, the value usually increases. Similarly, if the behavior has some inherent egregiousness, it is weighted more heavily and translates into bigger dollars. Even if the past verdicts in your state have been small, do not give up hope. Minnesota verdicts for emotional distress have historically been in the low five figures, with an occasional deviation up to low six figures. The recent $650,000 verdict for a male who had no wage loss is dramatic because the jury put a high value solely on his emotional pain.

Any corroboration helps. When witnesses confirm the actual suffering, it's easier to translate that into dollars. This is enhanced particularly by details of changes in behavior. They are much more powerful than conclusory opinions or subjective feelings. Medical records have value if they are clear and unambiguous. Roommates or family members who attest to dramatic changes in behavior will noticeably enhance the value of the pain. (See Before and After Symptoms Questionnaire on the CD/disc). Corroboration via contemporaneous notes and diaries will firm up the value attributed to the emotional pain. They are often self-serving, but a lengthy history with entries about feelings and pain before and during relevant time frames are credible.

An expert's persuasive power on the liability issues may be limited, but the effect of their testimony on the extent of pain is often significant. The opponent will often concede the expert's projection on the expected number of treatments. Although the cost of a few sessions is a form of special damages and relatively minor, the number of anticipated treatments has a ripple effect that can significantly expand the real value of general damages. Multiple treatments demonstrate a serious injury that geometrically multiplies the projected costs of treatments.

If the client is effective in communicating emotional pain, employers will experience more anxiety and even fear a jury's reaction. The employer will be more willing to value the emotional injury higher and increase the purchase price of settlement. The employer must have firsthand knowledge of the clarity of communications by the plaintiff. This can be the result of prior interactions or be conveyed in pre-suit negotiation; e.g., in a carefully selected presentation to a small group that focuses on the feelings of hurt, embarrassment, and shame. Counsel should not allow questions and answers. A felt monologue by plaintiff is sufficient to display the real hurt. You may want to script a list of topics to be covered, but the feelings should emerge naturally.

If there is evidence of a pre-existing condition, the thin skull concept should be seriously considered. In traditional tort cases, the tortfeasor takes the victim where they find them and prior notice is not required. In employment cases, however, courts have generally required the employer's knowledge of the pre-existing condition. The focus historically was on the aggravation of the injury and the pivotal point was often the burden of proof.

New case law is opening the door to claims that employer misconduct aggravated the prior suffering and thus, the "thin skull" equivalent can dramatically increase the value.[29] The Eighth Circuit's recent reallocation of responsibility to the employer to show that it is possible to distinguish between the prior pain and the subsequent pain and carry the burden of proof on how much of the pain is attributable to the prior causes opens a new future. If the employer fails, all pain is presumed to be recoverable for the plaintiff.

To be plausible, there must be a strong, almost tangible, argument that the employment setting was the proximate **cause** of the aggravation. With such evidence, the argument is an enormously powerful lever toward settlement.

---

[29] *Jensen v. Eveleth Mining*, 130 F. 3d 1287 (8th 1997) reversed special master trial judge, in part, because the amount of the award for emotional distress was inadequate and the court used the wrong burdens of proof where there was a pre-existing condition.

> ## CAUTION
>
> Proving sufficient causation in aggravation of pre-existing injuries is diffi-cult in settlement. Unless you can show the condition was relatively obvi-ous and that there were periods of reliable functioning after the prior traumas and before the incidents involving this employer, it will have lim-ited leverage.

Factors which decrease value

Major factors that can decrease the value of emotional injuries include:

- ❖ Similar symptoms
- ❖ Similar incidents
- ❖ Limited communication skills
- ❖ Family/friends failed to notice changes.

If there is a prior history of *similar* symptoms, you must be realistic. Such symptoms have a strong tendency to dilute damages. It has been the rare excep-tion that enables "thin skull" to apply. Similarly, if there was prior therapy for similar symptoms, there is a higher risk of dilution because the prior symptoms were documented. Moreover, they were serious enough to have led to therapy.

Even more critical is a prior history of *similar* incidents. Similar incidents have a strong tendency to dilute both liability and damages. They make it easy for the employer to psychologically "blame the victim". The prior incidents make it easier for the employers to legally defend themselves; i.e., if it has happened before, it must be her fault, not our fault. It also removes any psychological guilt the employer may have felt for causing severe pain.

If the plaintiff has only limited skill in communicating emotional pain, the employer will usually discount the value. For example, many employees, left to their own vocabulary, will say things like, "It just hurts," or "I don't like it." This can kill the case's value in depositions. The ability to elaborate and provide var-ied descriptions of the suffering is crucial to mega-settlements as well as mega-verdicts. Unless you anticipated these communication deficits and helped create a meaningful vocabulary, the value must be discounted based on impaired com-munication. There is one notable exception: a plain, simple person or a person with a low IQ will create a *Billy Budd* scenario and have the opposite effect.

If roommates or family didn't notice any meaningful changes, it is usually dev-astating to the value of the emotional injury. They sometimes say, "She was always like that." Others explain away their own guilt for doing nothing, by proclaiming, "She's had a lot of problems in her life." These observations require reducing the value and discounting the price of settlement. The discount is often neutralized when third parties are provided a detailed questionnaire that provides a vocabulary for their observations. (See Before and After Symptoms Checklist).

REPUTATION DAMAGE

Reputation damages are seldom evaluated in employment cases. The exception is defamation claims, but they are proportionately few. As "self-publication" claims have become viable, defamation claims are growing. For 20 years, reputation loss has been an appropriate measure of damages in certain civil rights cases; e.g., 42 U.S.C. § 1983. When Title VII was widened to encompass compensatory damages, injury to reputation fit under the expanded version of compensatory damages—42 U.S.C.§ 1981A, §2000. In recent years, it has become interwoven with lost earnings capacity.

It can be difficult to demonstrate reputation damages, however. Close friends will be, or at least say they are, unaffected by rumors. They don't want to admit doubts about their friend. They want to support him or her. Enemies who did not trust or like the plaintiff before the accusations are unlikely to be affected. Occasionally, enemies will admit that the accusations confirmed their suspicions. The middle group of casual friends, acquaintances and co-workers are an opportunity worth investing your time.

During the witness-interview phase, it is critical that you or your private investigator abandon either-or thinking. The assumption that reputation is either good or bad will destroy most evidentiary opportunities. Changes in reputation should be viewed along a continuum. Evidence should be gathered from the point of view of "fuzzy logic"; e.g., viewing reputation as a dimmer switch, rather than a switch that is either on or off.

The search for evidence should proceed in little increments; e.g.

Did the *rumors* make the witness pause and wonder about the plaintiff?

Did the witness wonder if plaintiff was possibly capable of the *accusation*?

Did the witness feel the need to protect himself or herself by distancing himself or herself from plaintiff, just in case the *statements* were true?

Then apply reverse logic. Did the company do anything to reduce the witness' apprehension; e.g., send any memo explaining what was going on? Did management try to neutralize the harm to your client's reputation? Did managers talk to the witness about the need for confidentiality, the potential consequences of the accusation or provide encouragement that your client would survive with the company? The failure to protect the accused can open witnesses up to the harm that might have been avoided.

Methods of eliciting reputation injury will vary by the type of claim. Essentially, each claim focuses on specific words, general reputation information, and legally important audiences. In good defamation cases and civil rights cases, plaintiff's counsel can assert "per se" damages. The bold assertions, however, do not carry much persuasive power in settlement. Groups of potential audience members need to be segregated because the words carry more legal weight, if given to prospective employers than to members of the community. Similarly, the employer's republication of defamatory statements to past co-workers and managers without a need to know has greater impact than the same self-publication statements by the plaintiff to neighbors, kids, or friends.

An example may illustrate this method of proof to enhance settlement. In an early negotiation of a defamation case, the slander was not really particularly clear cut, but it was arguably per se. The potential witnesses had previously been gung-ho supporters of my client, but now they seemed ambivalent. They proclaimed his innocence, but their hesitation was clear. I explained a quirk of the law: If the statements had no effect on the reputation of my client or if it had no effect on their attitude about my client, then he was not injured. If they had experienced even a little bit of hesitation or a little doubt, then it was important for them to tell me. We discussed how reputation is built up over years and how it is easily ripped away by a single blow. We discussed whether these statements might have affected other people who didn't know the plaintiff. If people only knew him by name, was it probable that these strangers might believe the accusations? Would they feel that he was capable of such behavior? The witnesses confirmed the reactions of others, then admitted that, for a few moments, they too had had their doubts. Since the accused was not present in the workplace, they saw his absence as confirming the allegations. They were holding onto a reasonable doubt about his guilt. They had a nervousness—they were no longer sure they wanted to be associated with him or be seen as his backers. I asked about their former feelings and if the rumors and statements had caused them to pause just a little bit. Did they wonder if the plaintiff might have done what the rumors declared? I obtained seven handwritten statements of persons who had heard the alleged defamation. This helped generate a half million dollar settlement.

Retaliation Evidence Is Powerful

Retaliation is strongly disfavored by most people—jurors and judges alike. It doesn't matter if the decision-maker is liberal or conservative, all can relate to someone being punished for doing the right thing. Admittedly the dispute often centers on what was in fact the right thing to do. Most of the time, however, all audiences become angry about retaliatory motives. Employers know that they may be punished for acts of a manager indirectly in the compensatory damages or more directly with punitive damages. Serious whistle blower cases command a premium. If any facts have an overtone of retaliation, the value is often quadrupled or even magnified by ten times its normal settlement value. Retaliation is an extraordinary opportunity for mega bucks. It is more fruitful than a frontal attack seeking punitive damages. Believable patterns of revenge can multiply the value at trial by ten or even a hundred times the hard damages. Even though the egregiousness of behavior is not a requirement for punitive damages, it remains a major consideration in compensatory damages.[30]

Retaliation Evidence Enhances Prospect of "Implied" Punitives

Egregious injury is a not major requirement for punitive, but egregious conduct is a strong influence on damages. Evidence of revenge or retaliation satisfies this de facto requirement of egregiousness. The evidence must be solid to achieve settlement value, but it is feared more than most other types of evidence. The conduct must relate to the causes of action at issue. It is not the suffering as much as the ugly motive and ugly behavior.

Although the existence of skeleton evidence can be a potent factor in speed of settlement, you must be exceedingly careful about the appearance of extortion. Special facts that the employer wishes the plaintiff did not know and does not want others to know are better left as a backdrop. Such special facts are often like new paint for selling a house: It may not increase the value, but its presence makes the house sell faster.

Punitive Damages

In terms of settlement value, arguments about punitive damages usually have low, often negative, impact on an employer's incentive. But, the same facts can make a great silent backdrop for the fear of punitive damages.

---

[30] *Kolstad v. American Dental*, 144 L Ed, 2d 494, ___ U.S. ___ (1999).

Few humans can recognize their own misconduct, much less see a deliberate disregard of other people's rights. It is psychologically improbable that any wrongdoers will admit misconduct. The lawyer's perception is altered if a court has approved punitive damages, but client's mind-set is only modestly affected. Corporations are fictions, but they consist of humans. In theory, it should be easier for a corporation to recognize the misconduct of a "bad apple" than any systemic decay. Recognition of individual misconduct, however, tends to make the corporation feel corporately immune from responsibility for the misconduct of a bad apple. In such situations, the corporate attitude is instead, "Go after the bad actor."

As a practical matter, leverage in settlement will be enhanced only if you show ratification or adoption of the acts of the bad apple and the elements of respondeat superior. Recently, I have asserted that a corporation's post-suit agreement to indemnify a bad actor constitutes a ratification. The success of this tactic is unknown, but keep it in mind. If you are careful from the beginning to show that the actions of the bad apple were in the course and scope of duty and related to the performance of the job, your prospect remains strong.

Employers usually assume that there is no realistic risk of punitive damages. Proclamations by plaintiff's counsel have little scare value. Unless there is clear-cut third party evidence, intelligence suggests backing off this issue in settlement. On the other hand, if there is clear-cut evidence, don't waste time trying to settle. Let them to come to you.

CAUTION

If an insurance company is involved, de-emphasize or avoid claiming punitive damages.

Punitive damages are almost never covered by insurance. If you make a claim that's covered by insurance, the assertion of punitive damages is counterproductive. Instead, plaintiff's counsel should focus the money into compensatory damages, where the insurance company may be on the hook.

Arguments about punitive damages do have some power when addressed by a third party—either a mediator, magistrate, or judge. The third party has the opportunity to skillfully educate the employer about the real prospect of punitive damages. In Minnesota and many other states, a judge's approval is needed to add punitive damages. Once approved by the court, punitive damages become powerful leverage to settle—an independent outsider has rendered a formal opinion that there is **enough** evidence to justify letting a jury decide the amount.

In the phase of *evaluating* punitive damages, you must be vigorously **objective** and only minimally a client's advocate. The act of mentally assuming the role of an impartial third party, as if a judge, will facilitate a more thorough examination of whether these behaviors really go beyond minor misconduct and really look like deliberate disregard. Rather than attribute a value to punitive damages, it's more effective to coax defendants into heightened uncertainty on liability and use the prospect of punitive damages as a cocked pistol.

Leveraging Evidence into a Punitive Damages Posture

On occasion, the power to convince employers of the risk of punitive damages may be obtained through cumulative affidavits. The affidavits must be clear. They must create a strong momentum through the right kind of allegations. They must focus on deliberate disregard of rights at issue, more than the misconduct of the bad actor.

If the liability case is clear-cut, you may choose to emphasize punitive damages in settlement negotiation. But in the process, you must judiciously stage the delivery of information justifying punitives. The employer may not be negotiating in good faith, but rather trying to elicit your case in advance so they can modify their position in later litigation. You must be selective about sharing details and delay providing affidavits until you have solid reason to believe they are serious. One method of assessing their seriousness is the amount of money they have put on the table. In the words of Neil Mullin, "Make them pay for the proof of lies and fraud that you possess. Don't give it away for free." If their offer has not approached at least one third to one half of your compromise value, you should hold back. The risk of tipping them off is too high.

At the same time, you must balance the clarity of your liability position against the client's interest in early settlement. For less clear-cut settlement negotiations, there is little benefit in throwing your punitive damage justification in the employer's face. Let the threat hover. Commonly, it is more powerful as a shadow, where it does not evoke defensive posturing. Instead, let it enhance your claim of lost earning capacity (compensatory damages). As noted above, this is peculiarly compelling if you are negotiating with an insurance company who won't cover punitive damages.

If you genuinely believe that punitive damages are justified during early settlement posture, the values must be realistic. Meaningful values will require substantial discounts. The following examples reflect values that were obtained in trial of certain types of cases. They must be discounted for settlement purposes.

Amounts against Employers

Employment juries have awarded as high as $80 million dollars in punitive damages against employers,[11] but Congress has imposed limits in discrimination claims of $100,000-$300,000, depending on the employer's size. The caps on punitive damages are in conjunction with other compensatory damages. Back pay and front pay are **not** included in these caps.[12]

For tort claims, there are no fixed limits. NELA members have pushed the numbers and their successes are published in the Employee Advocate. A common rule of thumb for modest sized corporations is an amount based on assets at time of trial (typically 1/2 of 1% of assets) or a measure of net revenue last year (commonly 5% of net annual revenue). These percentages have been most frequently applied to mega-corporations and tiny ones but less often to medium-sized companies.[13] In publicly held companies, these asset and revenue figures are generally available to the public. The percentages and the numbers are premature, however, for early settlement. This is horse trading, not a jury. Unless you have facts that make the employer really thirsty, there is limited negotiation value in alleging corporate liability for punitive damages.

Amounts against Individuals

Historically, the amount commonly awarded for punitive damages against individuals has been an arbitrary sum of $10,000, but recent cases have been higher; e.g., $50,000 and even a million dollars. Minnesota courts have decided that two-and-one-half times the net annual income of the individual was too high for punitive damages against an individual police officer, but the court did authorize one year's income. The punitive damages reduction from two-and-one-half to one is significant, but the award was still $30,000 against a cop.[14] There is one great, published decision involving sex harassment in Florida where the court published an award of $1 million in punitive damages against a *solvent* individual.[15] It is well worth reading and citing. The evidence that supports punitive damages against an individual may justify a negligence claim against the entity and punitive damages for its own, but not the individual's, negligence.

---

[11] NELA member, Roxane Conlin obtained this mega verdict against *UPS* (S.D. IA 1998).

[12] *Martini v. Fanny Mae*, 178 F. 3d 1336 (D.C. Cir. 1999).

[13] *Baker & Mackensie. Individual liability for punitive damages.* $7.5 million with compensatory damages of $50,000.

[14] *Rosenbloom v. Flygare*, 501 N.W. 2d 597, 602 (Minn. 1995).

[15] *Stockett v. Tolin*, 792 F. Supp. 1536 (S.D. Fla. 1992.) The case also contains a great five-page discussion of the factors and a listing of other cases.

SUMMARY OF VALUATION PRINCIPLES

Until your opponent perceives your claims as possessing weight, your dispute will remain an annoying mosquito. Until they have experienced uncertainty, they do not need your product. The more they see and fear your power, the more they want to buy the settlement you are offering to sell. Once the shadow of the jury as a competing bidder feels real or imminent, your settlement demand is valued.

> ➤ Contrast hard losses (actually suffered to date) with hypothetical future losses.
>
> ➤ Compute trial values and discuss the real bottom line.
>
> ➤ The demand value should find equilibrium between trial value and bottom line.
>
> ➤ Recognize that employers are usually willing to pay approximately three times hard losses for early settlement. They won't pay more, **until** you have shown strong damages facts in addition to solid liability facts. You cannot expect to increase the sales price above the norm without substantial effort.
>
> ➤ If the employee's situation has stabilized, the demand should rarely exceed 4-5 times the hard losses.
>
> ➤ If the situation has not stabilized, the unknowns likely have maximum value in the early stages, but only if the unknowns are clearly recognized.
>
> ➤ Recognize that *some* fees at the outset are actual, the rest are hypothetical. You must make them real. Many in-house counsel and most insurance adjusters do not realize that our claims have fee-shifting provisions. You must educate them. The fees for trial don't carry much negotiating weight, **until** the employer recognizes the probability that you have the clout and stamina to go all the way.

EVERYTHING IS TIMING.

In theater, comedy and sales, the statement "everything is timing" is common. This is also true for lawsuits and negotiations. Timing is an art, not a science. While it may be instinctive for some, others acquire it by experience and reflection. Often, timing is interwoven with hunches and intuition. Both sharpen your sense of timing.

"Waiting is fullness" is a phrase first popularized by Robert Heinlein in *Stranger in a Strange Land*. This phrase has unparalleled application to clients in lawsuits. They are invariably eager to get it over now. If you prepare them at the outset that patience is a requirement for maximum settlements and remind them periodically, they will find it easier to wait. At some point, negotiation becomes an issue of something reasonable now or something larger later. There is no right answer.

Valuing Experience

A daily journal of experiences in life and law is a precious source for insight. Reflections on my successes and failures in negotiation, litigation and trial have enabled me to improve and prepared the foundation for this work. The act of writing keeps me concious of competing priorities and alert to the flow.

We lawyers often allow the pressure of deadlines to create lives of quiet desperation. The act of writing prevents a preoccupation with "doing" and revives the other dimensions. If you conciously keep your mind moving through the following cycle, you will find more enjoyment, productivity and success:

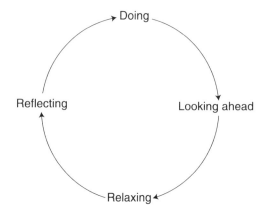

Chapter Fourteen

NEGOTIATING VALUE

Strategy: Do Not talk $$$ until they show some respect for your product.

Tactic: Explain that you want to hear their version first.

You cannot command a compromise by the force of your will. You must negotiate. Facts alone do not persuade; the meaning of those facts must be negotiated. Even if your liability facts are persuasive, they do not determine the sales price of your "product"; i.e., your damages. Good facts can make an employer thirsty to settle, but they do not assign a value. The sales price of a settlement is never inherent and seldom obvious. You must negotiate to create agreement about the value.

The skills of successful negotiation are demanding, but fortunately most can be learned. The most essential skill is the ability to place yourself in the opponent's position and to see the situation through their eyes. This is more than merely being objective. Until you can see their point of view, you will probably be ineffective in understanding their weaknesses, strengths or needs and addressing the issues that are important to them. You cannot make them truly thirsty until you understand their leverage points.

Your opponent's skepticism about your facts and the value you assign to your case is natural. You are, in effect, asking the employer to accept blame for what happened to your client. Since the employer wants to believe that the decision to fire was rational, the employer's advocate will usually echo that perspective.

Generally, you should not negotiate with the original decision-maker because he or she is too psychologically invested. The optimal negotiation involves a higher level decision-maker. Once a lawyer is involved, the employer, however, is rarely present at least until mediation or a court ordered settlement conference. Thus, you are left with negotiating with the employer's lawyer, who will translate your arguments to the employer. Your arguments will be filtered either through an incentive to litigate or a motive to keep a client happy by resolving disputes. To persuade the defense lawyer that your case has merit, you must supply the ammunition s/he can use to explain to the employer why your client is likely to win. The defense lawyer must also be able to communicate how much the plaintiff might win. (If you assert winning is a certainty, you expose your naivete and weaken your credibility.) You can sit back and let your opponent figure it out for themselves, or you can take the initiative to provide the justification for them, and in the process, help them understand your point of view.

This chapter divides this process of negotiation into three phases: Initial overtures, preparing postures and the negotiations. But first, we will examine the primary elements of negotiation.

COMPONENTS OF NEGOTIATION

In *You Can Negotiate Anything*, Herb Cohen elegantly identified three primary components of negotiation:

- ❖ power
- ❖ time
- ❖ information.

Awareness of these simplified components will keep you focused and sensitive. At each stage of the negotiation, ask yourself:

What is the source of my power at this stage?

What time frame has optimal impact?

What information will enhance thirst? What should be withheld?

POWER

Many lawyers see power in the money and resources of the other side.[36] A few like Gerry Spence recognize power, but describes it in terms of what we give to the Other. For example, Spence states that "The power I face is always the power I perceive." Still others look at sources of power that may be used to enhance the negotiation process. For example, lawyer Herb Cohen identifies 14 sources of power in *You can Negotiate Anything*. They include:

Power of competition	Power of legitimacy
Power of risk-taking	Power of commitment
Power of expertise	Power of knowledge need

---

[36] For an updated version of Machiavellain principles of power, see Robert Greene and Joost Elffers pronouncments in *The 48 Laws of Power* (New York: Viking 1998).

Power of investment	Power of reward/punishment
Power of identification	Power of morality
Power of precedent	Power of persistence
Power of attitude	Power of persuasive capacity

Familiarizing yourself with the distinctions between these differing sources of power can enable you to identify your true strengths and use them to improve your ability to negotiate successfully.

TIME

Time refers to both timing and patience. You must be acutely aware that the particular times for discussing settlement will influence both the prospect of settlement and the amount of settlement. As plaintiff's counsel, you are usually the catalyst, but you must be patient in waiting for the response.

Each negotiation round typically has three cycles—a demand and an offer make up one cycle. Then, you have a series of successive counteroffers constituting cycles two and three. If negotiations fail, you may engage in another round of negotiations later. Remembering this series of offers takes some of the pressure off the first interaction. You may feel that an initial offer is an insult. More often, it is a posture or a position adopted to ferret out your resolve. You can walk away or you can use the occasion to probe their perspective.

Patience does not mean passivity. It means waiting a reasonable length of time. It also means building in some outer limits. A two-week gap between the first and the second rounds is reasonable. Then the intervals should get smaller— perhaps 7 days between the second round and the third, 3 days to the fourth and 1 day to the final agreement.

> ### TIME IS AN IRREPLACEABLE RESOURCE
> When you say yes to one thing, you automatically say no to all others.

INFORMATION

Information is always imperfect. Even if you know the "facts", the opponent's view of the "facts" is frequently different. You and your opponent will invariably disagree about the inferences drawn from the facts. Moreover, you will usually have incomplete information about your opponent's strategy. Unforeseen events can dramatically alter the risks. Gerald Nierenberg uses a metaphor of erecting a building for the concept of communication: Information corresponds to the supplies for the building and communication is the blueprints for its use. If the supplies arrive without the plans, any type of structure may be built without knowing what the architect had in mind. If the plans are in place, the supplies or information can be used intelligently to pursue the negotiation. Organized information impacts the risk.

The difference between stupid risk taking and intelligent risk taking is information and its blueprints. As Daniel Keher points out in *Successful Risk Taking*, "successful risk takers have supreme confidence in their own ability to exercise *control* over the risks they take." Information increases your control by enhancing your awareness of the choices available. You cannot control the outcome, but you can control many of the steps leading to the outcome.

Calculated risks are different from self-destructive risks or playing the lottery. Those who feel their lives are ruled by luck, chance, judges, astrology, institutions and outside forces tend to avoid risk. Persons exercising control over their lives know that risk-taking is inherent and that risks are reduced by facts. Information about the facts is a start, but information about the process is also necessary. Learning the fundamental principles and strategies of negotiation can increase your sense of control.

STAGE ONE: INITIAL OVERTURES

One source of power in the initial overture is surprise. Unfortunately, it is short lived unless accompanied by something that has more enduring emotional impact. The first overture to the employer should be selected by the likely value of the case. Large values require large amounts of effort. Smaller values can be achieved with less effort.

METHODS FOR MAKING AN INITIAL OVERTURE:
Four methods for making an initial overture are:

- ❖ Send demand letter
- ❖ Telephone in-house counsel
- ❖ Start an actual lawsuit
- ❖ Send a "friendly" cover letter with a draft complaint.

Each choice has its own pros and cons.

Send a Demand Letter

A demand letter is typically full of sound and fury and signifying nothing. It has the appearance of a bluff and worse, a hollow one. Demand letters may be useful in small cases—under $10,000—but they are almost worthless in larger cases. The hidden message of the demand letter is that the lawyer doesn't think the case is worth enough to put in the extra effort. Even if the demand threatens an imminent lawsuit, it seldom conveys seriousness. During my five years as a defense attorney, most demand letters were treated as waste-basket material.

There are two exceptions when a letter may suffice: a) if you have that rarest of cases where the facts are truly one-sided, liability is clear-cut *and* damages are obvious; or b) if you have a positive history with the opponent or the opponent's counsel. In the first exception, the employer is probably awaiting your call. You need only to value the injury in a reasonable manner. In the second exception, your positive history gives you credibility, but it only carries you so far. Either of these situations may be sufficient for a demand letter to get the ball rolling toward settlement. As noted earlier in Chapter 2, ghost writing letters can be a powerful alternative.

Telephone In-House Counsel

Where the situation likely involves simple correction of a mistake in COBRA or personnel records, mild sexist language or very mild sexual harassment, a call to in house counsel to apprise them of the situation often suffices. In the self-interest of the corporation, they will often act promptly to correct the situation. If it is more complicated, details are important and a detailed letter of even draft lawsuit may be necessary.

Cliff Palefsky has demonstrated that a sizable verdict on a cutting edge theory can open the door of in-house counsel and accelerate settlement talks in other cases.

Start an Actual Lawsuit

A real lawsuit is a declaration of war. If the facts are *truly* great, declaring war can be a good strategy for a settlement. There are other times when you has no real choice; e.g., a statute of limitations is about to run or a prior settlement attempt was mediocre, botched, or received a hostile reception. [It doesn't matter if the attempt was pro se or with counsel. The failure has created a psychological barrier.] The real thing, however, seldom facilitates fast settlement.

Send a "Friendly" Cover Letter with a Draft Complaint

By contrast, a draft lawsuit looks real and has most of the power of a real lawsuit, but it stops short of declaring war. A draft lawsuit has the realness of a formal lawsuit, with one major difference: the draft is **not** signed. Normally, a draft complaint should be attached to a cover letter. The cover letter should invite exploration of settlement before the actual lawsuit begins.

The meta-message of an attached complaint is that a lawyer cared enough to invest time and effort in this matter. If it is cogently written for the employer-audience, it will have an impact. If it has blatant errors or obvious gaps, it will be discounted and impede settlement.

EFFECTIVE APPROACHES IN INITIAL OVERTURE

No matter what method is selected for the initial overture, the following approaches are essential to make the first message effective:

- ❖ Write to grab a specific audience
- ❖ Be businesslike, but not standardized
- ❖ Identify probable causes for the harm and a simple working theory
- ❖ Be specific about selected facts in your attached draft complaint
- ❖ Do **not** communicate a demand in your overture.

These approaches establish your first impression, similar to the first four minutes of meeting a person.[37] You will initially be judged in the first few minutes and that perception will linger indefinitely. People tend to maintain their original perceptions, regardless of contradictory information. Your impact is based on the picture as a whole, more than the details.

Write to grab a specific audience

Your primary audience with the first cover letter is the CEO, but you must be sensitive to the secondary audience of in-house counsel or out-house counsel. The two documents must have 'grab' appeal for both audiences. (See sample cover letters on disc/CD.) The first communication to CEO is often pivotal. It is usually the only time you get to communicate to the CEO without the intervention of counsel. The letter or other communication must be business-like: You cannot appear to be a screamer. A calm deliberateness gains credibility. The contents of a thoughtful letter starts planting doubt about the decisions in dispute, the personalities at play and the candor of subordinates. The hidden logic is simple: If the subordinate manager had handled it properly, no lawyer would be writing letters to the CEO.

---

[37] Pat Zunin, *Contact: The First Four Minutes.*

Be businesslike, but not standardized

To be credible, the initial overture should be straightforward and to the point. It must succinctly identify the problem and suggest a solution. The problem is a dispute that may become a lawsuit, the solution is to explore settlement. If you haven't condensed it to one page, redo it.

The cover letter must be straightforward, but not overtly threatening. It should have set time boundaries; e.g., invite a response within seven days. The letter should also specify the alternative: "If I don't hear from you by _____, we will assume you prefer litigation."

Identify a probable cause for the harm and a simple working theory

The cover letter should *tersely* summarize your theory of causation; i.e., why the employer is to blame for what happened. No seasoned trial lawyer goes to a jury without a theory; there is no reason to assume your opponent is any less open to logic, common sense and emotional reactions. He or she is a jury of one (or a committee of three). To be persuasive, the letter should show, in succinct simple terms, a working theory of the case. This theory is not the legal conclusion, but a focused explanation of how you connect the facts. If you have isolated verifiable facts, your inferences are stronger. If you show how a few facts will be pivotal, you leverage the maximum power. Much power is demonstrated when your cover letter identifies one incident that acts as a microcosm for the whole—a nugget that illustrates the big picture of the conflict. The microcosm is the core and facts should be presented in layers around it in the details of the complaint. If you have a meaningful method of connecting facts at this first overture, your opponent will be thirsty.

Consider a creative approach such as acknowledging the logic of their decision, but then contrasting it with a different point of view. Alternatively, you can identify points of likely agreement but then contrast it with points of disagreement. Many executives will not know the motives you are imputing to their staff. Others already know that causation is there, but they doubt your ability to prove it. You can let their guilt about getting caught work for you and enhance settlement. This does not refer to their guilt about doing the wrong thing, but their guilt about getting caught. The guilt didn't stop them originally, but at that time they didn't think the employee would seek or find a lawyer.

You should anticipate that at the first negotiation, defense counsel will be barely familiar with the basic facts. If you have a coherent theory, it can give you initial control of the turf. At this point, the theory need not be comprehensive. It is not necessary to fill in all the gaps, but you should point in a specific direction. If you have one legal hook that appears valid, the fuzziness of other claims need not hold you back. Defendants often know their real motive. Their anxiety about getting caught often has more scare value than your threats.

Be specific about selected facts in your draft complaint

It is logical to assume that the employer will solicit a lawyer's opinion. The cover letter carries little power without a fully developed complaint attached. The lawyer's opinion may be disregarded or given only a small weight. The employer is usually aware of the out-house lawyer's self-interest in billable hours and incentive to litigate to the hilt rather than pursue early settlement. This incentive is less applicable for the in-house counsel, who prefers quick resolution but who has issues with rapport and deterrence of future claims. Smart executives are savvy to in-house counsel who may be preoccupied with backing management, deterring other suits as well as justifying prior advice or existing policies written by the lawyer.

The complaint should simultaneously demonstrate a set of facts that provides an alternative point of view and lets the lawyer know that this suit won't be dismissed on a Rule 12(b) motion. Even better, draft it to show that a Rule 56 summary judgment is unlikely. This demonstration will put the defense counsel into a defensive position. They will begrudgingly admit to the employer that this suit will not be tossed out of court, *cheaply*. The enhanced cost factor will increase the employer's thirst for compromise. This first salvo shows the lawyer that you are serious and very competent. Despite their bravado and economic interests, most defense lawyers hate to lose. A carefully crafted product will blunt their arrogance.

As the contents of the cover letter start planting doubt, the CEO may read the complaint and develop skepticism about the decisions, the personalities at play and the candor of his subordinates. The complaint can help executives see possible deception by his/her subordinates. It won't be admitted to plaintiff's counsel, but the skepticism starts.

Language must be specific

In a lawsuit, the weapon is words. Vague or general statements in a letter or in the complaint have little impact. Specific facts that spell out nitty-gritty details have clout. The complaint should break the facts down into tiny pieces. The act of laying the evidence out line-by-line will improve your thinking in drafting the complaint and enhance its persuasiveness.

Notice pleading is undesirable at this stage. It may preserve maximum flexibility in litigation, but it is rarely effective for settlement. Remember, the option of changing the complaint to notice-pleading remains available at the time you commence suit.

When a lawyer is trying to be persuasive, conclusory language is almost useless. Someone who yells "discrimination" or "harassment", often turns off the reader or listener—the brain shifts to neutral and no one pays attention. It is far more powerful to talk or write in terms of behavior. For example:

* ❖ Compare "Employees were discriminated against." with
  "Only 7% of the women were promoted, but 30% of the men."
* ❖ Compare "He sexually harassed her." with
  "His hand was on her breast."
* ❖ Compare "The company was unfair to older employees." with
  "In each department, only the oldest employees were laid off."

Compare and contrast facts have real power, but only if supported accurately by the actual facts.

DO NOT COMMUNICATE YOUR DEMAND

The first letter is *not* the place to communicate a dollar demand or even information about damages. Wait until you have seen their thirst.

The liability facts must be real to the employer before they will have an interest in the harmful effects. The effects (or emotion facts) are rarely made real until they are translated into behaviors. Emotional facts, in particular, should not be conveyed in an initial overture. Most descriptions of emotional pain will be perceived as blatant sympathy ploys and they will ring hollow until liability begins to be perceived as real. There are occasions when the carefully constructed description of emotional injury can whet the employer's appetite, but they are exceedingly rare. As a general guideline, don't mention your emotional facts until the employer asks for a demand. Even then delay in quantifying the injury. Once the negotiation process is underway, a detailed letter can demonstrate the pain of your client's injury.

Although the first overture should **not** mention a specific purchase price for settlement, casual references to savings or future costs may be useful. Occasionally, I provide a footnote reference to *Huffman v. Pepsi*, where defense counsel billed over two million dollars to fight a case where the demand was only one hundred thousand.[18] The actual verdict was over five hundred thousand and the trial court awarded David Duddleston of Minneapolis almost one million dollars in fees.

STAGE TWO: PREPARING YOUR POSTURES

The preparation phase includes identifying goals, ensuring they are plausible, identifying strategies for achieving the goals and preparing levers for settlement. Optimally, it revolves around checklists that remind you of the range of possibilities. This preparation assumes you have completed a review of values similar to the process in Chapter 13.

IDENTIFY GOALS

Presuming you have completed the process of identifying the financial goals, you should also clarify the client's intangible goals. These might include:

- ❖ Continued employment or temporary "reinstatement"
- ❖ Agreement not to contest unemployment
- ❖ Converting terminations to resignations
- ❖ Continued insurance coverage at employer expense
- ❖ Discipline for bad guys
- ❖ Policy changes
- ❖ References or Acknowledgements.

Continued employment

Over the years, one fact has proven a powerful predictor of success in applying for new jobs. The fact is "having a job". This makes an applicant the most attractive. Even the appearance of being employed is simply a very good way to get another job. Therefore, it is valuable to consider the option of continued employment, real or on paper. Alternatively, temporary "reinstatement" on the payroll can be helpful. If the employer declares that it would never accept the employee back, you can drop the issue, use it as a trade-off or use to justify an increased demand.

Agreement not to contest unemployment

This is worth only $6-7,000, but it is cash to plaintiff. Unemployment has a negligible cost to employers and most will forego contesting it. If the employer declares that it would never "participate" in a "dishonest" statement to unem-

---

[18] Such References should be discreetly used because they may look like hyperbole or even tackey. *Huffman v. Pepsi*, 1995 Minn. App. LEXIS 943 (Minn. App. 1995) unpublished.

ployment agencies, you can drop the issue or use to justify an increased demand. Their agreement or refusal also gives you additional information to assess the constructive discharge claim.

Converting terminations to resignations

Economically, this costs the employer nothing. But it can help your client get a new job and this benefits the employee in a small, but significant way by reducing the risk of a suit. A few employers act self-righteous and oppose this issue. Usually, it is a bluff.

Continued insurance coverage at employer expense

This is a very modest cost to the employer and a great benefit to most clients.

Discipline for bad guys

This one has huge political overtones, because it admits wrongdoing. However, it also has significant trade-off value. If they do it, it may necessitate a reduction in your demand. If they don't discipline the manager in question, it can justify raising the demand.

Policy changes

This intangible also has some political overtones, because it concedes inadequate policies to begin with. A blatant deficiency, however, makes a new policy a must, but policy changes impact many other employees and employers will be guarded. However, it too has some trade-off value.

References or Acknowledgements

These are usually worthless for the plaintiff's job search, but a discussion of the contents can elicit useful information about how the managers really view your client. If they flatly refuse to consider references or continued employment, their sincerity may be deeply felt or a cover up. If they consider saying positive things, it is psychologically harder for them to backtrack later. Even if no agreement is reached on a reference, the psychological effect is beneficial because contradictions look unprofessional.

Some long-term employees sincerely want the acknowledgement of a job well done. If this is important to your client, it must be considered. It should not be done too early; pursue it only when the dollar gap has narrowed and it can function as a gap filler.

These intangibles should be weighed for the good of the client. A contingency fee does not pay you for these gains, but they enhance settlement and advance the good of your client. You must either set aside the fee issue or quantify it in some reasonable method. No matter how you resolve it, the intangibles remain useful as negotiating chits to be traded for something else of value.

Ensure Goals are Plausible

By this time you will have identified the three key values: 1) trial value, 2) the bottom line your client needs to get on with life, and 3) a demand that balances the two. You still have flexibility in how you express the trial value. Your choice is a realistic estimate, a slightly inflated value or even a deflated value given to the employer for strategic purposes.

Keep in mind that big dollar demands have little scare value. Unless it's a great case, you run the risk of ruining your credibility and wasting a window of opportunity. Bluffs are usually transparent. If your client is willing to take a lot less, you may blow the opportunity with an inflated demand. Excessive demands may even constitute malpractice. If your objectively recoverable dollars are low now, they will likely be low later.

Before meeting with your opponent, it is wise to check out the proposed value with respected peers. We typically brag only about our good facts or only our bad facts. To get valid feedback, give your peers the facts favoring the defendants first—get valid feedback then add your good facts one at a time.

There is new data on trial verdicts to help guide your assessment of plausibility.[39] The new Bureau of Justice Statistics Bulletin reveals that the **median** verdict in employment discrimination in 1996 was $200,000, while the median contract verdict was $37,000, fraud was $47,000 and *other* non-discrimination employment cases was at $53,000. [Median means half were above and half were below.] At the same time, 48 percent of the employment discrimination verdict were over $250,000 and 13 percent over $1,000,000.

Be wary of mentioning punitive damages in early settlement negotiations. They are often overrated by plaintiffs, underrated by defendants and rarely provide negotiation value. As mentioned in Chapter 13, the arguments about punitive damages must be tailored to the audience. Keep in mind that because punitive damages and intentional torts are rarely insured, they should **not** be mentioned if the paying audience is an insurance company. Instead put the big bucks in compensatory damages. Let the willful misconduct be a backdrop for higher compensatory damages. If you don't get a settlement, you can still go after punitive damages for negligent supervision later. In general, back off punitive damages unless the evidence is clear-cut. Focus on leveraging uncertainty.

---

[39] *Lawyers Weekly* story 11/29/99 p.1-12; Republished on the Web at www.lawyerweekly.com.

If, however, the facts realistically justify punitive damages, don't dilute your presentation by delivering all the evidence at once. Gradually offer clear affidavits, piece by piece, to convince the employer that the risk is real. It is not enough to allege bad facts, they must be organized to show deliberate disregard of rights. The egregiousness of behavior is not a legal requirement, but it is a major consideration in compromise. Temporarily suspend your role as an advocate and evaluate the evidence from a third party perspective, like a judge.

CAUTION

Before revealing the compromise demand, be sure your opponent understands the relative strengths of your liability. If you mention your compromise sum before the anxiety of uncertainty is established, any power in your damage evidence is neutralized. If your number appears extreme because of the lack of proper education, you lose the opportunity to convince the buyer of a nearby price.

STAGING STRATEGIES TO ACHIEVE YOUR GOALS

To maximize settlement opportunities, facts must be delivered in stages. Facts must be valued by the audience. This cannot happen until they recognize which facts can leverage the outcome. Facts have more value when the listener has asked for them. Facts have more value when they are not diluted by the quantity.

- ❖ Decide what additional evidence to share
- ❖ Decide what evidence to hold back
- ❖ Anticipate worst facts and create a context.

DECIDE WHAT ADDITIONAL EVIDENCE TO SHARE

Counsel should tentatively decide, in advance, what **additional** facts or evidence, if any, will be shared during the initial negotiations as well as subsequent meetings. You have laid out your important facts in the complaint. The opponent will place higher value on something he or she has asked about. If they identify a gap in your case and you fill it immediately, they will appreciate your skill of anticipation. Foresight will enable you to decide when and how to stage the delivery. Corroborating evidence should be presented in layers. Your prompt response also builds momentum.

DECIDE WHAT EVIDENCE TO HOLD BACK

Serious negotiation must proceed in stages. You may withhold only a few statements, affidavits, pages of evidence, facts or inferences, but it is strategically wise to be guarded. A fallback position is a key ingredient to any successful battle. Awareness of the ratchet effect; i.e., your fallback position, is also a major skill of persons widely perceived as lucky.[40] You must remain conscious that the facts, inferences and documents that you are sharing may remove your strategic advantage. Until the opponent shows increased seriousness—e.g., by the size of their offer—you should not be delivering all your major facts or supporting evidence. Often defendant's theory of the case is non-existent at the onset. You need to be cautious that premature disclosure of how you will prove your inferences and conclusions may be turned against you.

After all, you may end up entering litigation. If you have laid all your cards on the table, the employer may circumvent your facts with a new theory. Think of negotiation like a game of seven-card stud: Four cards are showing to everyone, but three are unknowns in your hand. Some power is in what you hold in your hand, but most of the power is in how you bid against the others based on what is visible and what you know of your audience.

When you have information that impacts your overall case and you want to block its delivery consider the ideas of Charles Craver. In his CLE materials, Craver identifies blocking tactics that must be limited to crucial information. For example, he mentions:

❖ Simply ignore the inquiry and move to another area
❖ Answer only the beneficial part of the complex question
❖ Over or under answer the question
❖ Answer a different question
❖ Respond with a question of your own
❖ Rule the question as out-of-bounds or improper.

Any of these techniques must be planned in advance. It is too difficult to improvise on sensitive areas. If you fail to plan, there may be nonverbal leakage.

ANTICIPATE THE WORST FACTS AND CREATE A CONTEXT

You need to be brutally honest and anticipate your worst facts. Your opponent won't miss the opportunity to raise them. Your best strategy is to create a context that explains them either by the immediate context or by universalizing them. If the opponent is likely to trivialize your sex harassment facts, be ready

---

[40] Gunther Max, *The Luck Factor.*

with an example to put it in perspective. For example, I anticipated a female lawyer denigrating the significance of a spanking a boss gave my client at a holiday party. She tried. I made my point by asking if she would be humiliated if a senior partner spanked her in front of her peers.

It is invaluable to write out a script of what you will say and to predict what your opponent's response is likely to be. This allows you to anticipate what evidence they will need and request. You can plan your reply, whether it is sharing, contexting or deflecting until later.

PREPARE LEVERS FOR SETTLEMENT
- ❖ Clarify demand in Writing: Deliver in person at second meeting
- ❖ Prepare anchors and shorthand statements
- ❖ Identify verdicts in your state which are similar
- ❖ Refer to cases by one name only.

Prepare Written Demand But, Delay Delivery
Prior to the first meeting you should prepare a one-page description of your demand in the form of a comparison chart.

> The purpose in preparing the demand, but delaying delivery is to organize your thinking. You should **not** deliver it at the first meeting, unless things go unexpectedly well or liability is almost a consensus.

For analytical purposes, it is useful to prepare the chart for your use only. The break out of damage categories will often enhance the credibility of your numbers and indirectly reflect your objective assessment of risk. If the evidence is strong and the category valued highly in your community, only a small discount is necessary. On the other hand, where your evidence is spotty or the category has an automatic discount (e.g., lost earning capacity has a present value discount), the discount reflected in your compromise values demonstrates your thoughtful objectivity and risk factors. Big numbers are stupid, unless justified. When the hard losses are high due to big salary, stock options or length of unemployment, the dollars will be dramatically higher. When the emotional injury is severe, the dollars will be substantial. It is most plausible if you can tie it to recent verdict in your jurisdiction, e.g., I use the $650,000 emotional distress verdict recently awarded in Minnesota as an anchor and discount accordingly. Two examples:

COMPARISON CHART FOR LARGE CASES

Type of Damages	Trial Value	Current Demand
Lost salary, options & Benefits	$100,000	$75,000
Front pay 24 mo @ $2,000 gap	$ 48,000	$40,000
Lost earning capacity 60 mo/gap	$120,000	$60,000
Emotional pain	$ 50,000	$20,000
Humiliation & embarrassment	$ 30,000	$25,000
Attorneys fees to date	$ 30,000	$25,000
Value at the present time	**$378,000**	**$245,000**

If we go all the way to trial, the amount will further increase by the following:

Attorneys fees 5 days @ trial + preparation	$ 50,000
Likely Benefits to Plaintiff	**$ 428,000**
Defendant's attorneys fees	$ 150,000
Potential Costs to Employer	$ 578,000

The ratios communicate the desired message of a 65 percent confidence in liability, a sensible reduction for risks in evidence and display the final increase as attributable to attorneys fees—an avoidable event. The compromise amounts reflect which damage claims are viewed as the strongest. The display of potential costs to employer irritates your opponent, but jogs the awareness of the employer. Although you should not plan to deliver the chart at the first meeting, you will be able to improvise. You may later deliver it as an future trial exhibit without the compromise demands or a settlement proposal with trial and demand values. [The case settled for $200,000.]

COMPARISON CHART FOR LARGER CASES

Type of Damages	Trial Value	Current Demand
Lost salary, options & Benefits	$ 900,000	$ 650,000
Front pay 24 mo @ $5,000 gap	$ 120,000	$ 100,000
Lost earning capacity 120 mo/gap	$ 600,000	$ 300,000
Emotional pain	$ 500,000	$ 400,000
Humiliation & embarrassment	$ 100,000	$ 75,000
Injury to reputation	$ 100,000	$ 75,000
Attorneys fees to date	$ 100,000	$ 80,000
Value at the present time	**$ 2,420,000**	**$ 1,680,000**

If we go all the way to trial, the amount will further increase by the following:

Attorneys fees 10 days @ trial + preparation	$ 100,000	
Doubling of compensatory damages	$ 700,000	
Value at the present time	$ 2,420,000	
Likely Benefits to Plaintiff	**$ 3,220,000**	
Civil Penalty payable to taxpayers		$ 250,000
Defendant's attorneys fees		$ 500,000
Potential Costs to Employer		$ 3,970,000

The ratios communicate the desired message of a 66 percent confidence in liability, a present value discount for LEC but smaller discounts on emotional injury because of corroboration of medication and hospitalization for PTSD. The final increase is attributable to doubling of compensatories—a real risk in Minnesota and unrelated to punitive damages. The compromise discounts reflect which damages claims are viewed as the strongest—economic over emotional distress. [The case settled for $880,000.]

Often it is useful to present the information in narrative form and to write out the numbers; e.g., eight hundred thousand dollars. It reduces the visceral reaction and coaxes the reading of the whole letter rather than obsessing about the numbers. When the numbers are bigger, I do not to add up the totals. The act of doing the math can psychologically invest the defense lawyer in the numbers. The figures must be reasoned to have impact.

In the rare case where liability is so clear that defendant is foaming at the mouth to settle, don't bother with breaking out the damages—just select a figure that a jury would find reasonable and discount it for the time value of money.

You should plan to deliver your demand in person so you can observe their nonverbal reactions and guage the credibility of your numbers. These observations also allow you to adjust your attitude about how firm the demand should be characterized.

Occasionally, a half page narrative preceding the chart is useful. If damages are complicated, the terse narrative should display a list of your key factual or legal strengths, but candidly acknowledges your weaknesses. As you acknowledge the weakness, apply a judo tactic that turns it upside down and puts it in the best perspective. This isn't easy, so plan to commit some time.

Consider Advance Notice of Later Increases in Demand

You need to anticipate future developments. For example, if the dispute does not settle, will you withdraw your demand or increase it at a later round? It is wise to forewarn your opponent, but do it in writing. For example, I insert a postscript, in my first digit to remind me to make a choice at the time of actual delivery. For smaller cases I omit it.

> P.S. To insure there is no misunderstanding, I notify you in advance that our willingness to compromise is related solely to this round of negotiations. If we do not settle during this round, we will withdraw the offer and the demand will be increased during litigation.

The word "round" preserves your flexibility and indicates your continuing willingness to negotiate, for now. The message is clear: This is not your bottom line demand in *this* round, but there will be consequences, if we don't see your best offer during this round. Many lawyers are afraid to show flexibility. It is not a sign of weakness, but rather a sign of intelligence. Remember, you cannot be arbitrary. Some event, like new facts or stronger witnesses or occasionally, additional fees, must be used to justify the increase.

Prepare Anchors and Shorthand Statements

Modern lawyers, like most folks, have fallen victim to the 30-second sound bite. We have learned to think in nibbles. You can take advantage of this phenomena by thinking in shorthand. Be ready with lawyerly catch phrases; e.g., "True, but it's a fact question" or "It prevents summary judgment." Such statements can often shut off their arguments like a wave of your hand and show your confidence that it won't justify summary judgment. This keeps bargaining at a more equal level.

There is power in anchoring your arguments with core facts. These are statements that the employer cannot readily refute or readily explain away. These facts must also have grab appeal. For example:

"She had straight "A's" on her performance appraisals."

"There were zero warnings and no reprimands."

"Her numbers speak louder than your subjective deficiencies."

Comparison facts are powerful. It is crucial, however, to compare apples to apples. If you want the outcomes to be felt, the similarities must outweigh the differences. Shorthand references of these comparisons should be written and kept at your fingertips.

CAUTION

Last minute comparisons usually sidetrack the arguments. They invite vigorous arguments emphasizing differences.

Identify Verdicts that are Similar—By Cause of Action or Facts

Consider preparing a verdict history organized by cause of action for your jurisdiction. This will add legitimacy to your demand. If there are only a few verdicts in your area, look to neighboring states and check the NELA advocate. Separately list the favorable verdicts by local juries and footnote the appellate outcome. This allows you to focus on the juror sentiments, not the myopia of the appellate judges. You can point out that jury verdicts enjoy a presumption on appeal.

If you plan to use information on average verdicts (charts and graphs from Jury Verdict Research), wait until the opponent has mocked your demand before revealing your corroborating sources. Showing the data prematurely is counterproductive.

In arguing liability, refer only to cases that are on point and then make a passing reference to one name only; e.g., "Yes, but...under *Meritor*, sex harassment by the boss is more intimidating than a boss." Or "Under *Ellereth*, sex harassment is about power, not sex." Seasoned lawyers use a one word reference for a case—*Meritor*, rather than *Vinson v. Meritor Savings Bank*. Stating full case names makes you look like either an amateur or a pretentious preacher. If you are relying on new precedents or unusual holdings, you should have copies or the citations available. Once again, don't offer them until the defense has challenged the concept or requested authority.

Tailor Arguments to Your Audience

Settlement values are affected by the type of employer. If you are dealing with defense counsel at this first meeting, you must appreciate that your original audience has changed. Instead of the employer whose self-interest is usually resolution, the lawyer's self-interest may be to litigate. The lawyer is now in the foreground, but the employer is close behind in the background. Therefore, arguments should be tailored for appeal to the values of both audiences. Ordinarily, you can assume that the chart will be shown to the employer. As discussed previously, each audience has different leverage points. You should anticipate whether the defense counsel is billing-conscious, win-lose conscious or client-centered. This knowledge can dramatically influence the amount and type of evidence you share.

Prepare Checklists of trade-offs

Anticipate trade-offs. Often, it is advisable to prepare a master checklist of items you are willing to trade off and reasons to justify the trade-off. Reasons for the opponent are often different from reasons for the plaintiff. The heat of battle in negotiation can cloud our minds and this outline should be prepared in advance. You can update it on an ongoing basis and use it for susequent cases.

You must know your client's priorities. It is usually expressed as money, but not always. Often the money is symbolic of some other need, which if met will resolve the dispute. Usually, it is wise to ask for a few things you know are somewhat unacceptable and plan to trade them off for more money.

CAUTION

In 1986, my client, an ardent non-smoker, asserted that she was fired for her complaints about smoking. The employer laughed at us. No court in Minnesota, or elsewhere, had recognized any common law cause of action protecting non-smokers. Minnesota had not even recognized a common law exception for retaliation in violation of public policy. Instead, I invoked a private right of action based on the Clear Indoor Air Act. I also used it as a proposed source of public policy. After we survived motions to dismiss by a cigar-smoking judge, discovery progressed. As settlement discussions began, we asked for two years of salary and insisted that the employer go smoke-free. The smoke-free aspect was intended as a bargaining chip. We anticipated their refusal to go smoke-free and planned to double our demand when they refused. But they agreed to go smoke-free and removed a major bargaining chip from our quiver.

My fellow smokers repeatedly remind me of this case, because it was the first major corporation in Minneapolis to go smoke-free. The year was 1987.

STAGE THREE: THE NEGOTIATIONS THEMSELVES

During the negotiations, the primary focus is the interaction with opposing counsel. In any sizeable negotiation, there will be a series of demands, offers and counter-offers. Commonly, big cases involve six or seven meetings, while smaller cases may involve only two or three meetings and the latter may be collapsed into phone calls. In general, the larger the purchase price, the more negotiations are needed. The meetings sort out in the following fashion:

First Session: ideally, restrict discussion to liability only

Second Session: convey first demand, both monetary and intangible

Third Session: employer communicates first offer

Fourth Session: plaintiff reduces demand

Fifth Session: employer conveys counter-offer

Sixth Session: plaintiff makes counter-offer

Seventh Session: employer accepts counter or moves closer…

During these meetings, it is helpful to draw upon your experience in other endeavors. The game theory insights of John McDonald in *Strategy in Poker, Business and War*, written in 1950, are worth repeating:

Your moves alone do not dictate the outcome—the opponent's moves are equally important;

No single move has meaning in itself; it makes sense only as part of the whole;

You have to make assumptions about your opponent's strategy: his or her reactions are not mere chance events.

The game also provides insights because bidding and "bluffing" are major components of the game. In negotiation, you do not bluff about the facts, but bluffing about the bids is expected behavior. Phillip Hermann in *Better Settlements through Leverage*, provided useful insights on the principles of uncertainty and poker into negotiations. He points out that poker players look for obvious clues from other players and probe for more information by observing how the other players respond to bets. Likewise in settlement negotiations, you probe by making a demand at the high end of the reasonableness range and observing how your opponent's react. But keep in mind that a demand that is too high can destroy negotiations and weaken your credibility.

A poker player can win, with a minimum of good hands, because s/he observes the opponent's reactions to the betting, the cards dealt, and the effect of uncertainty. The benefit of observing your opponent's response during the give and take of negotiations is to obtain more information about their strategies and tolerance for uncertainty. Multiple offers and counter-offers are anticipated by experienced negotiators. The starting points and changes downward or upward are sending signals toward the desired end point. Savvy negotiators are likely to be conscious in their signaling, but most others appear either unconscious of the process or else assume their bottom line is somehow a secret.

You should be prepared to watch for nonverbal cues in your opponent—some clues will encourage reliance on your opponent's candor, but others may alert you to deception. Charles Craver in his numerous CLE materials has identified several nonverbal forms of communication in the negotiation process. These nonverbal disclosures are often inadvertant or subconscious. The important test is whether they are consistent or congruent with the verbal message. You should attend to your own gut feelings about these nonverbal disclosures because your brain is processing them more adroitly than your mind can consciously absorb them. They cannot be viewed in isolation, but must be "felt" as a whole.

Nonverbal Ambiguities

Common forms of nonverbal disclosure include facial expressions, but these are the most easily manipulated expressions. Watch for inappropriate smiles that suggest hidden agendas. Leaning back with hands on the back of the head or steepling gesture with fingers often exudes confidence, but also dominance. Casual touching may reflect sincerity or paternalism. Hands touching the face is often a meditative contemplation to buy time, but hands covering the mouth suggest deception. People cover and rub one eye when they find it difficult to accept the message. This is a useful clue. Open hands often express honesty and openness, but crossed arms or legs may be combative and reflect defensiveness. Intense staring is the opposite of warm eye contact and should cause you to be on guard. Wringing the hands, gripping arm rests or drumming their fingers usually reflect frustration, but they may reflect a normally nervous opponent. Head nodding is usually simply an acknowledgement and should not be interpreted as agreement.

Nonverbal Forms of Deception

Craver and others[41] provide samples of deception:

- ❖ Signal words, like "to be honest"; or "to be truthful"
- ❖ Changing gross body movements to look less shifty or more believable

---

[41] Paul Eckman in *Telling Lies* (New York: WW Norton paper 1992) and Williarm Majeski in *The Lie Detector Book* (New York: Ballantine 1988), provides pragmatic tools for detecting dissembly by others.

❖ Casually placing one's hand over your mouth to prevent uttering mis-representations

❖ Contradictions between the direction the head is shaking and affirmative or negative words spoken

❖ Involuntary raising of inner portions of the eyebrows, more frequent blinking or dilation of pupils

❖ Tightening of the red margins of the lips just before speaking

❖ Speaking more deliberately and in a higher pitched voice

❖ Clearing his or her throat more frequently

❖ Increasing number of speech errors—broken phrases, stuttering, more adjectives

❖ Making an obvious effort to look the listener in the eye.

You should recognize that skillful opponents will be attempting to read your nonverbal signs at the same time. If you can pair up with another lawyer for the negotiation, one of you should focus on the nonverbal communications while the other attends to the words or content.

First Session

Strategy: Your purpose is to listen. Delay talking money until they show respect for your liability position.

Tactics:

A. Limit first discussion to liability
   1) Coax out their version of facts
   2) Let them play their lawyer games

B. You should feel out the opportunity

C. Don't threaten publicity—let it hover in the background

Your primary purpose in the first negotiating session is to listen. In an ideal first session, you keep the discussion on liability only. You already gave your version of the facts in the draft complaint. Say little. Do not be expansive. Let them bluster and be self-righteous. Don't be hasty to argue. Power often resides in silence. Your thoughtful pause puts pressure on them to respond more fully.

Don't expect too much the first 30 minutes—both sides are testing the water. It's likely that they are trying to extract information from you about the sales price;

i.e., what you "really" want. This is the flip side of your goal: To extract information on what defense is considering as an offer.

Is defense counsel sharing facts and defenses? Does it appear to be a genuine exploration or a fishing trip? Unless information is being exchanged, **stop**. If they stonewall, exit. Sue them promptly, if you feel strong enough about the facts.

It is important to appear pragmatic, **not** self-righteous. Rather than seem rigid, you should appear as a knowledgeable, practical lawyer who has an interest in settlement. Power is also evidenced by a willingness to challenge their inferences and especially uncertain legal issues. If court cases are unfavorable to you, you must show a willingness to change the law where it is wrong. If defense counsel does not know you, drop hints about appeals you've won or discuss your eagerness to create precedent on novel issues.

If you can limit the first meeting to a discussion of only liability facts, you show great power. Everyone is eager to hear about the money. It takes enormous discipline to wait, but your silence conveys your clarity and patience. Jumping into the topic of money shows urgency. It weakens your position.

Ask relatively neutral questions in an effort to identify the underlying assumptions, values, personal needs and goals. It is useful to informally ascertain any external pressures that may be operating. Focus on the underlying needs and interests of both sides, rather than locking into stated positions. Avoid the temptation to talk dollars or stated positions. Stated positions rarely reflect all of the underlying needs and interests. Your goal is to discover the undisclosed motives that can enhance settlement that are mutually beneficial.

In advance of negotiation, you should have carefully planned out your "concession patterns." At this time, I am referring only to liability fact concessions. When is it prudent to stand firm on your facts and when should you concede that an issue is less than clear-cut in your favor? In this situation, you should step back—but only one level—conceding that the fact may not be clear-cut, but simultaneously pointing out that it is still a question of material fact. Since you are starting from a "principled" position, your fact concessions should also be "principled", not unexplainable leaps. Make the employer earn the concession by showing its direct evidence or by clearly explaining indirect inferences.

Listen for distortions and misdirections. Employers will lie. Our strength lies in knowing that they do. Defense lawyers will circumvent and may deceive. Our strength lies in knowing that they might. Some lawyers will outright lie, but few will jeopardize a career for a single case.

Listen especially to what is NOT said. Pay close attention to how the hard facts are handled. This will provide clues to whether the interest in compromise is genuine or if there is a hidden agenda. Concessions usually come out sideways. You must be alert to the signals. If the defense attack is solely subjective or focused on plaintiff's personality, you can generally feel more confident. If they had defenses on the merits, they'd be focused there. At the same time, measure their comments about personality against your own gut reactions to your client.

By this time, you should have a working theory that connects your liability facts to the legal conclusion. Be prepared to test it out. Notice their nonverbal reactions to your theory. Do they flinch? Is it because your working theory makes sense, has intuitive appeal or is so far out as to be ridiculous? Does it pass over their heads or elicit a response suggesting your theory is transparent or bogus? Ideally, you will have a theme or visual image that is so clear and elegant that it haunts them—an image that they can't get out of their mind. Once, I articulated my theory as follows, "Let me understand this—you're going to tell a jury that the plaintiff was fired because the general counsel thought 'he was unhappy with his job?' They guy who had straight 'A's on his performance reviews for 17 years and had just received a huge bonus?" Or you can use a little hyberbole; e.g., "so your theory is that the employer is God. Anything goes at-the-will of the employer." Insights tinged with gentle humor have a wonderful power to haunt after they leave your office.

When defense counsel asks how much you want, deflect the question by explaining your need for information from them. For example, you can say, "I haven't heard your side." Or "I want to consider your version of reality." Or "I need to see your documentation before computing a demand." This suggests your open-mindedness and objectivity. It also encourages them to share their version, as well as their documents. It puts the ball in their court. If they are serious, they will provide more information.

If they provide some "impeachment" information, it is better to know now. If acquired early, you can use it later to take the wind out of their sails. If you had prematurely given a dollar amount, they would have used the information to deflate your numbers. Now you can factor it in ahead of time (or give that impression). If you can get their impeachment information pre-suit, it can keep you from awkward contradictions. It will also allow you to more realistically assess your case.

One goal is to learn your opponent's point of view and elicit their factual and legal defenses. A more crucial goal is to understand their real needs. It is not easy to go below the surface, but one insight allows you to stand under their arguments and their positioning. You can smile, knowingly, to yourself. The very act of looking for the needs of others opens you to receive information you might otherwise ignore.

You may have to reveal many of the strengths of your case, but the goal is to get all of the defense perspective you can. Unless all of your documents are secret and you want to hold them back, you should encourage a mutual exchange of documents. If they hesitate to give many documents, be skeptical. Try to view whatever documents they will share. Remember, they may have facts that would bear on your decision as to whether to make the plunge. From a true professional (and there are several on the defense side), your solicitation will also extract a psychological commitment. It is not legally binding, but it is useful.

Let them play their lawyer games. If they attack you or your facts, display a Cheshire smile. Remember, they called you. If they emphasize affirmative defenses, be grateful. Alternative defenses implicitly concede the liability facts, at least for the sake of argument. When they emphasize contradictory facts, respond somewhat cavalierly, stating only, "That's a fact question" or "Genuine issues like that won't give summary judgment." This opportunity will elicit information that can be used to revise your complaint if you end up suing. If they insist on debating legal issues, go with the flow, but watch for signs of wasted time or futility. If you learn about weaknesses that can be corrected, you may avoid a fatal mistake.

CAUTION

Delay talking money until they show respect. You must delay communicating a dollar demand until they have shown *some* respect for your liability issues or common ground on liability is reached.

Don't threaten publicity

Publicity is a powerful weapon, *until* it is used. Once used, it is worth little. Instead of threatening publicity, let it hover in the background. If you feel a need to use the press, consider implying it in reverse. You are safer and more effective, saying "Neither of us would benefit by press" or "I received a call from a reporter. Do you want to consider a joint statement?" [You don't have to disclose the reason the reporter called or when. Let their imagination fill in the gaps.]

The mention of publicity risks a request to agree to seal the complaint or worse an ex parte motion to seal. If they seek agreement, refuse saying "I don't want to prejudge my options" or even "I may need to run an ad to locate additional witnesses.

Once the complaint is filed, public scrutiny may be helpful in ferreting out witnesses, and the casual mention of this need may help keep negotiations moving. Press conferences, however, are perilous. The lawyers suing Michael Jackson lost their litigation privilege and had to defend themselves.

As the first session ends, schedule a definite date for your return with a demand. It should be at least a few days to allow for discussion with your client about these new facts or perspectives.

PREPARATION FOR SECOND SESSION

You must incorporate their facts into your analysis, adjusting your preliminary figures into a real demand. Your first demand must look credible. An excessive demand will freeze your opponent into a low or zero position. Once an extremist demand has polarized the parties, meaningful compromise is almost impossible. It will delay settlement for months, if not years.

In anticipation of the second session, you and your client should have evaluated the damages components of economic loss, emotional pain, injury to reputation, the impact of retaliation evidence or skeletons, and whether punitive damages are a realistic option in *this* case. The client's real 'bottom line' must be a primary factor in the first demand, but this concept should not be broached **until** you have educated him or her about litigation realities.

If the demand is more than triple (300 percent) your client's bottom line, you risk losing the opportunity to settle. If the demand is less than 150 percent of the bottom line, you deny yourself room to move and to let the opponent save face.

Counterbalances

There are counterbalancing ratios that suggest the amount an employer is willing to pay. *Employers are usually not willing to pay in settlement more than triple the hard losses unless there are special facts.* Higher purchase prices may be motivated by clear demonstrations of retaliation facts, objectively compelling evidence on causation of emotional harm or reputation damage, or the background presence of certain facts that the employer wants kept private. These type of facts increase the willingness to settle, but more importantly they geometrically multiply the value over and above the common measure of three times the hard losses.

Finalize your written demand

In anticipation of your second meeting, your one-page comparison chart should be finalized. It is critical that you watch the ratio between trial and compromise—it reflects your judgment about the risk of losing. If the demand is less than 50 percent of the trial value, too much liability is probably conceded. If the demand is more than 80 percent of the trial value, reality is being ignored. As a practical matter, the outer limits on the demand will rarely be more than 40-70 percent of trial value.

Ratios also help in determining the amount to seek in compromise. Trial value is a predictable, but a fungible figure. If you want to hold your demand down for prospects of success and you want to remain credible on liability, you should reduce trial value. This calculation allows you to send the message you want on your confidence in your liability position. Consider comparisons between what you will seek at trial and what you are seeking in compromise and make a chart. The following is for an employee making $36,000/year who wanted reinstatement because of good benefits. After two months of unemployment, he obtained a job at comparable pay, but no benefits.

COMPARISON CHART FOR **SMALL** CASES

Type of Damages	Trial Value	Early Demand
Lost wages		
2 months unemployed = $6,000; $2,000 year gap.		
(Benefits were $10,000/yr. for 2 yr)	$ 30,000	$ 25,000
Front pay—24 months @$500 differential	$ 12,000	reinstatement
Lost earning capacity 60 months @$400	$ 24,000	$ 20,000
Emotional pain	$ 20,000	$ 15,000
Humiliation & embarrassment (NIED)	$ 10,000	$ 7,000
Injury to reputation	$ 10,000	$ 5,000
Attorneys fees to date	$ 4,000	$ 3,000
Costs (service, filing, PI, Ld phone, etc. =)	$ 200-	
At the present time	$110,000	$75,000 + * Reinstatement
If we go to trial:		
Additional depositions, etc.	$ 3,000	
Attys fees for discovery + 3 days @ trial + prep	$ 25,000	
Doubling of compensatory damages	$ 66,000	
Likely benefits to plaintiff	$ 204,000	
Civil penalty payable to taxpayers		$ 25,000
Defendant's attorneys fees		$ 50,000
	Potential costs to defense	$ 279,000*

*When the numbers are bigger, I do not to add up the totals. The act of doing the math can psychologically invest the defense lawyer in the numbers.

Usually, you can assume that the chart will be given to the employer. The ratio expresses confidence in winning, but the amounts are modest because of the client's goal of reinstatement. Remember this is pre-suit settlement. You should note that the hard losses ($30,000) are less than one third of the demand because you seek reinstatement. Categories like civil penalty can educate the employer about unexpected sums that have avoidance value to the employer and trade-off value for you. If legal issues are still not respected or damages are complicated, a terse written narrative should precede the numbers. It should simply list your strengths and acknowledge a weakness or two, which are turned upside down (think judo tactics).

SECOND SESSION

In the second session, you are ready to convey your first demand, but only if you sense that they takes your liability position seriously. They don't have to agree with you or cave in to your legal arguments, but it is crucial that they appreciate that your case has some merit. Once they have shown *some* respect for your liability position, the time is ready. If they haven't, invest more time in educating them—provide your response to the strengths they articulated in their defenses or the weaknesses they perceived in your claims at the first session. If they didn't disclose some real facts with you at that first meeting, you shouldn't be there. You are wasting your time.

You should deliver the demand in writing and in person so you can watch their reaction. This instant feedback allows you to read between the lines of their stated position. In many smaller cases, they will have authority and will counteroffer on the spot. If not, acknowledge that they may need time to consult with their client or ask if they have authority to respond. Since one of your strategies is to accelerate the timetable, you should ask if X number of days is sufficient. [In small cases, X may be 2 days, but large ones will involved 10 or more.] You need to be specific on the number of days because you are narrowing their options, but reasonably.

One of your goals should be to have a decision-maker present, one who has no incentive to litigate. Where appropriate, ask if they are willing to bring the general counsel or an executive along to the next meeting. You should justify your aberrant request as a way to explore some of your intangible issues like reinstatement because this request may insult opposing counsel.

If you received an immediate response to your first offer, ask how they arrived at the number. Then, tell them you need to consult with your client and exit Otherwise, you should receive their first offer in the third meeting.

MEETINGS THREE AND BEYOND

The first offer is seldom based on the merits: it is a feeler, a positional statement to test your reaction. If the offer is truly trivial, just pack up your bags and exit. If you take offense, don't waste words. Don't say anything, just walk out. Silence is more powerful than any hyperbolic statements. Defense counsel usually know they will meet you again in another case and s/he will usually feel the urge to explain. It's ok to let them, but keep your bags packed.

If the first offer feels low, but more than nuisance value, hear them out. [Nuisance value is relative to the potential injury. When the cost of defense was twenty-five to forty thousand dollars, nuisance value meant one thousand to five thousand dollars. In 1999, nuisance value is between five and thirty thousand dollars.] Ask or allow opposing counsel to explain why they picked a low value, why s/he is giving zero weight to your liability position. They may be bluffing and you can pick up clues. Or they may have information that you don't. There **may** be sound reasons for their beliefs that could enable them to succeed on a motion to dismiss, without any discovery. You owe it to your client and yourself to listen and probe.

If the first offer is modest, but at least related to the cost of defense, hear them out fully. [Cost of defense value is also relative to the potential injury. It used to mean twenty-five to forty thousand in the Midwest but now is closer to one hundred thousand.][42] This is **not the real** cost, but an average figure generated over several years. Today the actual cost of defense varies between fifty thousand and two million dollars in cases with single person plaintiffs.

Whatever the offer, it is valuable to obtain their explanation of how they arrived at whatever dollars they did. They have two primary methods of attack: 1) challenging your liability or 2) challenging your damage calculations. If they focus their attack primarily on your damages, that's a good sign. They are recognizing liability, which is the easiest situation to leverage upwards. Whatever their offer, use it to work backwards in analyzing their attitude toward liability. You need to understand if they are denying all liability or merely discounting it. If you can focus on how they arrive at the numbers, you obtain indirect clues about liability.

On the other hand, if they focus their attack primarily on your liability arguments, your preparation is about to pay off. First, you should listen to all their arguments—don't respond in piecemeal fashion. Try to gather a collective sense of the whole. It's ok to take notes. You don't have to be macho and forego note-taking out of worry that noting an important point will expose your angst. Dilute the impact of writing a specific note by doodling, writing shorthand, taking a lot of notes or jotting things down at odd times.

You should be extremely selective in delivering rebuttal evidence. By revealing only a little piece at a time, impact is increased. If defense counsel identifies a fact that you can contradict, refer verbally to your contradictory evidence. But, don't offer statements or affidavits until they ask.

---

[42] Source: the Rand Study estimated the average costs of defense at $80,000 but this was data collected in the 1980 and eary 1990's.

> *Tactic*: Do not offer evidence until they ask for your proof.

If you prematurely brag about having an affidavit, you weaken its impact. First, lock them in on the importance of the fact that they have raised. Get their version of why this fact is pivotal. Then, if you have a statement or affidavit that fairly addresses their point, pull it out. If it isn't on point, you are probably better off to wait and get a revised affidavit, if possible.

If the opponent is focusing on an affirmative defense, remember that an affirmative defense is a fancy way of saying, "*Even if* you prove the elements of your case, we can escape liability." This is often a good time to remind them that an affirmative defense implicitly concedes liability. You can respond with "I like these "even if" defenses. It makes the juries' task so much easier."

Advise defense counsel that you need to consult your client before responding to their offer. Often, they don't believe you—they know your recommendation carries much weight. IF they ask if you will recommend this amount, don't tell them. You are not yet in a position to recommend. As you end the meeting, schedule a time to resume negotiations. You are still trying to accelerate the meeting schedule, but you want enough time to look reflective. Try to shorten the gap of the next meeting to three days in small cases and more in bigger ones.

MEETING FOUR

At this meeting, you are usually ready to present your first counter. You can reduce your demand by any amount you deem appropriate, but you must recognize that the opponent will read a great deal into the size of your reduction. It is not the size of reduction in terms of absolute dollars, but the percent of reduction. The percentage decline is a much stronger signal than the actual amount. If you cut your demand in half, you have either expressed huge doubts about the strength of your case or you have admitted the unreasonableness of your first demand. A reduction of 50 percent should be done only if they provided solid facts that exposed serious holes in your case. If their offer was low, but in the ballpark, then you should probably reduce your demand by 10 percent. If their offer was modest, but further into the ballpark, then you should probably reduce your demand by 15-20 percent. You should be sensitive to calendar events, like fiscal year end for insurance companies or holiday purchasing events.

It is not a sign of weakness to acknowledge that their evidence on liability or on damages had some effect on your analysis, but think carefully about which effect you choose to acknowledge. If you can focus the impact on damages only, you confine the implications of the reduction. If you admit that it weakened your liability position (risk of losing), there may be a secondary ripple effect on damages (amount at risk, which could have been avoided by your planning).

A separate sum for confidentiality

Consider negotiating a separate sum for confidentiality. Many defense lawyers assume confidentiality is a given in their offers; i.e., they silently assume you will agree it is "standard." A valuable strategy is to counter a respectable, but not quite adequate offer with two different figures, clarifying that the higher figure includes no confidentiality; e.g., you can counter with two different figures, $175,000 with confidentiality or $150,000 without confidentiality. This places a premium on their desire for silence. Be sure your client has expressed his or her point of view about confidentiality.

There are four types of confidentiality:

- ❖ terms and condition of settlement; i.e., usually the amount paid
- ❖ the fact of settlement
- ❖ all material facts related to the lawsuit
- ❖ all facts related to the workplace.

You and your client must decide which of these types, if any, is acceptable. I recommend that only the amount of payment be confidential.

Graduated fees

Another useful technique is "graduated" fees. My clients are fully aware that if we settle before the lawsuit starts, my fees are only 20 percent of the settlement, plus the retainer previously paid. Once we cross the line to a lawsuit, the fees increase incrementally to 35 or 40 percent. Thus, it is obvious that the client keeps a bigger chunk if we settle early. My client and I discuss how the kitty must be much larger at a later date to net them the same amount. A higher percentage is subtracted as we progress in the litigation. I show the client a chart like the following to clarify this point.

	Settlement Fees @ 20%	Trial Fees @ 40%	Settlement Fees @ 20%	Trial Fees @ 40%
Amount:	$ 50,000	$ 75,000	$ 500,000	$ 750,000
Fees:	$ 10,000	$ 30,000	$ 100,000	$ 300,000
Costs:	0	$ 5,000	0	$ 30,000
Net to Jane:	$ 40,000	$ 40,000	$ 400,000	$ 400,000

Without counting tax considerations.

The formula is x-4%(x) - costs = net   or   net + costs/60%

We have to obtain $250,000 more money in later settlement or at trial to net the client the same result and we take the risk of collecting zero. Whether the number is small or large, this additional fifteen to twenty percent is a factor in many decisions.

You can use the percent of fee increase as a lever with the opponent. Many opponents are surprised to hear that my percent changes. They assume plaintiff's lawyers can only divide by three. Once they realize that the client receives a bigger piece in early settlement, it justifies putting a more tempting offer together in the early stages. You should save this issue until ending negotiations, because the actual difference is usually modest. It translates into a gap filler of about 10 percent.

Charts with the net to the plaintiff were more impressive when emotional distress was not taxed; e.g., prior to August 1996. Because of current law, this is purely hypothetical until the law is changed, hopefully in early 2000. When tax consequences were factored in, early settlement of $100,000 was equivalent of verdict of $200,000, at least where the potential amount for punitive damages and reputation injury could legitimately be viewed as emotional distress.[43] Similarly, an early settlement of $600,000 is equivalent of verdict of $1,000,000, where the potential of other damage categories can legitimately be portrayed as emotional distress.

Comparison of Net Benefit to Client from Verdicts/Settlements in Discrimination and Tort Claims			
Deductions	Verdict	Settle early @ 20%	Settle later @ 40%
	$ 200,000	$ 100,000	$ 145,000
Fees @ 40%	-80,000	-20,000	-58,000
Tax on Wages/Reputat ($45K)[45]	-18,000	18,000	-18,000
Tax on Punitive Dmgs ($45K)*	-18,000	0	0
Tax on Emo. Distress ($110K)	0	0	0
Costs	-20,000	0	-5,000
NET To Client	$64,000	$62,000	$64,000

HYPOTHETICAL Comparison of Verdicts and Settlements In Discrimination and Tort Claims
(NOT FOR CONTRACT CLAIMS)

Deduction	Verdict	Settle early @ 20% Fees	Settle later @ 40% Fees
	$ 1,000,000	$600,000	$823,333
Fees[44] 40%	- 400,000	- 120,000	329,333
Tax on wages/Reput(A$240K[45])	- 96,000	- 96,000	- 96,000
Tax on Punitive D (A.$240K)	- 96,000	0	
Tax on Emo. Distress(Alloc. 120K)	0	0	
Costs	- 40,000	0	30,000
NET to Client	$368,000	$376,000	$368,000

If NELA's lobbying effort is successful, this flexibility may be restored. Watch Congress and the Employee Advocate. For now, it is purely hypothetical.

Each round of negotiation typically goes through three cycles. If settlement does not occur at the first round, there will be another round later, either voluntary or by court direction.

Watch increments of movement in offers

The more important gauge is the increments after the first increase. You should keep track of the increases in terms of percentage over the starting offer. For example, if the first offer was $50,000 and the second was $100,000, this doubling tells you there is a lot more money available. But an increase from $50,000 to $60,000, tells you the employer is not likely to move much more, without new facts. Thus, the twenty percent increase means they are slowing down dramatically and getting ready to stop. Unless you have some new information to alter their positions, they will move little. This observation is the origin of my

---

[44] For calculation convenience, I use 40% at trial. Personally, I charge 25% for pre-discovery settlement, 30% pre-summary judgment and 35% at trial.

[45] Assumes verdict of $400,000 for wage loss and damage to reputation, $400,000 for punitive damages and $200,000 for emotional distress/embarrassment/humiliation; Rates of 23% federal, Rates of 8% state, social security 7.5% rounded. The ratio of taxable/nontaxable should be applied to the amount left after the fees allocated to taxable income. Since non-taxable emotional distress was 200,000 and taxable part was 800,000, I use an allocation of 4/5 for tax calculations. After deduction for attorneys fees ($400,000), the 4/5 is applied against the whole amount remaining for the employees ($600,000) = $480,000 then 40% taxes is applied pro rata.

theory that information must be provided in stages, carefully calculated for best effect. Too much information at one time dilutes its value.

The entire negotiation process can be summarized:

- ❖ Tantalize with hard facts blended with inference
- ❖ Perform implied promise with reliable facts
- ❖ Until they are thirsty, risks are not real
- ❖ Protect against premature disclosures
- ❖ Wait for solicitation of confidentiality
- ❖ Don't dilute power with quantity
- ❖ Never give more, until they ask
- ❖ Subtlety arouses more intrigue
- ❖ Intrigue with the possibilities
- ❖ Anticipate audience needs
- ❖ Do everything in stages
- ❖ Build momentum
- ❖ SEIZE THE DAY...

EARLY MEDIATION

Mediation has become a popular and successful means of resolving many employment disputes. It allows the defense lawyer to remain a vigorous advocate for his or her client, while simultaneously providing thought-provoking questions and providing a third-party perspective that is more objective. Mediation also allows you to remain a vigorous advocate for the plaintiff, while simultaneously providing provocative questions and third-party objectivity to your side. You can also supply information to the mediator on your client's real needs and the weaknesses in your case that can be used to educate your client, without making you critique either your client or the case.

A very successful mediator, Joan Morrow, has succinctly stated that the goal in mediation is "to get the very best possible offer on the table. This allows the plaintiff to make an informed choice whether to accept the offer or go forwards with more litigation."

Litigation has a built-in incentive for the lawyer paid-by-the-hour to engage in costly discovery, but mediation has no such incentive. The self-interest of the mediator is in achieving resolution, not by failed mediations that lead to more litigation.

Traditionally, defense lawyers assumed client loyalty and recurring business by doing a good job. A good job was often equated with early settlement. The increased intensity in competition among defense lawyers combined with the diminished loyalty by a corporation for its lawyer has often shifted the goal from keeping clients "happy and returning" to a preoccupation with shorter term gains. Healthy profit motives have given way to maximizing your billing while you can.

A cottage industry of hiring outside auditors to scrutinize bills of lawyers was started in the 1980s, but it never really reached a trend. Law firms expanded their bill from a one sentence summary to detailed elaborate billings and used more hyperbole to justify exhaustive discovery. Instead of reducing hours or encouraging earlier settlement, the scrutiny resulted in a stalemate.

In the 1980s, I followed the lead of some academics and suggested that corporations hire two different law firms: one to litigate and one to evaluate settlement. The slight increase in up-front cost would be readily offset by the gain in objectivity. This solution has not been widely accepted. Mediation provides an equivalent and very workable alternative.

THRESHOLD ISSUES

Minimum Requirements for Mediation

A stake in the outcome

To make it work, both sides need a stake in the outcome. Therefore, all parties must initially agree to split the costs. The splitting does not have to be a 50:50 arrangement: Where individuals have also been sued, it can be divided by the number of parties. Similarly, if resources are widely disparate, the percentage up front can be adjusted. The costs vary from $150-300 per hour. The amount of time varies with each mediation, but time is usually estimated at six hours for a simple case and approximately twenty hours for a more complicated one. At the end of a successful mediation, the employer is often willing to pick up the mediator's entire bill.

Conflict must be ripe

A conflict must be ready for mediation. Unless the facts have been fleshed out by thorough investigation or by some discovery, mediation may be premature. If the real dollar value is small, it may not matter much. But if the potential value is high, it is usually not beneficial to invest the effort until enough facts are known to meaningfully clarify the conflict.

Decision-maker present

A key decision-maker must be present. Do not attend unless someone is present who has the authority to change the employer's position. If they have limits on their authority, insist on someone else coming to the mediation. Telephone participation is not good enough because the process requires involvement throughout the entire progression. You can't cut and paste the mediation experience to someone who is too busy or too important to be there. The process is close to being wholistic: The give-and-take process cannot be easily summarized to bring someone else up-to-date.

Threshold amount

Some defense lawyers may use alternative dispute resolution as a delay tactic, free discovery without rules, or worse, engage in mediation in bad faith. To ensure that you are not being duped or taken advantage of, it is occasionally useful to consider a threshold sum to show the defense is serious. Many lawyers, like NELA's Dee Rowe, have refined this special technique in big dollar cases. They won't agree to mediate unless the defense has placed a substantial amount on the table. There is no magic amount, but it should exceed the likely costs of defense for this type of case. An offer of that magnitude means the defense is indirectly acknowledging liability, the only remaining question is how much. The amount need not relate to your demand, but this threshold should be at least one-third of your secret bottom line. You may convey this threshold before the mediator is selected, but sometimes, it works better to go through the mediator. If you opt for this strategy, you should ask the mediator to exact a commitment to a certain minimum to ensure all parties are not wasting their time.

CAUTION

This threshold can be counter-productive. If defense counsel genuinely wants to settle, it creates an obstacle in the need to maintain client rapport. When the same defense counsel sees the need to compromise but is also the trial lawyer, the dilemma is aggravated. The need to persuade the employer to offer big bucks to meet the threshold requires not only candor about the strengths of plaintiff's case, but also the weakness of the defense. The necessary bluntness can diminish the relationship. If you have reason to trust the defense counsel, you can allow the defense counsel to wait until the mediation. Thus, the mediator can be the "bad guy" who points out the defects in the defense, the gaps in credibility and the barriers to selling the big picture to the jury.

You need to know the other side is serious. A threshold is one method. Sometimes, trusting your instincts about the other counsel's desire for settlement is often better than a numerical threshold. One way to test this situation is to simply ask the defense counsel if he or she needs a mediator to explain reality to his or her client. If you listen between the words, you can gauge their sincerity.

WHO TO SELECT

For most cases, I strongly recommend someone who is a good listener and a good communicator, someone who understands that feeling logic is a stronger driving force than legal logic.

Generally, a full-time mediator is the best. Part-timers can succeed, but a part-time defense lawyer is often cynical about persons who sue and protective of persons who are sued. Some former defense lawyers still see the world through thorn-covered lens. Their questions often insult sensitive plaintiffs, their arguments are premised on plaintiffs as gold-diggers and their style is subtle intimidation. Occasionally, an insurance defense background is a strong plus. They will have credibility with the defense, talk the jargon and understand the motives and values of both the corporation and the claims adjuster. But, be cautious.

Retired judges are seldom effective mediators: They are accustomed to making decisions, not negotiating mutually satisfying outcomes. There are exceptional judges who are wonderful mediators and there are some situations where a judge's opinion on liability issues is helpful, but you must be selective. Good mediators will seldom give their opinion on value, at least directly.

Savvy defense lawyers often want a former plaintiff's attorney as a mediator, hoping they will talk sense to this plaintiff's attorney who seems to have an exaggerated notion of reality. It is dangerous for you to assume a plaintiff's lawyer will be your zealous advocate. We are professionals and when we put on the hat of a mediator, we take our duties seriously and act as a neutral.

The relationship with a mediator is short-lived, but highly significant. Many defense lawyers assume that an "apology in green" is the only validation, but money is not the only victory. A mediator can fulfill some of the other needs— the emotional validation of being heard is often pivotal to achieving closure. Many plaintiffs really want someone, other than family or a hired gun, to listen to their story. If the listener validates your client's issue as important and helps s/he feel that fighting back did some good, your client will gain much satisfaction in early mediation.

The means of success in mediation are diverse. Joan Morrow, one of the premier mediators in the Midwest, has articulated Ten Commandments of Mediation:

- ❖ Thou shalt Prepare Thyself, thy Client and thy Mediator
- ❖ Thou shalt Shape the Process to the Dispute
- ❖ Thou shalt Not Exclude Naysayers
- ❖ Thou shalt be Patient and a Counselor
- ❖ Thou shalt Come with People with Real Settlement Authority
- ❖ Thou shalt Use the Process to Exchange Information
- ❖ Thou shalt Remember the Parties' Feelings and Meet their Needs
- ❖ Thou shalt Not Take the Name of thy Opponent in Vain
- ❖ Thou shalt Confide in the Mediator
- ❖ Thou shalt not Despair at Apparent Impasse.

These precepts are as essential to success as explaining to your client the boundaries of mediation: 1) no settlement can occur without his or her agreement; 2) values at trial are different from the mediation demands; 3) demands diminish and offers increase during mediation; and 4) the "real" bottom line should not be preset—it will evolve during the mediation.

PREPARATION FOR MEDIATION

Use the same degree of care in preparing for mediation that you use in preparing for trial. This does not mean that you prepare all of the exhibits and witnesses, but rather that you think through your case and the real needs of all the parties. Mediation is usually centered on the needs of the parties, but it also operates in the framework of the legal strengths and weaknesses.

Don't flood the mediator with tons of paper, like the complaint and discovery documents. Instead, digest the information and summarize it in five to ten pages. Only a few details really matter. Use your judgment to focus on those important facts. The following format is helpful to many mediators who lack the intimate familiarity that you have acquired over several weeks or months:

- ❖ A cast of characters
- ❖ The big picture
- ❖ The strengths and weaknesses of your primary legal claims
- ❖ A chronological list of key decisions that underlie the battle
- ❖ A history of settlement demands and offers
- ❖ A well thought out explanation of how damages are calculated and discounted for early settlement.

Identify all the central characters by his or her roles, personalities and primary decisions. If you have objective insights into what she or he will gain or lose by compromise, share your theory of motives. If you have a sense of the plaintiff's real needs, the mediator is the best person to tell.

Break the claims down into the elements, but only the ones that are truly disputed. Identify the key facts that enhance your claim, but also those that detract. Invest time in finding lynchpin facts that favor resolving the dispute in your direction. Make a conscious decision on what you want to deliver and what to hold back. You should prepare to demonstrate not only how you will disprove the defenses, but separately, how you will prove up your own case.

> For lawsuits, the central questions are who caused this harm and how much?
>
> For mediation, the central question is how can the needs of both sides be met?

You should provide a history of settlement demands and offers, sharing any newly acquired facts that influenced changes in your position on either liability or damages. For damages, you should prepare one or two simple charts as ammunition to be used in the other room.

You should enter the process in good faith and assume good faith by your opponent. At the same time, power is maintained by retaining "walk-away" ability. You must have the psychological willingness to walk away, but also to accept the consequences—more litigation, trial and heightened risk. Patience is critical: Often, it takes stamina to stay and mediate. Wisdom lies in recognizing when the potential for compromise is better than the risk.

STAGING THE DELIVERY OF EVIDENCE

Some mediators will ask you for all your strongest facts up front. The benefit of full disclosure is to maximize the mediator's expectation of value. The downside is diluting the impact of facts by revealing them in the aggregate. Generally, you need not fear that the mediator will make a premature disclosure to the opponent. You can usually rely on mediators to keep information segregated and confidential, but you must request it explicitly. You can control the best timing for later delivery of your strongest evidence through your instructions to the mediator. Sometimes, it is wise to trust their instincts more than your own.

To whet the opponent's appetite, it is necessary to explain your theory of the case and provide **enough** supporting facts at the beginning to start the interaction. Beyond that, I recommend waiting on disclosure of your strongest evidence. You should plan to stage the delivery as the issues narrow. You want to delay delivery of key corroborating evidence until the defendant has asked for it—or wait until they have declared that you can't prove something. Then produce your strong, factual statements and affidavits. You should wait until some movement is made that shows seriousness—until you reach some common ground or until they have shown some respect for your liability position. Some mediators are quick to get to the money issues. Hesitate, pause, slow down. Remember, liability is a fancy word for a reason to settle. Make sure a reason is felt, before talking numbers.

CAUTION

Forewarn your client that some mediators ask your bottom line early in the process. It is dangerous to comply.

The money

Everyone is eager to get to the money. This eagerness should not give way to disclosure of your bottom line to the mediator, at least not early in the process. Better yet, avoid the human tendency to pre-set a bottom line. It should not be fixed. You can't really know where the process will take you. This strategy presumes that you have followed a sequence of analysis similar to that set forth in Chapters 13 and 14 on valuing and negotiating.

If there is a reasoned connection between your real bottom line and your demand, be patient. Trust the process. Even if you tell your bottom line, few mediators will believe you and worse, whatever bottom line you identify will be seen as negotiable anyway. If you have inflated the demand, you owe it to your client to bring it down closer to the perceived bottom line. Otherwise you may be wasting a glorious opportunity to settle.

Generally, it is premature to advance to your dollar demands until you have made some progress toward the following criteria:

❖ Received some feedback from the mediator that the employer has shown **some** respect for your liability position;

❖ Isolated the points of agreement and points of disagreement;

❖ Narrowed the issues to those that are 1) pivotal and 2) where the evidence can go either way—i.e., too close to call. This means identifying the risks that each side is taking if you don't settle.

❖ Discerned that each side appreciates the needs of the other side and clearly appreciates his or her own needs. This may include your client's need to tell his or her story or a chance to refute the other side's accusations.

❖ Ensured that your client has recognized the benefits of settling vs. not settling as well as the consequences of settling vs. not settling.

The act of making demands and interpreting offers is like making bids in poker. The bid gives a clue about each player's position. Starting bids are usually positional, but good mediators try to mitigate that approach. The starting bids actually conveyed always have some meaning, but the ratio of increments is more significant. You should always expect that subsequent bids are not final, but involve some bluffing. You should not think in terms of absolute dollars. Instead, be cautious about the proportionate size of your reductions: They may be seen as expressions of declining confidence in your case rather than the give and take of negotiation.

Let momentum grow by reaching consensus on liability and needs. As the stakes increase, the tension builds–the bidding acquires more meaning and your stronger cards gain in weight. Staging the delivery of solid facts is crucial. Until they have put some serious money on the table, there is little benefit in showing all of your cards.

As noted earlier, negotiation shares certain elements with game theory because both sides are interdependent, no single move has meaning in itself, and it is essential to make assumptions about the strategy of the other because their reactions are not mere chance events. If you have credibility with the mediator, she or he may trust your judgment about the timing of disclosures. On the other hand, you can also solidify the mediator's expectations by showing the cards you are holding. Remember, in the other room, the mediator is your best advocate. You want to help him/her succeed.

If the parties have invested several hours in the process and a mediator asks your bottom line, it is wise to comply. The mediator is gauging whether settlement has any realistic prospects of success. Cooperate. It provides the mediator with a means to determine whether to make any last-chance efforts before calling off the talks. Unless the mediator is mediocre or biased, there is little justification for bluffing the mediator.

If you succeed in mediating a solution, write down all the material terms in detail. A handwritten document is fine, but you should get it signed before anyone leaves. Do not leave issues for later resolution. Finalization can drag out the event and impair closure. Review the terms set out in the next chapter. Mediation is also an extraordinary tool for getting the employer's very best offer on the table, but it works best when it is approached with the care of trial preparation. Then and only then can your client make a truly informed decision.

Chapter Fifteen

FINALIZING THE DEAL

"Never count your winnings till the deal is done."

Kenny Rogers, *The Gambler*

If the parties agree on a purchase price and other terms, you can wait for defense to draft the agreement or you can do it yourself. If you prepare the first draft, you control the turf and speed up the process. Drafting the settlement will also remind you of all issues you need to be attuned to for final compromise. If you wait for defense counsel, two to three weeks may lapse because they have achieved their goal of stopping the uncertainty. At a minimum, you should maintain a checklist that spells out your options. My checklist includes my options, but also a simple justification of the reasons for each option, a sample set of phrases and alternative trade-offs.

The settlement agreement should specify at the least the following elements:

1. Mutual releases
2. If confidentiality is proposed, make it mutual
3. If liquidated damages, they too must be mutual
4. Tax consequences and documentation
5. A short timetable for payment in exchange for signatures.

To ensure full closure, releases must be mutual. Where appropriate, other employees should be named as releasees and requested to sign the release, even if they were not parties to the draft lawsuit.

Personally, I oppose confidentiality clauses, especially anything beyond the amount of payment. Other employees know about the facts for which confidentiality is sought. The agreement should either identify them by name or at least by number—they could be sources of leaks for underlying facts. Since neither side had meaningful control over the dissemination by these other employees, you should be explicit about the approximate number with knowledge of core facts.

If one of the four forms of confidentiality is necessary, there will usually be a companion penalty clause. You should insist that any liquidated damages provisions are mutual. This usually results in the opponent dropping the penalty concept or narrowing the boundaries. The corporation lacks control over so many potential leaks and this opens the door to later litigation.

You should seek maximum protection on tax flexibility. Although NELA is close to success in lobbying to make emotional distress non-taxable in the 1999 tax bill, we don't know the final result yet. Presently, there are only a few areas of consequence where we can have an influence.

First, keep in mind that a W-2 payment will involve withholding, but Form 1099 income will not. Because employers must match the social security contribution on a W-2, but not on a 1099, employers have a 7.53 percent incentive to cooperate with a Form 1099. But, this may be a 7.53 percent detriment to your client who will have to pay both sides of the social security contributions.

Second, consider that Form 1099 income may be designated either non-employee compensation [box 7 is filled out] or other income [box 3 is filled out]. The latter should avoid Social Security payments since emotional distress can be treated as "other income." This may bypass self-employment taxes, whereas a 1099 for wages or salary [box 7] will involve federal, state income, and self-employment of 15.3 percent.

After trial you have less flexibility in defining these issues. Thus, the net income differences of trial income compared to settlement income means comparing tax consequences and fees/costs of trial vs. settlement. (A sample exhibit on the disc/CD contains a fairly comprehensive list of issues.)

END OF EARLY EFFORTS

If your efforts succeeded, the dispute is over. If they failed, you must make an independent decision about whether to start a lawsuit over this particular dispute. You need to re-think the complaint, adding or deleting in light of new facts, consider whom to service the summons and complaint, and consider formally notifying the employer's lawyer that your offer has been withdrawn. While you are pondering, you can file an EEOC charge or a charge with your local or state human rights agency. You may have evidence that warrants requesting a Department of Labor audit of jobs and eligibility for overtime or exempt status.

If you have decided to go forward, be bold. The thrill of creating new precedent or fighting for justice can give you the courage to leap buildings in a single bound. Go for it. Be Barry Roseman's "cop on the beat" and enforce the law.

MIDDLE-STAGES OF SETTLEMENT

Chapter Sixteen

STARTING THE SUIT

Starting a lawsuit is a declaration of war. Any negotiations that occurred or did not occur before you declared war are factors. If you exhausted vigorous settlement efforts, you are no longer at the beginning of a dispute: you are part way into it. Your strategies need to change. The employer may have assumed that you were bluffing. If you were, so be it. If not, the next step should begin with a BANG. If you are facing a statute of limitations deadline, you may have to proceed to suit without any settlement talks. If the facts are truly one-sided, a suit may be preferred over settlement overtures. Your initial attack may seem routine to you, but it can set the stage for the perception of subsequent settlement opportunities if you make a strong first impression.

It is essential that you be in the driver's seat when you start a war. Decisions should be based on thoughtful strategy, not impulse or revenge for their refusal to buy your settlement.

> Once war has been declared, forget about initiating settlement.
>
> Let the impetus come from the defense.

Once sued, the employer realizes that you were serious, not bluffing. They may abruptly appreciate that they screwed up by not accepting your last offer. They may want to reconsider. If so, let them call. If they offer to meet your last demand or put a better offer on the table, listen politely. Your response must depend on your client's needs and your assessment of the real strengths. Nonetheless, it's so much fun to tell the defendant who meets your last offer, "It's too late. The demand is now [last offer plus 20 percent]." The thrill of rejection must, however, be counter-balanced by sound judgment about the true value of the case. Do not let pride interfere with accepting a good offer. You can legitimately raise your demand because of additional attorney time, the additional retainer invested by your client or more facts.

At the same time, there are several exceptions to this strategy of going forwards vigorously. If one of the following events occurs, you must be flexible about resuming talks or even initiating settlement talks at some logical moment; e.g.:

- ❖ If serious factual weaknesses surfaced during negotiations
- ❖ If new precedent creates a major legal obstacle
- ❖ If the prospect of an adverse medical exam terrifies your client
- ❖ If your client's tax or financial records show major discrepancies
- ❖ When the magistrate is unwilling to suppress subpoenas your client's family, friends or neighbors…
- ❖ If your client insists he or she doesn't want to go to trial

Absent one of these dilemmas, which can arise early or later, your calculated displays of silence should begin to have the desired effect. Be patient.

COMMON LAW VS. DISCRIMINATION

Before you declare war, you must decide several strategic issues that will influence later settlement options. These strategies include:

- ❖ Deciding whether to file discrimination charges
- ❖ Choosing the forums
- ❖ Avoiding removal
- ❖ Identifying inhibitors to settlement
- ❖ Anticipate surprises
- ❖ Deciding whether to commence suit by filing or serving
- ❖ Maintaining momentum.

If the common law claims are strong unto themselves, there is no need to add superficial claims based on discrimination claims. Often, discrimination is tossed in without any meaningful evidence. This is a tactical error. Even if they open up fee petitions, bogus claims generally weaken your suit and your negotiating position. If the only discrimination facts are protected status and adverse action, dig deeper or forego them. If you have only common law (i.e., non-discrimination) claims you can skip this section. But, if discrimination is a significant possibility, you should consider whether the discrimination facts are strong enough to justify filing a charge with the EEOC or State Human Rights and whether to request an immediate right to sue, wait for EEOC to run its natural course or wait only 180 days.

CHARGES WITH EEOC

Before you can sue under **federal** discrimination laws, the client must have filed charges with EEOC. If the client has already filed charges, review them to ensure comprehensiveness and if necessary, amend them.

While exploring settlement, it was advisable to delay filing the charge with EEOC. The act of filing is useful to break a stalemate in negotiations or to show renewed vigor. Once settlement talks have stopped, the charge should be filed.

CAUTION

A hurried or sloppy charge will rebound to haunt you. Do not prepare it casually or your later claims may be restricted; e.g., omitting reprisal will often preclude later claims of retaliation.

The EEOC charge should be detailed enough for both state and federal jurisdictions and the claims you may bring later. Most court decisions hold that Title VII does not apply to individuals. If you want leverage over individuals and you are in a deferral state, list the individual under the state claim.

WAITING ON THE EEOC INVESTIGATION

Occasionally, there is benefit in waiting for the employer's written response to the charge. The reply can narrow the issues and lock in their factual and/or legal defenses. Occasionally, the subpoena power of EEOC will also generate more documents for inspection. Once in a great while, filing charges will cause EEOC to intervene and obtain a court order to stop the intimidation of witnesses or destruction of oral or written evidence. NELA's Dee Rowe of Minneapolis has almost created an art form of tapping the power of the EEOC to protect witnesses.

Historically, few experienced lawyers waited for EEOC to work its natural course. It happened only on cases that were exceedingly weak or where the lawyer didn't like the prospect. When I filed a charge, I simultaneously requested an immediate right to sue. The rules suggested that you either had to wait 180 days for the EEOC to conduct its investigation or receive a dismissal. Nevertheless, the EEOC would certify that it could not complete the investigation and issue an early right to sue. This was justified because the agency was so overworked and understaffed that delays of six to eighteen months were the norm. Reciprocally, their investigations were slim and often deferential to the party possessing the documents—the employer. Under the new regime, this may be changing.

Historically, my requests for a rapid right to sue were also based on the data that EEOC rules for the employer approximately 92 percent of time, on average. Most state human rights organizations have similar results. No matter what the explanation, the effect is the same. If you decide to wait on the EEOC investigation, it is crucial that clients are warned that EEOC rules for the employer 92 percent of time, on average. The "No probable cause," whether justified or not, has a demoralizing effect.

Recently, the 180 day "requirement" has been resurrected. In *Martini v. Fanny Mae*, 178 F.3d 1336 (D.C. Cir. 1999), the employee lost a seven million dollar verdict because her right to sue was obtained on day 21 after filing the charge. It was destructive, but fortunately not fatal. The dismissal without prejudice allowed her to sue all over again, if she waits an additional 159 days. The past verdict provided significant settlement leverage.

FORUM CHOICES

For some cases you should rush to federal court, but for many others you should avoid federal court. Federal court may be preferable in those rare cases when the facts are truly great, when undisputed facts are truly dispositive, when the employer is the dominant force in a small town or the judge is a good old boy from the local defense firms. The situations tend to be court-specific and vary by jurisdiction.

The choice of forum question has two sub-issues: one forum or two forums; and if only one, which court—federal or state. About 30 percent of the time, I choose two forums: bringing only federal claims in federal court and only state claims in state court. A careful allocation of claims and related facts should minimize anxiety about splitting a cause of action. Because the elements of the claims are different, you should carefully select facts according to elements of the federal claims or the elements of the state claims. It is stupid to copy all the same facts for both claims. There are subtle differences between federal and state claims and they have material consequences. This approach is particularly useful if the Eleventh Amendment presents a bar to a claim based on 42 U.S.C. §1983, FLSA, ADA or age claims against a state defendant. You must build on the differences. A lawsuit in two forums allows you to segregate the legal strengths of certain state claims from the legal weaknesses of federal ones.

Lawyers can no longer engage in judge shopping, either formal or informal. The new procedure of random assignment of judges has generally replaced the old method of hanging-around-the-courthouse waiting to see which judge was just assigned and standing next in line. Even the appearance of judge shopping has adverse consequences. But, a voluntary stay can provide an option. If you properly analyzed the claims and properly allocated the facts and claims, you decide whether to aggressively pursue the federal action or whether to stay it, and proceed aggressively in state court. You can create a meaningful alternative depending on which judge is drawn. Control is not totally in your hands, but you have considerable influence, if you take the initiative. You can either obtain the consent of counsel or make a motion to stay one action. It is imperative that you do *not* wait for the opponent, who will use the opposite selection criteria.

If you don't know the judge from personal experience, obtain "objective" reports of your peers. Invariably, I run the judge's name through LEXIS or WESTLAW. Some of the judge's opinions provide some flavor of his or her mind-set, but remember that the decisions are on cases that were dealt to the judge by "random chance". In theory, and usually in practice, the judges do not choose the cases before them. When a new judge is appointed, some systems allow the existing judges to transfer 10 percent of their cases to the new judge, thereby allowing a judge to selectively eliminate certain cases.

Below are some criteria to use in selecting a forum. They reflect the differences and similarities.

DIFFERENCES BETWEEN FEDERAL AND STATE COURT

	Federal	State
Jury selection	Judge controls. Very fast (may allow 15 minutes each)	You control 4-8 hrs
Precedent	Excessive, Locked in	Limited, Flexible
Speed for motions	Faster Magistrate's available	Slower, Judge works alone
		Special master
Court's research time	Lots, two law clerks	Some, if one clerk
Quality of opinion	Widely varied, often thorough	Widely varied
Early disclosure of info	Automatic	Discretionary
Disclose financial info	Automatic	Discretionary
Judge appointments	A local selected by national point of view	A local selected by local point of view
Predictability	If strong case, go for it	If strong case, yes
	If weak case, tossed out	If weak case, maybe
	If close call, tossed out	if close call, trial
Limits on depositions	Ten, usually	unknown

SIMILARITIES OF FEDERAL AND STATE COURT		
	Federal	State
Duration	12 months	12 months
Costs depositions	$2-15,000	$2-15,000
Expert depositions	Optional, likely	Optional
Day limit on Pl. Depo	None—5 days, often 2	Often no limit
Disclose medical info.	Rule 35 limited to some	Tradition allows

The folklore that federal judges are a higher caliber than state court judges is as mythical as the notions that many federal judges are ogres. Federal judges have perhaps more prestige and power, but they are not harder working or higher quality. Both groups are appointed from a pool of local lawyers. Federal appointees are scrutinized on a national basis, whereas state court judges are selected without much scrutiny and then only local or statewide. Lifetime appointments do create a hazard, but this situation does not seem improved by election of state court judges. Reportedly, this re-election process keeps state judges slightly closer to the electorate, but the reality is that most voters are more likely to react to their handling of highly publicized criminal cases than to their civil or employment decisions.

Most trial lawyers prefer to stay in state court because of the differences noted earlier and the beliefs that federal judges are quicker to dismiss claims outright or dramatically narrow the issues for trial. Whether this belief is true or not, the evidence appears strong that lawyers are more in control of the trial in state courts.

AVOIDING REMOVAL

When you segregate state and federal claims into two suits, you have maximum ability to avoid removal of common law or state law claims. For the last several years, a lawyer could also avoid removal by accelerating the 30-day clock on removal. If acknowledgment of the summons and complaint (including a *signed* summons and complaint) was mailed to defendant, the notice started the 30-day clock on removal. The employer or its lawyer routinely ignored these acknowledgments, assuming that responding would only save the plaintiff a few pennies. Then, on day 31, we delivered a copy of the exact same summons and complaint to the sheriff. It was too late for removal. Most federal appellate jurisdictions have held that the first delivery by mail was actual notice sufficient to start the clock.

This technique worked in many cases. We were able to have federal claims heard in state court, where we voir dired the jury and had more autonomy. Even under the gun of a statute of limitation, I delivered the summons and complaint to the sheriff on day 20 after service by acknowledgement. Defendants still failed to timely remove it. They were silent, probably hoping I had inadvertently let the clock run. Even when I did formally serve it, they assumed they still had at least 30 days to remove or 20 days to answer. By the time they did try to remove, it was too late. Sadly, the U.S. Supreme Court removed this strategy in 1999. The clock now runs from actual service, not from notice. You may no longer seek a remand under the old case law.

TIP

If you bury the federal claims in the middle of the complaint and don't flag them in the caption, defense counsel is often too busy to notice till it's too late.

INHIBITORS TO SETTLEMENT

By the time you commence suit, certain factors inhibit compromise. Even when you apply the early settlement strategies identified in the previous chapters, there are several reasons why settlement at the time of commencement is unlikely. The major ones are not related to the merits or the facts, but rather derive from peripheral needs. The inhibitors are:

❖ Settlement may undermine the managers who made the decision

❖ Settlement may look like a cave-in

❖ The employer wants to deter similar coattail suits or proclaim, "Millions for defense, not one penny in tribute"

❖ The employer believes that the judge will use summary judgment to cut his or her workload and toss it out

❖ If publicity has occurred, the employer needs to prove it was right

❖ The employer believes that plaintiff's version of reality is still contradicted.

ANTICIPATING SURPRISES

Depending on the type of lawsuit you are serving, you should anticipate that the defense will use certain surprise strategies. For example, in high profile cases the potential for sealing files is a significant consideration. When there are truly ugly allegations in the lawsuit, it is wise to anticipate that the defendants may seek an order to seal the complaint. Defense counsel commonly procures an ex parte order, subject to a hearing within 10 days. In resisting such motions, it is important to anticipate the defense arguments that exposing someone's reputation is damage that cannot readily be undone. This phenomena is given huge weight by some courts, albeit unofficially. All of the nice, aggressive arguments about open courts and public's right to know are offset by this potential for "irreparable" harm to the defendant's reputation.

In resisting sealing, it is better to shift the argument to a different turf. "Our courts didn't seal the file of the priest accused of sexual abuse, nor the doctor accused of battery on patients." You can also contrast it with the practices in malpractice and DWI, where reputations are also at issue, but the cases are not sealed. This defendant is not entitled to special treatment. He or she should receive the same protection that others rely upon—his or her rights in open court, not hidden from the scrutiny of the press."

COMMENCING SUIT

We lawyers are skilled in executing discovery, but we rarely take the time to strategize the content or the delivery of the complaint. If this is the first effort in this case, the prior chapters on drafting and revising will help you make a more powerful complaint. This will carry the case steps ahead into the settlement process to come.

Revise the Complaint

The audience is different now—the judge is now the primary audience of the complaint. Consider a simplified version. Notice pleading may preserve maximum flexibility, but it reduces the impact on the ultimate reader—the judge. The complaint must be fine-tuned using the information acquired during presuit settlement efforts. Invariably, this will improve the persuasive power of the lawsuit. Before proceeding, you should take a fresh look at a revision of the facts and revise the words. New claims that illustrate new contradictions by the employer can awaken a new perception or a corporate sensitivity. Finally, reconsider the pros and cons of "suing" individuals. Often, it raises new issues (immunities), but sometimes it enhances the opportunity to clarify who is the bad guy. Alternatively, the bad guy may become the corporate fall guy.

Analyze who to serve

You are not limited to the CEO or the registered agent. Often, a copy served on a friendly member of the board of directors will ensure the widest distribution of the accusations. Rarely should you accept the offer of defense counsel to accept service. Service on the lawyer dilutes the impact and lets the lawyer summarize the complaint. It further removes the CEO from the reality of a lawsuit. You can explain to your opponent who offers to accept service, "What if the employer changes their mind and hires someone else, I might get burned." Since your self-interest is the most credible of motives, this can create a small anxiety in defense counsel. More importantly, service is another shot at communicating with CEO, through an improved and formal complaint. It also lets you tell the CEO that his lawyer has failed. There are, of course, strategic exceptions to this tactic; e.g., your rapport with a trustworthy, opposing counsel. It's permissible if you trust the individual counsel, but even then you should request a signed authorization from the client to accept service.

The alternative may be a belated discovery that the client has fired them. If the statute of limitation has expired, this could mean a malpractice suit for you. Consider service by acknowledgment through the mail. Until 1999, if defendant failed to respond, it was great—the 30-day clock on removal had begun. Most circuits relied on notice (of a signed complaint) to compute the start of 30 days, but a recent Supreme Court decision has changed the rules. The clock now starts at actual service, not notice. (See strategies in next section for avoiding removal under the new rules.)

MAINTAINING MOMENTUM

Once they have serve the summons and complaint, many plaintiff lawyers choose to do nothing. They just wait. It is more powerful to maintaining momentum by following up with any witnesses you missed at the settlement effort stage. Identify a list of friendly co-workers who may independently corroborate your facts and contact them. When the employer's lawyer gets around to contacting witnesses, he or she finds that you have already been there. They are not accustomed to plaintiff's lawyers getting the jump on them and he or she will be unsettled by your thoroughness.

You have a golden opportunity to lock in the testimony that might have been "flexible", or even manipulated by defense counsel. It is wise to warn the witnesses who give you affidavits and statements. If they are still employees, you should have contingency plans on how to protect them. Some lawyers use a 'buddy' arrangement where a friendly co-worker forewarns the others of the commencement of the lawsuit. Separately, you should also anticipate a conflict if witness calls about retaliation—a lawyer list for referring the friendly witnesses.

Some defense counsel may berate you, asserting it's a violation of an ethics rule to communicate with agents of an adverse party. As long as you avoid current management witnesses, who can bind the company, you should be safe, but check your local rules. Historically, former employees have been fair game, even former managers. Current employees who are not management are almost always fair game, but check recent local ethics rulings. If the employer sends a memo directing employees not to talk to you or to notify the employer before talking to you, you should immediately seek an order to stop the intimidation. There is a strong argument to assert implied retaliation for such employer's misconduct. Alternatively, if the case involves discrimination you can ask EEOC to exercise its power to stop intimidation and retaliation.

If your case involves public employees, consider government data practice laws that allow special inquiries for public data on employees. These are usually independent of the lawsuit. If the request goes to a different person who is not familiar with your lawsuit, you often get different answers.

To maximize settlement opportunities, you should plan strategies to keep the pressure on. Your continued effort shows that you are factually aggressive and ready to engage in aggressive discovery.

Chapter Seventeen

LEVERAGING DISCOVERY INTO SETTLEMENT

D iscovery can generate real power, but only if you avoid standardized forms and carefully tailor the discovery toward specific narrow goals. Laziness or old habits often result in exhaustive discovery. This need not be. Defense lawyer may enjoy the luxury of costly efforts because he or she is getting paid. You don't have the same luxury. If you crank out form interrogatories, the time savings is easily negated by the worthless results. On the other hand, if the needs of your proof are carefully thought out, you can hone in on what evidence is really needed. The other stuff may be useful, but it is not necessary.

> Organize discovery explicitly around the elements of each cause of action.

The elements determine which facts are material facts. That is usually all you need to know. The rest is color and background. Discovery can build leverage toward winning, but it also enhances settlement efforts. Skillfully written discovery and thoughtful depositions can accelerate earlier settlements of issues that otherwise lie dormant until near trial.

To make the most of your power to leverage discovery into profitable settlement, you need to:

* ❖ Prioritize your discovery strategies
* ❖ Interrogate live witnesses
* ❖ Protect your client
* ❖ Resist Summary judgment
* ❖ Keep your perspective.

PRIORITIZE YOUR DISCOVERY

GIVE EXTENSIONS TO GAIN TACTICAL ADVANTAGES

At the outset, short extensions should be given freely—not because you are a nice person, but for tactical advantages. Defendants have the 30-day free window to take discovery under Rule 30. Plaintiffs are denied this luxury. By granting an extension, I have frequently been able to get the jump on defendant in discovery. Often I receive a call 19 days after service of the summons. The defense lawyer is requesting an extension to answer. I readily accommodate them and agree to two to three week extensions. Within a few days, I send a deposition notice, a request for documents, and occasionally a few interrogatories. The primary goal is to rob them of the advantage of taking plaintiff's deposition first.

The custom of first-to-notice-a-deposition has priority is well established in most communities. Even if not legally binding, it is usually a major benefit. Generally, I target either the bad buy or a key decision-maker for this early deposition. There is a trade-off between documents I don't have and the benefits of first strike in deposition. Even if I do not have all the documents, I gamble—I already have many from the plaintiff, the settlement exchanges, EEOC or my own investigation. When the witness admits that his or her memory could be improved by the missing documents, you may have a justification for not completing the deposition. But, you will not be able to recall the witness without careful planning or unless supplemental facts surface. The success of this tactic can be a powerful motivator toward settlement because defendant lost the advantage of hearing the plaintiff's details first, but be clear about trade-offs.

GETTING THE JUMP ON DEFENDANTS

In federal court, you usually have to wait to *serve* your discovery, but you don't have to wait to get it ready. In anticipation of the Rule 26 conference, you can prepare a request for documents, a deposition notice, and a few interrogatories. If you have them ready to go before the Rule 26 conference with the magistrate, you can schedule the document delivery on automatic fax; e.g., set it for one hour after the Rule 26 conference begins. When the opponent returns from the conference, your paper discovery is waiting for them. Defendants are rarely able to juggle their schedule to get their own discovery ready on the same day. They have been upstaged. You have gained a tactical advantage. Your foresight and execution also improves subsequent settlement posturing. Defendants frequently ask for an extension on the deposition date. You can agree if they produce the paper discovery by the rescheduled date or if it is past 30 days, they are obligated to delivery before the deposition begins. You have acquired priority.

CAUTION

Some defense lawyers will try to accelerate the date of plaintiff's deposition before your scheduled date. Join in the game, pick an earlier date for someone else's deposition. Then prepare to negotiate.

USE DEPOSITIONS FOR SURPRISE FACTOR

The power of surprise is most valuable in your first deposition. It will diminish in later depositions because they will read the first ones or receive summaries. Interrogatories rarely elicit any surprise information because defense counsel usually dictate responses to paper discovery. Depositions have a greater impact on both winning and settlement.

LIMIT EARLY INTERROGATORIES TO HARD DATA

Thoughtful interrogatories are good for hard data; e.g., dates, numbers, names and places, but seldom for soft data or inferences. There is no logical reason to give defense counsel the opportunity to think through your issues or create a bogus answer. Defense lawyers will be able to use your request for soft data or inferences to plan their defenses. They will educate the managers about the company line. This makes rehearsals easier for the defense. If you have a primary theory of the case, you may want to consider a few interrogatories that are a diversion.

If you have to negotiate discovery limits, always seek the maximum number allowed—usually 50. They have the information that you need. Early interrogatories can elicit useful basic information, but don't use more than half of your quota. There must be a balance between those questions that weaken their defenses, those that bolster plaintiff's claims, and those that elicit the employer information that impeaches or values plaintiff's damages. You seldom understand their defenses at the outset, so you should save at least half to clean up and to fill in the gaps. Later interrogatories should be tightly crafted to fill in the gaps narrowed by depositions. You should consider some catch-all interrogatories; e.g., "If you can deny any of the requests for admission, provide all specific facts and detail which justify your denial." Be sure to put them near the end where the maximum number won't wipe out other important questions.

PLAN SOME DISCOVERY FOR THE EYES OF THE JURY

Many lawyers fail to consider the jury when writing interrogatories or requests for admission. If the words of laymen are used in a simple straightforward question or admission, these tools make strong visual exhibits. A few interrogatories or requests for admission tailored for the jury can expose the nasty lawyers who use multiple and bogus objections. It can illustrate the stupidity or viciousness of a defendant's approach.

INTERROGATE LIVE WITNESSES

PRIORITIZE THE SEQUENCE OF DEPOSITIONS

No lawyer goes to trial without a witness list. Similarly, deposition analysis should begin with a list of prospective witnesses for depositions. Your fact development will be more comprehensive and with less redundancy. Most important, it allows you to make decisions based on priorities.

After brainstorming a master list of witnesses, go through each element of each cause of action. Then identify which people can help prove each element of each claim. *Organize all discovery around the elements.* Prioritize the final list by which witness can provide what is needed.

Traditional habits allow defendants to hear the plaintiff's version before defendants are committed under oath. This allows the defendant to modify his story. When they know the plaintiff's version, witnesses often adjust their story to offset the details elaborated by the plaintiff. Defendants can then weave a story that sounds plausible, fitting their facts with the framework of the plaintiff's story. This allows them to reduce the number of disputed facts, both material and immaterial. While some of these facts may involve credibility issues, most do not. They are peripheral facts. They add context and affect confidence levels, but they rarely impact summary judgment. When you rob the defense of the priority window, you are in control. Defendants have difficulty adjusting their story when plaintiff's details are unknown. If you have locked in the defendant's version before they hear your plaintiff's nitty gritty details, this alone provides a powerful incentive toward settlement.

If the defense schedules your client's deposition first, you'll need to shift strategies. Thoroughly prepare your own client (See Introduction). When you take defendents' depositions, assume that managers and co-workers will have read portions of plaintiff's deposition and that top management will have reviewed a summary of key points offered by counsel. Use this likelihood to your advantage with these witnesses. For example, consider the old mental exercise, "Try not to think of an elephant." The very act of trying not to see it causes you to see the elephant. The defense witnesses will probably be preoccupied with what their lawyer told them not to say. Verbally dance up to what they are not supposed to say, but digress. Their frustration will eventually cause them to blurt something out sideways. Then you attack.

CAUTION

The same phenomena may work against your client. A workable solution is to provide an alternative for your client's focus .

It is dangerous to cram last minute advice to client. It confuses and becomes the elephant dominating their point of view.

Keep in mind that most subordinates will read and study what the boss said, but most superiors will *not* take the time to read what their subordinate said. They will rely on summaries by their or the employee's counsel. The condensed version will rarely encompass the linchpin or key facts.

HUMAN FACTOR IN DEPOSITIONS

Discovery builds leverage toward settlement (and winning) partly by eliciting evidence, but also by how you are perceived by the employer and managers. Your willingness to improvise can also make your opponents worry that the jury will like this particular plaintiff's lawyer. You seem so relaxed and confident, not cocky or arrogant, but calm and in control.

USE A SCRIPT TO PLAN, BUT BE EXTEMPORANEOUS DURING QUESTIONS

You cannot set traps unless you have identified, in writing, your goals for each witness. Using the elements as anchors, identify what you need to get from this witness and the best possible facts you could get from each witness. It is most beneficial to word your goals as clear-cut affirmative statements, e.g. he will admit notice of plaintiff's complaint. Then plan how you *might* be able to elicit those best possible facts. Chronology is an option, but it is easily anticipated. Consider a topical question or approach at the scene by moving backwards in time or from an odd perspective.

Scripting is crucial when you are planning questions, but not when you are asking them. If you follow written questions, you often forget to listen. If you are well prepared, notes are unnecessary—at least for the first 30-45 minutes of deposition. After a few basic questions, the witness' answer can be used to develop the next question. If you seem to jump around in the next question, the witness will be farther removed from his or her expectations. This can only be done if you know where you want to go, and you have previously saturated yourself in the documents and by thinking backwards.

Rather than follow a written script, you skillfully improvise. You dance around core issues, but stop short of getting to the matters the witness wants to address. The tension builds along with the witness' eagerness. When he or she finally gets to say things that were buried, the relaxed tension often causes him or her to blurt out other information. It opens avenues that you can attack from the back door.

If the witness' tension level is obviously taut at the outset, you naturally suspect that he or she feels guilt about something. But the witness has been prepared to talk about it in only one way. Your informal, free-form questions can elicit clues about what the witness really wants to say. Then you can adapt.

RECENCY IN MEMORY

The phenomenum of recency often explains why listeners provide odd responses to ambiguous statements. They assumed the questioner was referring to the most recent topic mentioned. Moreover, deponents are eager to say the things that they have memorized and that are nearest in time to this occasion. The defense lawyer has often warned them about what "not to say", and witnesses are afraid of blurting that out. They are worried about saying the wrong thing. Many witnesses are eager to get "it" out while it's still fresh in their mind. They are usually prepared for an orderly sequence of questions and they expect a certain formality. Informality at the onset relaxes them a little. When it succeeds, it will diminish the tension that is holding the "right words" together and throw them off balance.

MANEUVERING WITH DEPONENTS

Usually, you score big points when the deponent opens up and blabs. It's easier to ferret information from a Chatty Charles than a Tight-lipped Tammy. Thus, one strategy is to start out friendly, even amiable. This is especially effective if their lawyer is a jerk. The deponent expects you to fight back, be nasty and dirty like they are. If you don't stoop to their game, it throws them off stride. Unpredictability can be your friend.

It is usually beneficial to elicit their best memories on record first, and save the documents until the second half. Their memories are less trainable than their eyes. They will more readily recall rehearsed meanings from documents.

Use Fuzzy Logic to Prepare for Live Interrogations

When preparing for depositions, apply the rules of fuzzy logic, the rule of probabilities and the process of thinking backwards. See Chapter 12 for elaborations of these techniques. Fuzzy logic is useful in dealing with a rule that looks objective; e.g., assume that your client was terminated for absenteeism based on a rule that five unexcused absences within 60 days results in automatic firing. Ask the following questions in preparation and in deposition:

1) Who applied the rule? Supervisor, manager, human resources?
2) Was the rule always applied?
3) If there were exceptions:
   a) Who decided the exceptions?
   b) What criteria were used?
   c) Who received the exception?
   d) What do those who received by the exception share in common?
4) Who decided which absences were excused vs. unexcused?
   a) Who benefited by the decision?
   b) What criteria were used?
   c) What do those who benefited by the decision share in common?
   d) Whose responsibility was it to gather the facts to determine if the criteria were met?
   e) Whose responsibility was it to provide the facts to determine if the criteria were met?
   f) Was notice clearly given to all employees on what facts were necessary to meet criteria for being excused?
   g) Was "Five minutes late" considered the equivalent of one day missed?
   h) Who decided "g"?
   Return to 4 b) through 4 f).

This approach should be used initially with your client to prepare the complaint and identify defendant's weak points. Frequently, it is most powerful in the deposition questions. Once the weak link is found, the sequence can be reconstructed going backward and forwards up the chain of decision-making.

This illustrates the benefits of focusing on the selection of dispositive facts and tracing their origin.

LYING WITNESSES

There is no polygraph more reliable than your own internal crap detector. Gerry Spence, in *How to Argue and Win Every Time*, points out that humans, especially jurors, have "psychic tentacles which wrap themselves around the speaker, palpate him measure him, test him…for that which is out of sync." Spence is not referring to psychic in the mystical sense, but to the mechanism by which we recognize the *ring of truth*. We hear it in the sounds and the silences, we see it in the hands and bodies and smiles—the physical words— and we often feel it through the eyes. In Chapter 14, we identified numerous examples of nonverbal communication in negotiation that indicate deception. These have equal application in deposition. When you recognize that a deponent is lying, do not assume that now is the best time to expose him or her. Often it is better to simply lock them in and move on. Save the exposure of the lie for the most impact. If you anticipated the lie and set traps to elicit it, take joy in it, but stop.

If the lie comes unexpectedly, move on until you can take a recess and evaluate how to circle back around the lie and close off all the avenues of escape. I have found it invaluable to remember the four horsemen that underlie the hearsay rule: perception, memory, narrative and sincerity. To truly expose insincerity, you must seal off the other sources of error. Attack each systematically.

PROTECTING YOUR CLIENT

It is absolutely crucial that you prepare your client for deposition. I usually have eight to ten hours solely devoted to client preparation in three sessions of about three hours each. *You need to teach your client a new way of thinking.* You need to help your client recognize that depositions are artificial re-creations of reality: The truth is repackaged in black and white ink stains. After the deposition, the truth is fixed about the topics questioned. The ability to expand is limited to questions that were not asked.

Usually, I play the role of the opposing counsel and ask nitty gritty questions— the ones we as lawyers dread being asked of your client. I help clients learn to think through the various possible responses. Sometimes, you need to maintain client morale and it works better to have a lawyer friend do the practice cross-examination.

During witness preparation, your client may ask you what he or she should say about a specific issue. Your response should be immediate, "Tell the truth, ... but remember there are many different ways of saying it."

> The truth is the truth, but it can be packaged many different ways:
>
> Some ways help your case, others destroy it.

Words are the only packages that count in depositions. You must discuss how the questions are going to come at them. One practical explanation I use is "You have lived through the reality, but depositions are not reality. There are at best little pieces, chopped up pieces. The reality of a deposition is the words on paper—black and white. If you don't answer the question, your reality doesn't exist." Because of summary judgment, it is often necessary to depart from traditional advice of answering only what was asked. Instead, identify and explicitly focus on the three or four important areas for expansion.

EXPLAIN REAL PURPOSES AND USE OF DEPOSITION

Clients are more ready to cope with depositions when they understand how depositions are used. Your client must understand how the defense hopes to use his or her deposition:

1. To learn what he or she knows and doesn't know (what he or she felt or not felt, seen or not seen, heard or not heard)
2. To put a box around his or her story so it won't change much at trial
3. To set up the posture for throwing the case out of court
4. To show contradictions at trial.

Client's must understand that former concept of genuine discovery has been largely replaced by a primary purpose to get the case thrown out of court without a trial. Remind them that the employer will ask the judge to make a judgment based on written summaries of their testimony and that they often succeed. Clients need to know that their own words will be used to show that they do not have the right kind of facts or not enough facts. They must realize that their depositions will be used to show obvious inconsistencies, nonsensical beliefs or ultimately to contradict their live statements in front of the jury.

It is essential that clients learn that a new vocabulary applies in lawsuits. This new vocabulary is almost a foreign language. No one in ordinary conversation asks if you know something from your "personal knowledge". If you've already explained that this phrase means "Did you see it?" or "Did you hear it?" or "Did you feel the grab?", your client is less confused by lawyer jargon. For us, this shorthand is second nature: for clients it's a foreign language.

TIP

Defense counsel often ask intentionally ambiguous questions. You can suggest that your client ask the lawyer to explain the word or phrase. With professional lawyers this works to obtain a clearer question. A clever opponent will, however, toss it back in your client's lap and ask for the witness' meaning and then wield it against the witness. If the client is well prepared, he or she will have a workable definition and it will be easier to control the flow of information.

Always prepare your client for the question, "What are your damages?" If the witness is not prepared, he or she will often give a baffled look and feel stupid. The word "damages" is second nature to lawyers, but it is a foreign term to first time clients.

You must also help the client separate cause from effect—if they don't understand the difference, their testimony often emerges as gibberish Clients often talk in conclusory language, but the conclusions are as often invalid as valid. It is critical to help them think through the clues that led them to their conclusions. This approach will enable the client to describe the underlying facts, and the observations that shaped his or her thinking. Clients often just "feel" the motives or causes that resulted in termination. You must help them go underneath these feelings to discern the statements or behaviors that triggered these feelings and beliefs.

Clients must rediscover the "obvious". If they saw something with their own eyes, they often take for granted that others know about it. If they read a document, they often assume you also know the meaning of what is in the document. It is essential that their memory be dredged for details and meanings. Similarly, what they heard a manager say is often buried deep in the recesses of their memory. Until triggered by your in-depth practice cross examination, it will not surface. Later, clients often say, "I didn't know it was important"—but often this is a covert way of saying "You're the stupid one, you didn't ask me about it."

You should not tell any witness what to say. You need only help your client learn how to think about the questions. No client is too stupid to learn. Some are stubborn; others are egocentric and trapped in one view of the world. Both need to be subjected to an incisive cross-examination. This will help them appreciate how foolish their myopia comes across. The probing questions and blunt feedback will clarify what they are taking for granted. It is true that we can never truly know their reality, but we can approach knowing it.

Let your client know that if the defense lawyer is obnoxious or offensive, you will object. It if continues, you will walk out. We won't take abuse. If necessary, you can videotape the interrogation or ask the judge to appoint a neutral to watch over the deposition. At the same time, you should point out that this rarely occurs—most depositions are not Hollywood style.

Your client needs to understand that your objections serve two purposes: a) for the future, to enable a judge to decide if the question was proper; and b) for the present, to point out defects in the question and afford the questioner an opportunity to cure defects. Objections also have an incidental benefit in alerting the witness to be sure he or she understands the question. You should explain that it is not proper for you to give speaking objections or put words in the witness' mouth. You are simply alerting everyone to the potential defects.

Your client must be forewarned that your objection will not usually prevent him or her from answering the question. If s/he understands the question and if you do not instruct them not to answer, s/he will be expected to answer the question. Tell your client it will be very rare that you instruct him or her not to answer. If you are silent, your client should think about the defect, then answer.

TIP

With obnoxious opponents, you can alter your words on privilege instruction. While looking at your client, say "Objection, and I instruct you not to ask it." Your opponent will assume you said "not to answer it." If they seek sanctions for instructing the witness not to answer, he or she will be embarrassed by the transcript. You should discreetly remind the court reporter of what you actually said or they too may assume the normal instruction.

Clients must know that feelings count, but more importantly, they need to know **when** feelings count. For example, if questions are asked about his or her emotional distress, your client needs to elaborate to give substantial details and use feeling-facts. It is a fundamental error to fail to explain the difference and the similarities between embarrassment and humiliation as well as the contrast between emotional distress and humiliation.

By the night before the deposition, you and your client should have reduced the complexity of hundreds of facts to the four or five issues that really matter. The client then feels more assured that the other stuff will not destroy his or her case, but mistakes on these four or five could. Your client must understand when replies must be thorough (e.g, when to drive a truck through the open door) vs. when to be tight-lipped.

USE OPPONENT'S INTERROGATORIES TO YOUR ADVANTAGE

Many lawyers dread answering interrogatories. There is an alternate view: Use them to help you think through your case and develop detailed answers especially on damages and liability facts. The thoroughness prepares both you and your client for the deposition. They are even more valuable when you place them on the deposition table for the client to consult, where appropriate.

USE ADMISSIONS LIKE LASERS

Admission can be a powerful tool to lock in specific facts. They can confirm simple direct actions or statements. They can be very powerful to build the evidentiary basis for some legal conclusions, like scope of duty. If you break complex facts into tiny steps, you restrict the defendant's freedom to evade. They cannot be conclusory. To avoid giving fudge room, these must be very, very specific and should be behavior-oriented. For example,

- ❖ ADMIT: "Defendant did not issue any written discipline to plaintiff from 1985 until 1997."
- ❖ ADMIT: During 1992-1995, Defendant did not provide any written communication to either TK or GM of its plan to ultimately eliminate the lab technician position.
- ❖ ADMIT: When Defendant promoted Bill S, age 32, out of the lab technician position on 3-16-93, Defendant was aware of its plan to ultimately eliminate the lab technician positions.
- ❖ ADMIT: From 1991 to 1996, X promoted salaried individuals, but did not promote anyone over age 45.

Remember that interrogatories may be limited in number, but that the number of admissions is **not** limited.

EXAMS BY ADVERSE PSYCHIATRISTS

There is no longer any reason to presume that plaintiff must submit to a Rule 35 production of medical records or medical exams. Do not refer to them as independent medical exams; they are adversarial and should be called adverse medical exams. NELA lawyers, especially Steven Platt, have done an incredible job of reshaping the law to eliminate the automatic entitlement to an AME. See 1997 issues of NELA's Employee Advocate where Platt demonstrates his methods and his success.

If there is a severe condition or a diagnosed condition such as depression or PTSD, a Rule 35 production of medical records and AME is likely, but in ordinary cases, it is *not*. When defendant demands an AME in *an ordinary case*, a letter will usually suffice. The following is one sample clarification:

Dear opponent,

…Under existing law, AMEs are available only under certain situations.

1. a claim for intentional or negligent infliction of emotional distress

2. an allegation of a specific mental or psychiatric injury or disorder

3. a claim of unusually severe emotional distress

4. the plaintiff's offer of expert testimony on emotional distress

5. the plaintiff's concession that her mental condition is "in controversy" within the meaning of Rule 35.

O'Sullivan v. State of Minnesota, et al. 1997 U.S. Dist. LEXIS 18943 (D. Minn. 1997). It should be clear that plantiff does NOT come within the above situations and no AME is authorized. Thus, plaintiff's mental condition in this case is NOT "in controversy".

The answers to allegations in the damage interrogatories address the facts and corroboration of his/her emotional distress. We are *not* seeking to recover for the physical injuries. We will limit our emotional distress claim to the ordinary emotional distress experienced by anyone in these circumstances.

At the same time, if your client has a strong basis for a severe condition or a diagnosed condition (depression or PTSD), it is unwise to resist the AMEs. Instead, obtain advance information on the tests selected and the proposed purpose. Discuss them with your expert who can also give your client some familiarity by walking him or her through a portion of the test. Even if the defendant's expert debates causation, the AME may actually help establish the extent of harm. It is better to challenge the structure of the exam, the selection of tests and the interview process.

TIP
Some states have medical boards with rules that declare the "victim" of an AME to be a patient of the examining doctor. Thus, you are entitled to **all** their notes and records and the materials relied upon. Request them directly from the adverse expert once the report is done. You often find lawyer correspondence that patently biased the evaluation by premature focus.

Taping or witness present during AME
If the adverse doctor has a history of acting less of a professional and more of a hired gun or is known for aggressive manipulation of plaintiffs, insist on boundaries. Seek an order for tape recording or a court reporter to take down the questions and answers. NELA members JoAnne Jirik-Mullin and Jeff Anderson recently squashed the testimony of an expert who refused to honor the taping requirement and did not interview the plaintiff. The expert's opinion was excluded because of a lack of foundation.

RESISTING SUMMARY JUDGMENT
Plaintiff's lawyers are too often intimidated by summary judgment. This is naïve and unduly cynical. Yes, it's a lot of work (50 hours of writing on average), but it creates another opportunity to make the employer thirsty for settlement. A well-written brief often educates my opponents and motivates serious settlement talks – sometimes shortly after it is served and more often, immediately after oral argument. If you voluntarily drop claims where the evidence is undernourished, you gain in credibility with the judge and sometimes your opponent. You should make this decision before your opponent prepares his or her brief. It shows your confidence in the claims that remain.

Your primary audience is the judge

Try to discern this judge's needs, fundamental values, mode of analysis and philosophy. Remember to invest some time thinking about this conflict from this judge's point of view. What does the judge need to know from both you and the defense to make an intelligent decision? How is it best presented in light of this judge's values?

Write out 4 or 5 genuine issues of material fact

Take the time to actually write out four or five genuine issues of material fact. Make it easy for the judge. Lead off with a list of the genuine issues that require a trial. It's silly to brazenly assert "There are genuine issues". Instead, **show** them what they are. It is stupid to simply restate the ultimate conclusions. Instead, focus on the elements in dispute and word the questions in a way that favors your viewpoint, but make it look objective; e.g.:

❖ Whether plaintiff's impairment substantially restricted his major life activities of concentrating, reading, writing and learning sufficient to receive protection under ADA?

❖ Whether purported reasons were a pretext in light of heightened scrutiny imposed only on plaintiff, imposed only after his complaint and where explicit reference to his requests for accomodation are among the stated reasons for termination?

❖ Whether plaintiff's requests for accommodation were reasonable and if the repeated denials constituted **discrimination**, for failure to provide reasonable accommodation?

Weave the standards into the body of your brief

Another powerful method is to weave the standards into the body of your brief, instead of merely setting them out in an early section. For example, I organize the brief around the elements and state the plaintiff's facts only on a specific disputed element. Then I note that "Defendant denies this fact..." or "Defendant contradicts plaintiff's fact..." At this point in the brief when you demonstrated the contrast, remind the judge that "On summary judgment, the court must assume that plaintiff's description is true." This structure and reminder is repeated on *each* disputed element of the claim.

When you are arguing an inference, that is the time to remind the judge that plaintiff is entitled to all reasonable inferences. Echo this reminder throughout.

Use judo tactics

In your brief and at oral argument, admit that the purpose is to get rid of frivolous cases, acknowledge that if there are no legally important facts in conflict,
the claims should be thrown out. Then you proceed to illustrate why the con-
flicts in *this* case are material, the dispute is genuine and live testimony is
required to resolve the conflict. Remind the Court that under *Celotex*, credibility and weighing evidence are a question for a jury. To subtly remind the judge
of your willingness to appeal, cite an appellate case where she or he was
reversed for weighing the evidence on summary judgment.

KEEP YOUR PERSPECTIVE—KNOW WHAT YOU NEED TO PROVE

You must continuously evaluate how the evidence is tipping of the scales—
adding weight to one side or the other. It is supposed to be *easy* to establish a
prima facie case.[46] Sometimes, it feels like an enormous burden, but actually it is
a light burden. If there is trouble, refocus your claims or consider compromise.

We all know that defendant's burden is very light—indeed, it feels nonexistent.
Some courts have even allowed defendants to put forth reasons that are created
after the fact. But courts are savvy and recognize that "Rarely will an employer
fail to offer a legitimate business reason for its actions."[47]

FOCUS ON PRETEXT

The core issue is almost always a variation of pretext, whether discrimination or
common law claims. The scales must be balanced to see the dilemma. The real
weighty factors are the defendant's version of causes weighed against the plaintiff's version of pretext.[48] A change in reasons is itself sufficient to show pretext.
The change of reasons in and of itself satisfies the pretext requirement.[49] As the
Eighth Circuit has stated, "Because [the employer's] 'nondiscriminatory reasons'
for not hiring [employee] were various and always changing, [the employer's]
motive becomes suspect."[50] At the same time, the underlying factual principle is
that plaintiff, in effect, has to prove that the cause of the decision was sex, race,
disability... Motive is simply another word for what caused the decision or
what more likely than not motivated the decision.

---

[46] *Dietrich v. Canadian Pacific Ltd.*, 536 N.W.2d 319, 322-23 (Minn. 1995).

[47] *Anderson v. Hunter, Keith*, 417 N.W.2d, 619 (Minn. 1988).

[48] The proposed new Restatement makes the norm, not the exception, for Jury instruction Guides.

[49] *Maschka v. Genuine Auto Parts*, 122 F. 3d 566 (8th Cir. 1997); *Newhouse v. McCormick Co, Inc.*,
110 F 3d 635, 640 (8th Cir. 1997).

[50] Id.

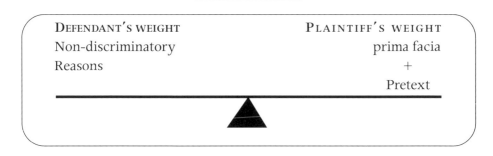

The more weighty the combination of prima facie evidence and evidence of pretext, the easier it is to outweigh the defendants' version of what caused the termination. Ultimately, the issue for the jury is which makes more sense: The defendant's explanation or your explanation? Do the defendant's explanation of other causes fit the facts better than your claim of pretext? On summary judgment, you merely need to show that the evidence presents a genuine conflict.

HIGHLIGHT THAT "INTENTIONAL" MEANS "NOT ACCIDENTAL"

Courts often say that we have to prove that "discrimination was intentional". This reference to "intent" does not mean the bad guy intended to cause the injury; it only means he intended to take the action, to do the act of termination. It is helpful to contrast intent with accidental or coincidental. Think of intent as the opposite of a true accident. In a true accident, no one would be at fault. The word "accident" in most vocabularies is misleading – e.g., we refer to car "accidents", but someone is usually deemed at fault. It has impact to say "This termination was not accidental." In discrimination, it is general intent, not specific intent that is at issue. Specific intent refers to the criminal concept of intent to cause the injury. This is not required for discrimination cases nor common law claims like tortious interference with contract. The spectrum of intent is important:

Truly Accidental → *Decision was Intended* → *Effect was Intended* → *Willful Injury*

Judgments based on written summaries are inherently offensive to our society's commitment to jury trials. At the same time, the frequency of summary judgment is unlikely to change, given the institutional benefits and the low priority of funds to handle the number of disputes created by the changing needs of society. Summary judgment will remain commonplace. The rampant losses of summary judgment are not automatic. If you are selective in pursuing full litigation, zealously research the changing law and write your briefs from the audience perspective, you can substantially improve the prospects of surviving summary judgment. I know lawyers, including myself, who survive summary judgment over eighty percent of the time.

Summary judgment can be viewed an opportunity to give a final wake-up call to the employer before trial. Only the lawyer will study the whole brief, but often the opponent will read the fact portions. Even though the motion's criteria is centered around legal issues, your summary of the key facts can enhance their appreciation of your story. How you connect the facts and inferences to prove your case is often their first awakening following discovery. If you are focused and lucid, it will magnify their yearning for settlement.

Chapter Eighteen

MID-STREAM COMPROMISES

Settlement opportunities often become more focused as discovery-generated evidence clarifies the relative strengths of each side. Simultaneously, the strength of one side usually mirrors the weaknesses of the other. Both perspectives provide incentives to compromise.

Almost everyone is willing to settle: The question is for how much?

For the plaintiff, carving holes in the armor of the defense is helpful, but **not** sufficient. Similar to trial, you should expect to affirmatively demonstrate your facts in settlement negotiations. You must create a clear image of strong facts, on liability and damages. As with the jury, the expectation of the employer audience is most demanding on issues where you have the perceived burden – you must justify altering the status quo or the inertia. Thus, during discovery your position must either get stronger or hold its ground. If the evidence does not bolster your theory of the case, you must reduce your expectations.

TIMING TO INITIATE NEGOTIATIONS

Mid-stream settlements can be initiated any time after suit commences, but certain moments are the most promising:

- ❖ After depositions of plaintiff and key decision-makers
- ❖ After all depositions have been taken, but shortly before summary judgment briefs are due
- ❖ When summary judgment is denied, partially or totally.

As with most other strategies, the first principle is necessarily focused on "Who is your primary audience—the employer or the defense lawyer?" Once you have answered that question as the defense counsel, you must still identify what kind of individual you are addressing." If the opponent is a pro, it's usually simple to initiate negotiations. Just remind him or her, "We've now taken the major depositions. Are you in a position to make a first round evaluation? Are we ready to talk?"

With others, you can use the end of key depositions as the occasion to posit that the dispute is essentially one person's word against another. When defense lawyers acknowledge your insight, you can bluntly point out, "Credibility is a jury question"[51] Since most of us think in terms of winning or losing, these reminders will bring the opponent back to the reality that summary judgment does not require you to win—only to create material fact questions. Persistent reminders will begin to wear them down because they don't want to lose at summary judgment.

If the opponent is arrogant, greedy or just stupid, it's appropriate to ask the judge's law clerk if the judge will schedule a settlement conference. Another option is to pause at recess in the deposition and ask the CEO or top management, in the presence of counsel, "Would you like to explore settlement now or wait until both sides have spent more money?" The defense lawyer usually becomes righteously indignant, but the CEO often looks puzzled. It's amazing how many executives assume suits can't be settled. For example, in response to the above question, I had one CEO state that he didn't know these disputes could be settled. He then fired his lawyer and we reached a compromise right on the spot. Predictably, I was subjected to an ethics complaint, but I won. Be sure to make such statements openly and only when opposing counsel is present. It's ok to embarrass a jerk, but don't completely unmask him or her in public—you will make an enemy forever.

Some defense lawyers engage in friendly banter that plaintiffs need an amount that divides easily by three. I laugh, and reciprocate, asking if he or she has billed enough time to justify talking compromise, but I only do so in private.

Before engaging in compromise overtures, you must ensure that you have invested a minimum amount of effort. You cannot be confident of the strengths of the case nor its value unless discovery diminished their defenses or has produced solid evidence favorable to your case. Initially, the focus must be on the exchange of evidence. You should assess if both sides have traded key documents and taken key depositions. In the early stages, we usually know the case better than the defense lawyers. We have a bigger stake in early compromise, so we are the ones who must piece it together. Defense lawyers will not begin to thoroughly educate their client until you have supplied the necessary ammunition. This does not imply that they are willing to educate their client, only that they are able.

---

[51] or "These contradictions are material fact questions," or "Who you believe sounds like a jury question."

We must discern the patterns hiding in the evidence. We must marshal the documents to support our position. Ultimately, most audience-focused persuasion is in your hands. If you have generated enough evidence to objectively respond to key defense arguments with "It is a fact question," you have set the stage. This cannot be done, however, unless you possess key documents and grasp their power.

ALLOW YOUR HUNCHES AND INTUITION TO INFLUENCE TIMING

Often timing is interwoven with either a hunch or intuition. Hunches and intuition sharpen your sense of timing—about whether to pause, move ahead, delay or act aggressively. You must learn to listen to these special sources of insight. Successful trial lawyers throughout the years have noted the power of following both hunches and intuition. At the same time, these sources should not displace rational logic or thoughtful analysis. They are companions.

Neither intuition nor hunches should be confused with what you want to happen or with guesses rooted in your rational thought. These sources have a different origin and method of communication. Hunches are thoughts that arise when you are working something else—a faint, ephemeral glimmer snapping into your awareness, seemingly out of nowhere. At first, it is usually only a nonverbal sense of something. It can evaporate rapidly. It is often vague at the onset, but you invite it to take shape by letting it enter your awareness. Sometimes, the faint message is a sense that now is the time to make a demand and other times the opposite, to wait.

Intuition, on the other hand, emerges while you are saturated in the problem at hand. Intuition is a gnawing sensation that permeates your being. Either in your gut or deep inside you, a still small voice makes you pause. It is fuzzy and vague, but disturbing. Usually, neither the image nor the message is clear. All you have is a vague sense of foreboding. Patience is required to let this "vague sense" percolate upward toward clarity. If you try to force it or speed it up, the sense will evaporate. If you ignore it, it may evaporate. Gently attend to it and let it come. For example, I have delayed making a demand because something vague didn't feel right. I could not identify any specific reasons but I felt an urgent need not to act at that moment. Later I learned that a key decision-maker had left the company. Later, I made a higher demand and it settled. On another occasion, the unknown event turned out to be an acquisition of defendant by an outside company. The new bosses had no loyalty to the decisions of prior management and eagerly negotiated an end to old litigation.

It can work both ways. In mid 1980s, I was defending a case mentioned earlier. Following a sizeable defense offer, the plaintiff almost doubled their demand. The insurer insisted on withdrawing the prior offer. While admitting that I didn't know why I thought it could still settle, I pushed for authority to offer 10 percent more in a structured settlement. I was faintly aware of marital tensions and instinctively felt that a short delay could make a divorce more imminent and financial needs more paramount. The offer was addressed to the plaintiff's long-term security, outside of the husband's hands. It settled.

TIP

Hunches and intuition are also useful in preparing for oral argument for the Court of Appeals. Using a combination of methods, I have heightened my awareness of the point of view of the judges listening to the case. I scrutinize a picture of the individual panelists and study individual decisions written by each particular panelist. Then, I pretend I am that panelist and let areas of inquiry float into my awareness. In one case, I anticipated 13 of 15 questions asked by the panel. In another, I identified and was prepared for all the questions they asked. This presumes a thorough saturation in the facts and law of your case.

Reciprocally, ignoring faint insights that seem to come out of nowhere but relate to your conflict can also be fatal. Attend to these moments.

One way to stay in touch with the inner self that provides hunches or intuition is to lighten up. We are so accustomed to warfare that we forget the delightful side of life—the fun of the battle, the thrill of the game and the joys of living. From your point of view, the world does not turn on this one case. Life will go on. There will be another case. From the client's point of view, the world should not revolve on this one case. You must help your client put this dispute on a shelf, and move forward with life.

With opposing counsel, it is always beneficial to banter about the fun of trial. If the evidence is well known to both sides, show them how much fun you will have exposing the contradictions of their case. A self-effacing style combined with confidence in the facts is more useful than self-righteousness.

Isolate Personal Urgencies

Today may or may not be a good time to compromise for the client. Sometimes, our personal financial needs may pressure us to settle. It is crucial that you be conscious of those influences and diligently try to exclude them. Establish a line of credit to carry you through the tough times. On the other hand, your client's emotional or financial needs may motivate you to push a settlement. These are proper considerations for the seller of settlements, but they are only one half of the picture – they do not address the buyer's needs. Re-think the situation from both points of view.

Hurry Not

There is a tendency to rush into settlement and to expect employers to give your dispute their immediate priority. Just because your side has become eager to settle means nothing unless the employer is similarly motivated.

Normally, you cannot expect a response to an overture in less than two weeks. Employers have on-going priorities and this lawsuit has been expected to drag on for months or even years. It is important to be sensitive to the political needs of the corporation—it will take time for managers and bad guys to adjust to the idea of compromise with the "enemy". It may take several committee meetings.

Defense morale has been wrapped up in fighting the war you declared on them earlier. You need to allow a few weeks to hear back if it is a good time to explore compromise. If you try to see the world from the defendant's point of view and not merely your client's or your own, you will see the obstacle course facing even a good defense counsel. Look at the case from what they know and what they do not know, yet.

PREPARATION FOR SETTLEMENT TALKS

If you are contemplating traditional one-on-one negotiation, review Chapter 14. If you are contemplating mediation, review the end section on negotiating through mediation.

Sift the Facts

By this stage, you have identified hundreds of facts as part of the investigation and discovery. Whether you pursue direct negotiation or mediation, it is time to search through the morass of facts and find the three or four key facts that really matter. These are *not* the basic facts, but rather facts that are pivotal in proving disputed elements or have persuasive power to tip the balance on the big picture. These key facts are *not* the elements themselves; they are *not* the ultimate conclusion. They are only key facts.

These few facts will be useful as your anchors in negotiation. Use them as a frame of reference when responding to defense arguments with, "Yes, but how do you explain the absence of warnings [or your key fact]?"

After you have identified the pivotal key facts, test them. One method of testing them is to ask:

- ❖ Is it reasonably clear and unambiguous?
- ❖ Will it be difficult to dispute?
- ❖ Is there little evidence that rebuts or contradicts them?

Once you have answered these questions affirmatively, the power of these key facts is enhanced if they also bolster secondary facts or other causes of action?

SIFT THE CLAIMS

You should sort through the claims for the ones with most impact on this employer. Employers usually know their real motives at the time of the decision. Their anxiety about getting caught can rebound to scare them. Self-generated fear is far more powerful than your threats. Defense counsel is rightfully most cocky when you do not demonstrate a clear-cut legal hook. If all your claims fall in the fuzzy category, settlement is seriously impeded. If you have at least one valid legal hook, the fuzziness of other claims need not hold you back. Gender discrimination is often difficult to prove, but a companion overtime claims will sharpen the issues and make pretext easier to show.

None of us would begin trial without serious preparation. Yet, many lawyers enter negotiations and mediation with only a few, last minute preparations. This is a good way to ensure failure. The alternative is to be thorough.

WEIGH THE FACTS

Whether you are pursuing negotiation or mediation, it is critical that you write out the bare bones elements of each cause of action—simple and straightforward. It is also necessary to list the elements of each serious affirmative defense.

Then you should prepare a comparison chart that fleshes out the strengths and weaknesses of both your case and theirs. The following format has proven useful in getting ready for serious negotiations. It highlights the point of view of the defense and allows you to anticipate their major arguments and develop rebuttals to their arguments.

	Our strengths	vs.	Their strengths
Key facts only			
Linchpins on credibility			
Contradictions			
In testimony or with documents			
Witnesses			
Witness demeanor			
Big Picture Feel/Microcosm/Theme			

First, you list the key facts (not basic facts or conclusions) for your case and do the same for their case as candidly as possible. These should be related to the main elements in dispute, not all the elements. Then, compare the competing sets of facts. This will allow you to find the linchpin facts—those that swing the balance on credibility or toward clear common sense.

Next, specify their contradictions of your case and your contradictions of their facts. It's often useful to organize by main issue and then by witness; e.g., plaintiff witness vs. defense witness.

Next, pause to consider how your client and his or her demeanor will sell to a jury. Repeat this for any witnesses you are relying upon for key testimony.

Finally, ask yourself "How does this feel? What is the big picture? Why should society make this employer pay for this injury? Is any of it the employee's own fault? How much?"

Part of this task is to clarify the big picture. You must reduce hundreds of facts to a short, simple sentence—one designed to tell a seventh grader what the conflict is about. This sorting and sifting of facts sharpens your awareness of your weaknesses and their strengths. It also allows you to winnow the dispute to its core. Then you can grasp the prospects of summary judgment and later credibility decisions.

RE-COMPUTE VALUE OF BEST CASE

You must update your assessment of value as the case progresses. Things change over the course of discovery. You must incorporate these changes to maintain credibility.

Adjust economic loss

The economic loss will be directly affected if your client finds a job, is hired, receives pay increases, bonuses or promotions. These must all be factored into the losses you claim. Some clients don't take mitigation seriously and make half-hearted efforts. Other clients may have been experiencing their first period of unemployment ever and did not know the importance of a paper trail. To make it easier to keep systematic records, you should give them job search logs to fill out. If delivered monthly, you will have the hard data for mitigation efforts. If you directed him or her to vocational rehabilitation programs or agencies that will help with revising resumes, acquiring interview skills and providing career counseling, their attendance records will be valuable corroboration.

Your new calculation will be based on information that has fewer unknowns than at the commencement of suit. You now have six or twelve months worth of data on actual losses and on mitigation. Your estimates of loss and projection can be more solid and credible. Be sure to consider all economic impact including:

- ❖ lost salary and wages or the differential
- ❖ lost raises at the old job vs. new job and eligibility for more raises
- ❖ lost or delayed eligibility for 401(k) or 403(k)
- ❖ value of lost benefits [usually = 30% or more of salary] or the actual projected differential
- ❖ lost pension or profit sharing or the differential
- ❖ lost stock options or the differential
- ❖ lost retirement bridges.

Your adjustment must be realistic about mitigation and its effects on back pay, front pay and lost earning capacity.

Adjust emotional distress claims

The information from the treating therapist or other health care providers needs to be updated periodically. If the diagnosis or prognosis remains dire, a request for a favorable written report may be appropriate. If the diagnosis or prognosis is no longer dire, you may forego a written report. If the condition has improved dramatically, however, it is better to know because reality must be admitted. If improvement is only marginal, you may be able to explore settlement before submitting supplemental answers to interrogatories or expert reports. It's foolhardy and probably unethical to assume that the improvement can be minimized for long. When disclosure is appropriate, you can maintain some uncertainty due to temporary amelioration of symptoms or the recurring nature of certain types of problems.

If an expert evaluated the current problems and recommended future therapy, it is essential that you obtain proof that the client pursued it. The defense is usually sliding scale programs, so you should be ready to explain any failure to do therapy.

Adjust Intangibles Claims

By this stage, the option of continuation on payroll is usually dead. The employee may express a desire for reinstatement, but it is the rare employer who shares that interest once it has been sued. Be cautious about your client's expressed desire to return unless the client has a clear self-interest—a great pension, great benefits or only a few years to retirement. Otherwise, it may simply be desperation and loneliness. Look to other alternatives and consider a trade-off identified below. To be eligible for front pay, the complaint must have demanded reinstatement and thus the remedy remains on the table.

Pragmatism dictates against simplistic offers of reinstatement. Instead, they should be restrictive by requiring evidence of protection from later retaliation and the purging of false, disparaging or negative information. The liquidated damage clause, commonly used in confidentiality, can be tied to retaliation. It makes reinstatement less attractive to the employer. Reinstatement is more viable with a large employer who may have various departments for assigning employees and small employers present awkward obstacles.

Sometimes, a short-term reinstatement for an agreed upon interval of three to six months appears as a valuable tool since it will fill in a gap on a resume. It is usually symbolic, but may get the ball rolling. It is most pragmatic to view reinstatement as a trade-off. While preserving the claims to front pay, you can gently and plausibly push reinstatement. Your hidden agenda is that reinstatement is something that you can later drop because the employer won't ever accept your client back. If your opponent does not immediately reject reinstatement, but appears willing to go to bat for you on that issue, backpedal quickly unless your client really wants to return. Don't betray your opponent by misrepresenting your client's interest in returning. It will make your opponent look foolish to his or her clients and destroy your trustworthiness.

References remain worthless for job searches. Earlier, they may have been useful to lock in a friendly manager's assessment. Now it's too late. If a reference finds interest, offer the employee's version of a reference and ask the manager's attorney if the company can live with it. If the answer is yes, it helps to corroborate your feelings about the case and could still become the basis for five to six requests for admissions. Similarly, some long-term employees (e.g., 30 years with same employer) want the recognition and validation of job well done.

You should update your analysis of the tax issues, but do not plan to raise them early in the mid-stream negotiation. The issue suggests you are on the road to consenting. Remember, the issues can be used as trade-offs as the money moves toward you. Re-examine the section on taxes in the valuation chapter.

CAUTION

Deductibility of fees may be limited to wage preservation/production, while fees for obtaining emotional distress are usually **not** deductible.

CALCULATE "WORST CASE", AND "MOST LIKELY" CASE AT TRIAL

Your client will once more need perspective. Demonstrate the value of the most likely case and the worst case at trial. Be sure that you exercise objective judgment in determining the most likely value at trial. It will influence your client's expectations. The "worst" case is usually zero, but occasionally a negative value may arise from costs incurred after an offer of judgment or taxation of costs. Remind your client of what cannot be achieved through lawsuits; e.g., the Bobbit solution.

You must again explore the differences between the bottom line and the demand. The simple, elegant question used by Joe Golden can significantly shape your client's perspective on settlement.

"What do you **need** from this settlement to get on with the rest of your life?"

Once again, do not ask, "What do you **want** from this case?"

The bottom line must factor in the client's immediate survival needs, the anticipated short-term future, and in many cases, the long-term future. It must assess their fear of trial, fear of losing, risks of delay in the trial itself, risks of reversal, risk of more delay if you win and the defense appeals. Your own assessment should be tempered by discussion with trusted peers.

It is also essential to weigh the prospects of success to determine what the most likely value at trial is. The prospects of success can be 50:50, or 40:60, or on rare occasions possibly 75:25. Your estimate of percent of success will establish the client's sense of the appropriate discounts on trial value and sharpen his or her sense of what is realistic.

Most clients need to be reminded that courts can take away a jury verdict. Because of quirky appellate court decisions, thoughtful settlement discussion must include mention of the costs, necessity and consequences of an appeal. Your client needs to understand that appellate courts generally favor the jury's verdict on the facts, but that questions of law could cause a reversal and require a new trial.

You should remind your client that settlement is not about justice. It is about the maximum that the employer is willing to pay and the minimum your client is willing to accept—a middle ground. It is not about what is right. It is not about their personal needs, mortgage payments or debts. (See handout on disc/CD.)

SET THE DEMAND

Comparisons are a concise way of measuring relationships. It is helpful to apply certain ratios to your computations to determine the larger message you are sending. Chapter 14 described these ratios in detail and they are not repeated.

Determine the appropriate ratio of demand to trial value

The ratio between demand and trial value sends a message about your confidence in this case. If you say the trial value is worth a million dollars and you make a demand for $100,000, you are expressing ten percent confidence in your case. By contrast, a trial value of $250,000 with a demand equal to $150,000 tells your opponent that you believe you have more than a sixty/forty chance of winning.

Generally the demand should be 55 percent to 60 percent of the trial value because this shows confidence in your liability position but also objectivity. On rare occasions, a demand at 35-40 percent of the trial value is a candid admission of a tough case on liability, but the honesty in admitting weakness enhances the credibility of your large damage claim. Generally, this strategy should be limited to cases with high potential damages.

Determine the appropriate ratio of demand to bottom line

The ratio of demand to bottom line remains flexible, but the mid-stream demand should not exceed double the bottom line anymore than early demands. If the demand is more than double, you are losing an opportunity to settle on terms compatible with your client's bottom line. Ethically, you probably can determine the demand on your own, provided you give due consideration to the client's bottom line. However, it is usually wiser to involve the client.

The demand must build in some negotiating space. It must also allow the defense counsel to save face by allowing her or him to pull you down. The demand should maintain a carefully thought out relationship to **both** the trial value and the bottom line as set forth in Chapter 14.

At this stage, theorizing about punitive damages may be helpful, but usually it is unpersuasive. Despite the client's feeling of outrage at what happened, most cases are not legitimate punitive damages material. Moreover, the threat carries little weight in a reality-based negotiation.

Often, it is helpful to create an outline summary plus footnotes to back up your formulas and details. This approach works in small and large cases alike. In the following example, my client had only lost two month's of pay but her lost benefits were much more significant. The size of benefits was the result of an unusual package of benefits by her former employer, lag time for her pay to catch up and the delay until trial due to the two-year human rights investigation. Because of her success in mitigation, the differential for front pay and lost earning capacity is modest. She had no therapy, medications or counseling so we used the self-help values of emotional distress. She insisted on a bottom line of $50,000.

# 1 Summary of Damage Categories	Trial Value	Compromise Demand
Lost wages + benefits over 2 years	$ 42,000	$ 30,000
Front pay 3 years (mostly benefits)	$ 28,000	$ 12,000
Lost earning capacity (includes reputation)	$ 60,000	$ 12,000
Emotional distress (Humil & Embar)	$ 20,000	$ 10,000
Attorneys fees and costs to date	$ 12,000	$ 10,000
Subtotal for Compromise	**$162,000**	**$ 74,000 ***
* taxable income		
If we succeed on discrimination claims, we will add:		
Attorneys fees for discrimination hours only	$ 40,000	
Costs (depositions, experts, subpoenas)	$ 12,000	
Civil penalty	$ 25,000	payable to taxpayers

To accommodate her very modest bottom line and desire to avoid trial, we adjusted the demand downward in relation to her bottom line. The extent of reduction for each compromise category shows the weight we afford our evidence for that type of damages (backpay and fees are the least discounted). We adjusted the trial value in relation to demand value. The original trial value felt high because it included a doubling of compensatory damages for an additional

$ 130,000. We didn't want to make our liability look weak by discounting it so much. Thus, we adjusted trial value downward in relation to demand. We added future costs, but segregated them to gain a balanced ratio without detracting from trial value. The threat of a higher number was thus distinctly communicated. You should prepare a separate chart that omits the compromise amount. If you first deliver the chart with trial values, you can gauge their response before committing yourself to the planned demand. Then, improvise. In large cases, you may provide the written trial values, but make the demand orally. The paper version will have more impact on the employer, but the figures must be realistic to have impact.

> Sometimes a narrative is more effective than a chart. If you use a narrative, spell the demand amount in full words, not numbers (e.g., five hundred thousand dollars). This inhibits the reader who races to see the number. It facilitates examination of the whole letter.

REVIEW YOUR STRENGTHS AND WEAKNESSES

Skillful preparation requires that we think about our weaknesses, also known as their strengths. These observations should be filtered through a judo perspective. You must invest energy converting the weight of their strengths into a weapon you can use against them, but it usually pays dividends. As with early settlement negotiations, you should know one or two cases that support your liability and damage positions at your fingertips.

In recent years, a new style of negotiating has proven useful where my opponent is a thoughtful and intelligent professional. Suggest an experiment where each takes turns describing the other's case with a goal of finding common ground.

> First, you articulate the strengths of the opponent's case and invite the opponent to elaborate on what you missed.
>
> Second, your opponent identifies the strengths of your case and you elaborate on what they missed.
>
> This approach demonstrates candor among "equals". It accelerates the narrowing of points of disagreement and points of consensus.

If you decide to play this experiment, be candid about your weakness that are known or obvious, but you don't have to spill your guts about things they don't know or strengths that have not been appreciated.

You should evaluate in advance whether this audience is appropriate, but wait to mention this approach until the actual meeting. This will elicit more spontaneous responses, even if they are not as comprehensive.

ACTUAL NEGOTIATION

All human interaction requires some routine bonding activities. There is no reason to treat a negotiation any differently. Before you shift to the merits, you might deflect the usual battle over weaknesses by playing the "strengths experiment" set out above. It changes the turf and shows professionalism. If you are apprehensive about this new experiment, you can still follow the traditional approach but it's time to sharpen the narrowing process.

Follow the guidelines set forth in Chapter 14 on Negotiation in Early Settlement. Delay your dollar demand. Identify common agreement on liability issues. Spell out the fact questions. Don't simply hear their argument, really listen to them. Notice which arguments are spoken in solid, even tones and which are put forth more hesitantly or where the tone of voice falters or drops or raises. This is a poker game and cues are rampant. Signals can be deflected and diverted, but they cannot be totally suppressed. Notice which arguments are made first, which are last and which seem to be omitted.

When they ask what you're demanding, begin slowly and describe the process you went through to arrive at trial value and the basic assumptions you made. Explain your basic considerations. Then pull out only your one page chart or summary of *trial value*—(without revealing that you have a second chart with compromise numbers) and show it. Watch their reaction.

If your opponent is silent, focus on the face and body. Is it poker-faced or responsive? Don't offer, sua sponte, a copy of this chart. Wait until they ask or start to take notes, then tell them it's their copy. If they take it in stride without vigorous opposition or laughter, use the trial values as a base for discussion. If they take issue, then give them your second chart with compromise figures and tell them your compromise amount.

If they are amused, be patient and admit it's best case scenario. Ask them what problems they see, assuming it's a best case scenario on liability. Their selective illumination of your weaknesses will give you major insights. Notice what they don't point out. This will show you what they see as your selective strengths. Then, tell them your compromise figures and show them your second chart.

If they throw it back at you and say it's ridiculous, don't be defensive. Admit it's best case scenario. Ask if they recognize the possibility that you *could* win some of your claims. Then, ask what values they would apply, assuming you won. Once again, pursue their illumination of your weaknesses. This will show, by reverse logic, what they see as your major strengths. Then, tell your compromise figures and show them your second chart. If they disagree, but don't argue vehemently, consider proposing mediation. It is a great tool for closing a gap when the parties are disposed, but unable, to end the matter.

At mid-stream, mediation is an even better tool for getting the employer's very best offer on the table. As noted in Chapter 14, mediation works best when approached like trial: A thoughtful analysis conducted around the needs of the audience, a theory of the case simplified for clear communication and charts and exhibits prepared. Then and only then can your client truly make an informed decision on the balancing act between settlement or continued litigation.

SETTLEMENT AT OR NEAR TRIAL

Chapter Nineteen

SETTLEMENTS NEAR TRIAL

Competition does not make people successful:
Success makes people competitive.

Hon. David S. Doty, Federal Judge in Minnesota

Many lawyers seek trial with the fervor of our ancestors pursuing wild animals. The challenge of doing battle with "the wild thing" is awesome and thrilling. Risk-taking is invigorating. If your case is one of rare, truly great cases, ignore settlement. Let the defendant broach the subject of compromise. If there is nothing significant on the table and you want to try the case, go for it. Big rewards do not come without big risks.

When the employer offers zero or peanuts, it's easy to decide to plunge ahead. You have nothing to lose. Nevertheless, such risks are often painful, stressful, and often counter-productive for the client. If the employer offers something reasonable, however, it should be difficult to say "no". This chapter is focused on how to amplify the employer's thirst for settlement at the edge of trial. Before discussing the moments primed for settlement, withdrawing and increasing demands, bifurcation and trial notebooks, we illustrate the factors propelling or inhibiting settlement.

RISKS, ANGST AND GOALS

As trial nears, both sides start experiencing the maximum impact of the force of uncertainty. Standing at the precipice of trial revives the significance of the Jack Benny scene where a thief puts a gun to his back and says, "Your money or your life." After a long pause, the thief jabs the gun into Benny's back and again says, "I said, your money or your life." To which Benny replies, "I'm thinking. I'm thinking."

Trial may not be that dramatic, but the risks of losing the money on the table are heightened by the roller-coaster ride of trial and the delays in closure. You must probe your client to learn his or her real goals, but you must also be alert that your attitude toward the risk shapes a major part of the client's perspective.

RISK TAKING BY WHOM

The issue of who is taking what risks at trial is a pragmatic issue worthy of your examination. The client's emotional risks during trial will substantially exceed the emotional investment of the experienced lawyer, but it may equal that of the novice. The client has already experienced injuries—lost job, emotional pain, reputation damage—and is trying to recoup those losses. You have made a major investment of lawyer time, but you may want to cut your losses before putting more time at risk. The plaintiff's time commitment at trial is probably less than 20 percent of the your time commitment. Most trial lawyers estimate that for each day of trial, there will likely be two days invested in preparation. Thus, a five-day trial will require approximately fifteen days of law practice and these are likely to be fifteen hour days. Thus, you are investing an additional 225 hours of your time (roughly ten percent of your yearly quota) in this trial. (This estimate does not count the time later invested in opposing post-trial motions, submitting fee petitions and the appeal). In addition, you typically subsidize the financial cost and take the risk of non-reimbursement.

Client Wants Trial

If the client wants trial, the ethical decision is easy. If the client insists that there be no settlement and that "we" go to trial, make considerable effort to educate your client. He or she must be reminded about the risks of losing, but also the consequences that they are giving up in voluntary compromise, including reduced flexibility on taxes and the intangible remedies. (See Chapters 12 and 14 on educating the client and values.) You must ensure that your client's stake is high enough to counterbalance the emotionalism that demands vindication. One tactic is to require your client to make an advance deposit for the expert's testimony and/or trial subpoenas and witness fees. Though the amount is modest, it will bring home the financial reality and test the commitment, presuming a your fee agreement provides this flexibility. I frequently remind clients that if they believe in their own case, they can borrow small amounts from several relatives and friends. Lawyers should quit being macho—admit that you can't carry the costs for **all** your clients. The psychological commitment also requires demonstration of financial commitment.

No matter how clearly you think you have communicated the iffiness of winning and collecting money, many clients persist in assuming that once the jury has spoken, the money belongs to them. These clients need to be reminded that even if you win at trial, the money won't likely come for another year. You must repeatedly re-educate them that there will be post trial motions, petitions for fees and appeals. They must be fully aware of the risk that what the jury giveth, a trial or appellate judge can taketh away.

Client Does Not Want Trial

On the other hand, if the client does not want trial, you must honor that sentiment regardless of the reason. You should explore your client's angst, but ultimately it is his or her call. If the client insists on avoiding trial, you must pursue the settlement options. The issue remains how to make the employer thirsty, without appearing weak or afraid of trial. Strategies must be softened to ensure that you don't forfeit opportunities by bravado.

Client Unsure About Trial

Some clients express nervousness about trial, but this should not be confused with a desire to avoid trial at all costs. Anxiety must be addressed and morale built up. Sensitive confidence building is appropriate, but do not artificially inflate client's expectation. Be patient. If the client is not a little nervous, you should be the one who is worried.

Stirring the employer's desire to settle near trial follows the same framework identified throughout this text, but strategies must be tailored for the occasion and the changing audiences. The principles of timing, audience, inertia, uncertainty, fuzzy logic, the lawyer factor, and basic concepts of leverage must be applied but with a different subtlety of mind.

BUILDING LEVERAGE NEAR TRIAL

Strategies for increasing value in settlement are distinct from strategies for increasing your opponent's fear of losing. Some tactics, such as motions for punitive damages, are interwoven with both aspects.

TACTICS RELATED TO VALUE

The timing of the precise tactics for increasing the value of a settlement will vary by the peculiar rules of your jurisdiction, but the strategies are essentially the same:

- ❖ Withdraw the existing demand
- ❖ Realistically increase your demand
- ❖ Add punitive damages
- ❖ Subpoena financial records.

The act of withdrawing your last demand is less threatening than increasing your demand. But, its ambiguity also dilutes its power.

Withdrawal of existing demand

If you and the plaintiff are gung ho for trial and do not intend to settle without it, then you should send a withdrawal of demand letter shortly before the scheduled start of trial.

Alternatively, you may decide to leave the last demand on the table or to withdraw a demand at a later moment. Let timing and the gap be your primary guide. If you are seriously trying to get their best offer *before* trial, the withdrawal should be prompt—before trial preparations are full speed ahead. This means *at least* two weeks before trial. You must give the defendant's lawyer time to educate the employer about the risks of trial and the pros and cons of compromise. The withdrawal should always be verified in writing.

If you previously gave a written notice to expect an increased demand, you can simply withdraw the demand and remain silent about a new demand all the way to the court-house steps. I usually do not identify a new demand at the time of withdrawal. It's a power play—I want them to ask about the new amount. If your withdrawal is silent, defense counsel will invariably call to talk settlement. They will use the guise of getting a better copy of an exhibit or questioning your witness list, but then bring up the new demand in an off-hand manner.

When, however, the client is eager for settlement, you should identify the new demand. Let the defense know what amount will buy the package. Pragmatically, it should be 20-50 percent higher than the prior demand.

Sometimes, it is advisable to wait to formally withdraw the demand until the jury is picked. Then, at a break, remind counsel that the offer has been formally withdrawn and provide your documentation. By tying it to the actual jury, now selected, it magnifies the anxiety effect.

CAUTION
Withdrawal demonstrates cockiness—be certain it is warranted.

Follow your hunches on timing.

Realistically increase your demand

If you are eager to take this case to trial and the client agrees, it is entirely appropriate to increase your demand. This tactic assumes your prior demand was reasonable and that the increase is justified by some intervening events.

My first experience with the power of thoughtfully increasing demands occurred by accident over 15 years ago. At each interval of settlement talks, I instinctively doubled the demand. Over time, the defendant raced to catch the last demand.

> The first plaintiff's lawyer on the case had commenced suit in 1982 based on a breach of contract for non-delivery of the client's stock options. The defense counter-claimed for a related breach of contract. The client's first lawyer then demanded a $10,000 retainer. The client was unable to pay and the plaintiff's lawyer withdrew. The client was so intimidated that by the time she came to me, she just wanted out of the lawsuit. She had tried three other big firms in town. Each had turned her down because her potential damages were too low. She hired me to end the case by offering a mutual dismissal. My settlement effort failed when the defendants arrogantly asked her to pay for their time in counter-claiming—an amount equal to $3,000. She had no money to offer.

> After some investigation, I threatened to amend, adding a claim for misrepresentation based on a conflict of interest. The defense laughed at my bravado, but they offered a mutual dismissal. I said, "No, this time she needs $5,000 to bail out." They refused. After the motion to amend was won, the defendants offered $5,000. I said "Too late. The demand is now $10,000." They refused. After some discovery, they offered $10,000. My response: "It's too late. Now, it's $25,000." After more discovery and motion practice and after we survived summary judgment, they offered $25,000. My response "Too late. It's now $50,000." When the jury retired, they handed me a check for $50,000. I laughed and said, "Don't you guys ever learn: it's in the jury's hands." The jury came back at $110,000. Defendent finally paid up. The year was 1983.

Intervening events must justify the increase

Time alone justifies very little increase. Surviving summary judgment, acquiring new evidence, or a new perspective or newly available witnesses, a new judge or new law can all justify increasing your demand. It is crucial to appreciate that intervening events must be used to justify the increasing demands.

Increases of double or triple magnitude will not be a commonplace experience. More often the raises will be 20-30 percent. If the only event is an increase in lawyer's fees, it justifies a small, but noticeable raise. Other events (new witnesses, found documents) are more beneficial.

When you increase the demand, you must be sensitive to the timing issues and particularly to the existing gap between the last cycle of offer and demand. If the gap is proportionately small, your increase may mean you lose the offer. At the same time, a failure to increase it may result in a defendant belatedly, accepting your offer before you can increase it.

> ## CAUTION
> Arbitrary increases backfire. The other side may withdraw.

Once I was defending a non-profit entity. Liability clearly favored the plaintiff, but her demands felt extreme, even in 1987 dollars. Her wage loss was only ten thousand dollars per year, but her demand was $900,000 because of a PTSD diagnosis. I worked hard to persuade the insurance company to offer $200,000. Plaintiff's counsel then raised his demand to $1,500,000. The insurance company became angry and instructed me to withdraw all offers. Before taking that rash action, I asked plaintiff's counsel why he raised the demand. His response was, "That's what you do." I explained to him that you have to have a reason for doing it—some event that justifies it. He offered no new evidence. Despite the huge increase in the demand, I sensed insecurity in the plaintiff based on rumors of marital discord. I revised the settlement approach to address her personal needs for future security. We offered an annuity that guaranteed her expected annual income for 20 years. For less than $225,000, I was able to satisfy her needs and put fees on the table for 500 hours of lawyer time. The arbitrary increase almost cost his client a good settlement.

Adding punitive damages
Certain issues should selectively be incorporated in the planning strategies and addressed some weeks prior to the last two weeks before trial. One strategy is adding punitive damages. This is a pivotal motion. It should not be brought unless you have a good prospect of winning under local rules. The motion has sizeable scare value, but if it is denied, employers see it as a huge victory. Even though it is legally distinct from your case, they read it as an omen on the merits of your case.

Some jurisdictions allow punitive damages without any motion, but others require court authorization in advance and even requirements of service. Jurisdictions also vary on whether a motion to add punitive damages is a non-dispositive or dispositive motion. You must check the controlling jurisdiction. Commonly, they are viewed as a non-dispositive motion and discovery cut-off orders must be monitored in advance. You must be certain to make this motion in a timely fashion. If the motion is still acceptable shortly before trial, a motion to plausibly add punitive damages can itself provide a powerful incentive for settlement. In some jurisdictions, you can still make motions to amend at trial, as the evidence comes in and even after the evidence is all in. Do not be afraid to make oral motions. You don't always need a paper motion. If you do, you can sometimes submit a handwritten motion so there is record. In such case, you must rely on the strength of the evidence and be sure your motion is based on what actually came in, not what you think came in.

When briefing the issue of punitive damages, it is important to remember that the evidence that justifies punitive damages is different from the evidence for compensatory damages. Usually, courts require only a prima facie case and the rules often negate consideration of the defense's facts. It is often useful to analyze the facts using opposition thinking; e.g., what would the facts[52] be if defendant had "regarded" or shown proper "regard" for the rights of others?

Although we usually feel the employer's conduct is egregious, cases that justify punitive damages under *existing* common law standards are not common. Historically, they made up less than five percent of the cases. With the Civil Rights Act of 1991, society decided to significantly expand the use of punitive damages to punish past discrimination and deter future discrimination. Individual cases usually have the appearance of being isolated decisions, not likely to recur, but Congress directed research on how juries assessed employer conduct and tabulations of data on punitive awards as well as the caps. The Department of Justice in 1999 issued its Statistics Bulletin "Civil Trial Cases and Verdicts in Large Counties, 1996," which demonstrated that jurors awarded punitive damages in 19 percent of the employment discrimination cases.

Based on the sizeable verdicts of NELA members like Roxanne Conlin, Mary Ann Seday, Joseph Posner, Nancy Erika Smith, Neil Mullin and others too numerous to mention, the prospects of raising the caps or segregating punitive damages are significantly improved. You can cite these NELA jury verdicts in your correspondence and post-trial motions, but not in your briefs in support of punitive damages. It may worry a judge about the prospects of a so-called runaway jury.

---

[52] *Swanlund v. Shimano Industrial Corp.*, 459 N.W. 2d 151, 153 (Minn. 1995).

Subpoena financial records

You should also consider what documents to seek after winning the motion. If this defendant is a publicly held company, you can get a copy of financial records from your broker. If you do it and discreetly let them know you have the records, you will surprise the other side with your foresight and due diligence. You can justify a subpoena for their financial records; e.g., their balance sheets or profit and loss statements for last three years. Like adding punitive damages, this should be planned in advance and served a few weeks before trial.

Offers of Judgment

A popular defense tactic has become offers of judgment. The effect is not merely on costs incurred after the Rule 68 offer, but can also affect your fee petition. If the verdict comes in less than the amount offered, the Rule 68 offer not only precludes plaintiff from recovering his or her costs, but also will usually impose liability for the opponent's costs after the offer. *More significantly, it can foreclose attorneys fees under certain statutes even if you win.* One crucial question is whether the statute defines fees as part of the "costs" (e.g. Title VII) or fees as separate from "costs" (e.g. ADA, FLSA, ADEA). In the latter group, plaintiff's fees are recoverable even if the Rule 68 offer was greater than the verdict. But watch the flip side argument about defense fees. Another question is whether the offered amount specifies fees, thus allowing them to be added later to a small verdict. Some courts will include the value of injunctive relief. [53]

A counter strategy.

Some jurisdictions view an offer of judgment differently than a settlement offer, which are inadmissible under Rule 408. Offers of judgment may be admissible into evidence as an admission of liability, if duly filed and thus part of the pleadings. Timing is important. If you decide to offer it before plaintiff rests or refer to it in closing statement, you should inform the court and cite authority for its admissibility. If it comes prior to trial, educate your client that the opposition is admitting that you win. It is a public admission and you quote it in public and even in the media.

---

[53] *Local 32B-32 v. Port Authority of N.Y and N.J.*, 180 F.R.D. 251 (S.D. N.Y. 1998).

Tactics Related to Winning

There are several tactics you can employ to increase your opponent's fear of losing. If you use these tactics effectively, they can magnify settlement opportunities.

- ❖ Witnesses previously mentioned, but underemphasized
- ❖ Order of witnesses at trial
- ❖ New documents on exhibit list
- ❖ New co-counsel
- ❖ Bifurcation
- ❖ A trial notebook

Witnesses previously underemphasized

If your witness list includes a person whose identity was previously disclosed but was not emphasized, you can add uncertainty to defendant. The employer will often ask defense counsel why this person was not deposed. Defense counsel must backpedal and either admit your cleverness, your deception, or his or her own failure to appreciate the potential importance. Once I hired a private investigator to find a witness who had disappeared four years earlier. Through four unlisted telephone numbers, she traced him to a little eating establishment in Michigan called the Last Chance Saloon. When I notified my opponent that he was available to testify, they met our demand.

Order of witnesses

The order of witness can also unnerve the defendant. It is not simply the merits that sway settlement. As noted elsewhere, a sizable number of cases will settle promptly when the CEO is scheduled to testify. Often, the CEO had zero involvement in the termination decision, but the company adopted it. Their testimony may be relevant on applicable policies that exist or did not exist as well as on corporate practices of investigation before termination and ultimate responsibility for managers who made the decision. Most CEO's hate to be subjected to cross-examination, much less exposed in public. Moreover, they often feel ignorant of the details or do not want to defend someone else's decision. At the same time, do not be cavalier about issuing a subpoena to a CEO. If the CEO is too remote, you may irritate the judge. In addition, you may find that a CEO like Lee Iacocca has enormous persuasive power with the jury.

New documents on exhibit list

Occasionally, documents not previously disclosed will surface. Sometimes we receive such documents anonymously in the mail or clients find them at the last minute. It's usually wise to disclose their existence promptly and include a cover letter affirmatively setting forth their arrival. On the other hand, if the belated documents that surprise the opponent are caused by their own poorly drafted requests for production that did not cover this evidence, identify them as exhibits without advance notice. They enhance settlement leverage because of the alternative, defense malpractice.

New co-counsel can make a difference

Sometimes the addition of co-counsel can impact settlement values. In one recent case, a third year lawyer was getting ready to start trial on his first sexual harassment case. The top offer on the table was one year's pay. He asked me to try the case with him. I showed up at the trial settlement conference and gave written notice that I would be lead counsel. Within one hour, the employer's offer jumped to six years of pay. This offer was too good to turn down and the matter settled. These moments are wonderful strokes to the ego, but more likely they represent the power of uncertainty on the edge of trial.

Bifurcation

You should vigorously resist attempts to bifurcate the trial. Employers often try to separate the trial into two issues to be decided separately: liability and damages. Any serious attempt to unsettle the employer into settlement must involve the threat of simultaneous presentation of damage evidence in the same stage as liability evidence. Jurors are ordinary humans: they tend to be effect-oriented. Lawyers, judges, and appellate judges tend to be causation-oriented. Thus, the employer will be unsettled by the situation that allows the jury to consider the impact on the plaintiff while deciding who is to blame. Moreover, there is a strong tradition in America for juries to hear both liability and damages facts simultaneously.

A LEXIS search will usually produce authority to oppose bifurcation on grounds of judicial inefficiency. You should anticipate an advance or last minute request by the defense to bifurcate to "save the court's time, when the plaintiff loses." Be prepared in advance with court decisions disfavoring bifurcation and supporting the tradition and efficiency of a single trial.

On the other hand, it is acceptable to bifurcate the amount of punitive damages. In fact, it is common to have the punitive damages portion bifurcated. If defendant does move to bifurcate liability and damages, you should remind the court that it's customary to bifurcate punitive damages, but not to chop up the liability and damages issues. It is not wise to call it a compromise—simply present it as the norm.

If the amount of punitive damages is bifurcated, you should nonetheless push hard to have the issue of entitlement to punitives decided in the first stage of the trial, unless your statute dictates to the contrary. Stated differently, you usually want the jury to decide if there was deliberate indifference, at the same time they are deciding liability questions. There is a risk of confusion, however, on the standards for liability.

As noted earlier, there is a window between a jury's decision on entitlement to punitives and its award of the amount. It provides have a great window for settlement. The certainty of punitive damages is now clear, but the amount unknown. The uncertainty provides enormous leverage for settlement.

Preparing a Trial Notebook

Creating a trial notebook is gospel—it should be your bible. At all times in the two weeks before trial, you must carry it with you. It is critical to thoughtful planning. It is the only way to capture the brainstorms that emerge spontaneously. Insights will evaporate rapidly if they are not recorded immediately. It is essential to organizing your brilliant ideas and being organized in general. Strategically, a trial notebook is an absolute must. In many jurisdictions, it is a requirement.

Your trial notebook will also impress your opponent. When you come to a settlement conference so well organized that everything you need to know is contained within a single 1.5-inch three-ring binder, the impact is considerable. You are prepared, organized, and ready to go. Most lawyers are not. It unsettles your opponent, especially trial lawyers who hate to lose.

To be useful, the trial notebook must be organized. There are many variations, but one sequence that I have found useful is:

- ❖ To-do list (listing necessities on one page; e.g., get and serve subpoenas, do JIGs, pretrial brief, witness preparation…)
- ❖ Voir dire questions
- ❖ Opening statement
- ❖ Closing statement
- ❖ Witness list (and variations in sequence of presentations)
- ❖ Exhibit list (by number)
- ❖ Direct exam: witness 1 (exhibit #s you plan to introduce through them) witness 2, … expert witness
- ❖ Cross examination: witness 1 (exhibit #s you plan to introduce through them) witness 2, …expert witness

- ❖ Jury instructions—crucial ones only
- ❖ Hot evidence issues: (anticipate objections and find cases organized by exhibit or topic)
- ❖ Arguments against directed verdict.

STRATEGIES NEARER TO TRIAL

As you enter the final two weeks before trial, additional levers can maximize settlement opportunities.

SUBPOENA KEY WITNESSES

The key witnesses should be subpoenaed without asking opposing counsel to cooperate. On less important witnesses, courtesy, negotiation and patience can prevail. Let counsel agree to produce them voluntarily and coordinate their arrival two hours before they testify. At trial, be sure to let the judge know you are relying on defendant's offer to voluntarily produce certain employers. Cooperation usually works, but don't take chances on important witnesses.

SUBPOENA NEWLY APPRECIATED DOCUMENTS

Often, the saturation of trial preparation brings new theories to mind. These theories may create evidence not foreseen during discovery. There is no need to be shy about subpoenaing these documents to be produced at day one of trial.

On day one of trial, you will likely be preoccupied with jury selection and the opening statement. Therefore, you should ask another lawyer to come and examine these documents for potential inferences. If you don't have staff available, don't be afraid to reach out to your peers. Occasionally, these last minute documents were hidden by defense, not improperly, but because your request was not precise enough.

In one case, for example, the trial subpoena served on the parent corporation produced yet another personnel file (three distinct copies had already been produced in discovery). This new file had additional negative reports about the plaintiff. It was likely that the corporate defendant had papered the file after the fact. Rather than supress the file on grounds of non-production, we used its creation and belated discovery to show deliberate disregard of the law. The creation of belated documents was magnified by our original discovery instruction that asked defendant to exhaust all possible sources. If any sources were not checked, they had been asked to identify what sources they exhausted and the reason any others were not explored. They neglected to respond.

At universities, it is almost commonplace to have four or more personnel files: official personnel office, department file, department chair's file, benefits file, even former supervisor's personnel file. If you didn't know to get all files during discovery, you should try to get them now.

CAUTION

It is crucial to think through the likely evidence. In one case, neither side had considered the possibility of phone logs to corroborate complaints. We issued last minute subpoenas to retrieve a phone log. We assumed it would confirm the 20+ calls our client claimed he made in complaints about the service. The records showed only 3 calls. While the records may have been falsified, they appeared neutral and untampered. Thus, our brainstorm backfired. Since credibility was crucial, this was a linchpin fact and the case was lost.

The issues in the weeks before trial are critical if you are pursuing settlement. They should be anticipated and analyzed carefully to obtain maximum leverage. In addition, there are other strategies, essential during trial, that should be considered.

Chapter Twenty

SETTLEMENT OPPORTUNITIES DURING TRIAL

You don't learn anything when you win.
You only learn something when you lose.

Hon. David S. Doty, Federal Judge in Minnesota

T he moment of trial crystallizes all of the events that came before. Since plaintiff goes first, the need for final preparations must be balanced against the settlement opportunity at trial. Some defense counsel will sidetrack you with the last minute requests for new demands. Unless your need to settle is paramount or they make an offer that is substantial, you should generally ignore these diversions. Let them put another offer on the table even if it means bidding against themselves. You are in control.

Trial lawyers often focus on being warriors, while employment lawyers focus on being pragmatists. Many employment lawyers become timid on the eve of trial. Whether the origin is in the fear of losing, the fear of looking foolish, concerns about clients losing whatever is on the table, or a fear of sanctions, the reticence is very real. You must reshape the settlement posture by using a strategy of disciplined boldness.

If this is one of your first trials, you can't fully hide your fears. But you can apply judo tactics to turn your inexperience around. Show excitement about your first trial experience. This approach suggests that you will try harder, be more prepared and hopefully, be willing to make mistakes. You can create anxiety in your opponent by commenting, for example, "I hope the jury will forgive my mistakes." If you also show an eagerness to learn, it will be unsettling to a seasoned opponent. A veteran knows that jurors (and judges) will be unpredictable, but even worse is the fear that the jurors will forgive the mistakes of a novice, but not those of an old timer.

After a few trials, you can brag about how much you love a jury trial, but mentioning the results is optional. The mere fact that you brought up the trial kindles the listener's assumption that you wouldn't have done so if you had lost. If defense counsel asks who won, tell them. If you lost, your candor shows your ability to "go on ticking". It can unsettle them. You can also echo your love of jury trials by discreetly weaving it into the topic into settlement talks. It unsettles many opponents who have the equivalent of the lay public's fear of public speaking. My opponents have occasionally complained to judges that "Heikens doesn't care if the damages are low. He just loves to try cases. He's crazy."

It is tacky to brag about past achievements [unless asked], but if you can weave in a war story it enlarges their fears. Let your exuberance spill over. Timing is everything. You can mention a recent verdict as the reason you didn't get discovery done on time, neglected to call them back or had to reschedule depositions.

KNOW YOUR AUDIENCE

Know your defense-lawyer audience. You should talk to your peers about the opponent. While many defense counsels are wimps and terrified of losing, there are some who zealously pursue trials. The zealous ones may be oblivious to their client's needs or in hot pursuit of the need to prove their manhood or womanhood. The primitive quest for risk-taking is probably buried deep in our genetic structures, but it provides a compelling force when matched with certain personalities.

CAUTION

If defense lawyers are in a district where recent verdicts have been tiny, their cockiness may be justified. Reciprocally, you can be bolder if high verdicts have occured recently.

Some defense lawyers are cowardly lions who have obtained the maximum billings and now want to settle to avoid losing. On the other hand, good lawyers know when their own client's story is shaky or based on distortions, exaggerations, or lies. They don't lightly bite the hand that feeds them, until it's necessary. Necessity arrives when the risk of uncertainty and losing becomes too high. Thus, an attractive offer may sway the defense counsel to become blunt with his or her client and amplify the prospect of compromise.

Plaintiff lawyers frequently banter that defense lawyers go to trial to raise billings. Some no doubt do. But in my five years as defense counsel in the early

1980s, revenue for the firm was not a consideration on whether to settle or go to trial. Winning was an issue. Losing was an issue. Cost was also an issue, but not revenues to the firm.

To keep a paying client happy and returning, defense lawyers need to keep the bill low. If the verdict is a resounding loss, they know they will lose the client. They will be blamed for poor judgment in not knowing the case or not settling earlier. If, however, the defense lawyer knows the client is leaving their law firm anyway, revenues could become a consideration. Historically, that particular beast was rare. Now, with changing loyalties and intensified competition, the selection of law firms has often become more like a beauty contest. The real difference of short-term gains vs. long-term relationships is often overlooked.

If fiscal logic controlled these decisions, employers would settle disputes early, before discovery or at least before trial preparation time. It does not make economic sense to pay more than minimal defense fees to find out you will lose. Yet, it routinely occurs. Your preparedness can crystallize their fear of uncertainty and lust to avoid losing.

You also need to know your judge-audience. Talk to your peers about the judge. At a minimum, learn about the judge's quirks about procedures, handling voir dire, marking exhibits, approaching witnesses, accepted duration of opening and closing statements. Listen to war stories about this judge. Most are one-sided and a little distorted, but you can sort out the common nucleus in any collection of stories. These insights will be useful in your arguments opposing a directed verdict and also on post-trial motions. [Review the section on judges in Chapter 3.]

TIMING FOR SETTLEMENT

With knowledge that only 10 percent of cases filed will actually get to trial, it behooves you to consider settlement options as you finalize trial preparations. There are several major points when disputes in trial commonly settle:

❖ Night before trial
❖ Day before the CEO has to testify
❖ When a surprise witness is called; e.g., general counsel
❖ When the jury retires, if evidence has gone in well.

Remember these critical turning points and stay alert to opportunities to build on the occasion. If the CEO's testimony is plausibly relevant, subpoena him or her for early testimony. Their risk-avoidance behavior can provide the extra incentive for early settlement. There are additional events that can trigger settlement, but they are very rare:

- ❖ After an opening statement that is truly extraordinary
- ❖ When a "smoking" gun document surfaces unexpectedly
- ❖ When a directed verdict motion fails and the employer had seen it as a certainty
- ❖ When defendant's key witness testimony is excluded
- ❖ When your rebuttal witness presents a huge surprise, but this works only if defendant has opened a door.

OPENING STATEMENT

"The form and content of the winning argument may stem from the logical, intellectual, linear progeny of the mind. *But the energy, the power, the stuff that excites and moves, that makes us credible and eventually convinces, is born of the soul.*"

Gerry Spence, *How to Argue and Win Every Time*

To enhance settlement, your opening statement must be clear and simplified. The opening allows the employer to appreciate, often for the first time, how the big picture of the evidence may be viewed to favor plaintiff's case. This is often effective in making an employer more thirsty to settle. The employer begins to appreciate that your package may be more attractive to the other bidder–the jury. The fear is real—employer's competitor may place a higher purchase price on your case.

If you think in terms of a big picture, you will speak of the big picture. But it must be rooted in crucial details. Your evidence should be presented in *layers* that flow from your theory of the case. The opening must reveal your road map, the organizing principle for the morass of facts. Remember, you have lived with the case for over twelve months. The jury will have only a few days. They cannot process the data you are throwing at them unless you give them a map or model to help filter through this new information.

Jim Kaster of Minneapolis convincingly describes the power of your belief in your case, "If you don't believe it, the jury won't either." If your opening statement makes the jury want your client to win, they will listen to the evidence, selectively attending to the favorable evidence and disregarding the other. The reverse is also true. Many employers and their counsel are alert enough to observe a jury that is leaning in your direction. This observation whets their appetite; making them eager to have their bid to be accepted before the jury puts a higher sales price on the case.

CALL SURPRISE WITNESSES

Another strategy in calling witness involves surprising the defense by calling someone at the counsel table as a witness to material facts. In several cases I have called the general counsel, sitting there unsuspecting, on the ground that he was carbon copied on a document. This provides settlement intrigue. For example, at the start of one trial, the demand of $100,000 looked reasonable, but defendants were offering less than half that amount. When a working class jury was selected, the demand was raised to $200,000 but Defendant only raised their offer to plaintiff's earlier demand. On day two, the court authorized a claim for punitive damage and the demand was doubled to $400,000. Defendants once more moved up, but only up to the *prior* demand of plaintiff. The demand was then withdrawn. At the end of day five, a surprise witness was called—in-house counsel sitting at the defense table throughout trial. This presented a major shock to defense counsel who had not anticipated such a bold move. The request was justified because in-house counsel had been present during the sex harassment investigation. Witnesses had testified to conversations, thereby waiving the privilege. The judge, apparently disturbed by the prospect of a lawyer on the witness stand, wavered on admissibility. That night defendant offered $500,000, but the demand had already been raised. The next morning to avoid testifying, defendant met plaintiff's new demand and the case was settled.

This technique obviously requires forethought and discipline not to tip your hand. It may also require some justification for not appearing on the witness list. Rebuttal witnesses usually do not need be disclosed, but be ready to show that the witness really is rebutting something.

Minneapolis attorney Stephen W. Cooper had an extraordinary experience with a surprise witness who wasn't even called to the stand. He was cross-examining a CEO on reprisal and a defamation claim without direct evidence. A person wandered into the wrong courtroom by mistake and sat in the back. The CEO recognized the person and apparently remembered that he had slandered the plaintiff to this witness. The CEO assumed the witness was there to impeach him. To avoid perjury, the CEO contradicted her prior deposition testimony and admitted making a defamatory statement. The jury awarded almost twelve years of pay.

A DAILY TRANSCRIPT

Occasionally, a great case will warrant requesting a daily transcript, but it is very costly. If you make this request in front of defense counsel, it may have a small scare value, but usually, it is advisable to keep this request private until closing argument when you can quote the actual testimony.

FOCUS ON CAUSE TO SHARPEN THE BIG PICTURE

While we plaintiff's lawyers are busily trying to impose liability on the defendant, we must not lose sight of the jury's need to see the world as rational. If they don't see the defendant as the cause of plaintiff's harm, they are likely to see the plaintiff as the cause of his or her own harm. We humans tend to quickly identify a cause for the effects we see. Whether the connection is coincidence, superstition, the scientific method, rational thinking or common sense, it happens. You must recognize the very real human need to blame someone for what happened, to feel that someone is at fault. We want the world to appear orderly where cause leads to effect. Identifying a "cause" is simply another way of attributing blame for the effects that include your client's suffering.

No matter what the legal issues, it is wise to recognize this "felt" burden of causation in opening statement and again in closing. The employer will be listening and comparing explanations. In contract cases, you must show the broken promise is the cause of the injury and likewise the statement in fraud and defamation claims. In discrimination, you effectively have to prove that the cause of the decision is the employer's view of the plaintiff's sex, race and disability… Motive is simply another word for what caused the decision. Pretext is really a battle about the causes for termination. The jury will decide which makes more sense: the defendant's explanation of other non-discriminatory reasons or your explanation of pretext.

The truly accidental event is rare, if at all. It may be an Act of God or a random event, but in a true accident, no one is at fault, or at least no one is accountable. Juries can blame the employer or blame the employee for his or her *prior* actions that triggered or "caused" the employer's response. The primary choices for the causes of termination are:

❖ Employer's hostile motive
❖ Employer's view of employee's conduct
❖ Employee's "misconduct"
❖ External forces—e.g., the marketplace "required" layoffs.

These causation theories are different in negligence cases, where a hybrid version applies: The employer may not have caused the injury, but it could have prevented it. At the same time, concepts of comparative negligence[54] and the last chance doctrine are an important new trend. They reflect the reconciliation of real social needs and felt theories of causation.

To obtain settlement during trial, you must have a better theory of causation than the employer and it must be lucid. To maximize the purchase price in settlement or a verdict, you must have hard data on economic loss, solid evidence on emotional injury, and evidence of real damage to reputation. If you seek punitive damages, you must have evidence that makes ordinary folks angry.

CLOSING ARGUMENTS

Your closing argument wraps together the pivotal evidence, but only the evidence that was actually received by the jury. Nothing else matters. While your opening statement helps you win, closing summations have more impact on damages—the how much question. If the jury hasn't seen the justness of your cause by this time, it's probably too late to win on closing. Nonetheless, your closing must remind the jury of your promises at the outset and the evidence that fits your theory. It must demonstrate how the employer's key evidence was neutralized or negated.

Asking for Money

Gerry Spence in *How to Argue and Win Every Time* provides compelling illustrations of how to ask for just amounts of money. You must be credible, and to be credible you must openly reveal your feelings. To be heard, you must speak truth from the heart. You must show, not tell, how the jury's power to do justice is limited to awarding money.

A powerful closing can scare the hell out of an employer. It can make them want to avoid the risk that the jury will place a higher value on your injury than their last offer or even your demand. If you have a final demand on the table and it still meets your client's needs, it may be stupid to gamble. But, at this moment, you must trust your feel for the jury. If they are paying rapt attention, feel emboldened. But you watch your own delusions—while you psyched yourself up to be convincing, you may not appreciate the usually objective point of view of the jury.

---

[54] See *Phillips vs. Taco Bell*, 153 F.3d 844 (8th Cir. 1999) which effectively applies the last clear chance or avoidance doctrine to constructive discharge. A proposed new Restatement makes this the norm, not the exception, for JIGS.

At their roots, all decisions are essentially emotional—our personal priorities and needs are repackaged as values and logical decisions. Emotions have their own rationality. They are not irrational, simply different from sequential logic. Education of the jury is the critical final step. For settlement purposes, you must educate both the employer and your client. The first step is to educate yourself. I hope this book has enhanced your starting point.

CONCLUSION

Employment lawyers can be both crusaders and profit makers. This emotionally intense area of human disputes is complicated, but also an enormous amount of fun. Its challenges are provocative—intellectually, emotionally and spiritually. Taking risks is invigorating: intelligent risk-taking is profitable. When you understand your audience, you can better control the outcome of the game.

In 1996, Neil Mullin and I were discussing the essence of trials. At one point, we simultaneously expressed the same insight about what causes magic during trial. The same concept applies to finding the balance between settlement and trial:

"It ain't the words; it's the music."

PRIORITY READINGS

NEGOTIATION STRATEGIES

Phillip Hermann, *Better Settlements Through Leverage* (New York: Lawyers Coop 1965)

Gerard I. Nierenberg, *The Art of Negotiating* (New York: Barnes & Noble Books, 1968 reprint 1995)

Herb Cohen, *You can negotiate anything* (Secaucus: Lyle Stuart, Inc. 1980) (New York: Carol paper 1994)

Charles Craver, *Effective Legal Negotiation and Settlement* (MN CLE 6/96)

Roger Dawson, *Secrets of Power Negotiating* (Hawthorne, N.J. Career Press 1995)

GENERAL STRATEGIES

David Rogers, *Waging Business Warfare* (New York: Zebra 1987 reprint 1995)

Daniel Kehrer, *Doing Business Boldly: The Art of Intelligent Risk-Taking* (New York: Random House-Times Books 1989).

John McDonald, *Strategy in Poker, Business and War* (1950) reissued (New York: W.W. Norton 1996)

DAY TO DAY LITIGATION PERSPECTIVES

Gerry Spence, *Trial by Fire* (New York: William Morrow & Co. 1986)
How to Argue & Win Every Time (New York: St. Martin's Press 1995)
The Making of a Country Lawyer (New York: St. Martin's Press 1996)
From Freedom to Slavery (New York: St. Martin's Press 1993)

Louis Nizer, *My Life in Court* (Cutchague, N.Y.: Buccaneer 1993)

Melvin Belli, *Ready for the Plaintiff* (New York: Popular Library 1956)
My Life on Trial (New York: William Morrow 1976)

Morris Dees with Steve Fiffer, *A Season for Justice* ((New York: Charles Scribner's Sons 1991)

Stanley Rosenblatt, *Trial Lawyer* (Secaucus: Lyle Stuart, Inc. 1984)

John Jenkins, *The Litigators* (New York: Doubleday 1989)

Barry Reed, *The Verdict* (New York: Bantam 1980) (a true story and movie)

Chester Oksner, *Punitive Damages* (New York: Tudor 1988)(Fiction)

PUTTING PRECEDENT IN PERSPECTIVE

Norman Cantor, *Imagining the Law* (New York; HarperCollins 1997)

Jerome Frank, *Courts on Trial: Myth and Reality in American Justice* (Princeton: Princeton University Press 1950)

Michael Walzer, *Spheres of Justice: A Defense of Pluralism and Equality* (New York: Basic Books, Inc. 1983)

Richard A. Posner, *Sex and Reason* (Cambridge: Harvard 1992)

COMMUNICATING CLARITY

Ronald Tobias, *20 MasterPlots* (Cincinnatti: Writer's Digest 1993)

Barry Tarshis, *How To Write Like A Pro* (New York: New American Library 1982)

Cheryl Reimond, *How to Write a Million Dollar Memo* (Des Plaines: Dell Publishing 1988)

Sol Stein, *Stein of Writing* (New York: St. Martin's Press 1992)(on fiction)

Peter Elbow, *Writing with Power* (New York: Oxford University Press 1981)

Bert Decker, *You've Got To Be Believed to Be Heard* (New York: St. Martin's Press 1992)

Karen Berg and Andrew Gilman, *Get to the Point* (New York: Bantam, 1989)

LIVING IN FLOW AND THINKING NEW WAYS

Mihaly Csikszentmihalyi, *Flow*, (New York; HarperCollins 1990)

Creativity (New York; HarperPerennial 1996)

Milton Fischer, *Intuition* (New York: Dutton and Greens Farms, CT: Wildcat Publising Co. 1981) (a lawyer author)

Laurie Nadel, *Sixth Sense* (New York: Avon, 1990)

Alan Lakein, *How to Get Control of Your Time and Your Life* (New York: Signet 1973, but reprinted more recently)

Max Gunther, *The Luck Factor* (New York: Ballantine 1978)

BIBLIOGRAPHY

INTRODUCTION

vi   David Rogers, *Waging Business Warfare, Negotiating* (New York: Zebra 1987 reprint 1995) 94-96

      John McDonald, *Strategy in Poker, Business and War* (1950) (Reissued W.W. Norton 1996)

vii   Daniel Kehrer, *Doing Business Boldly: The Art of Intelligent Risk-Taking* (New York: Random House -Times Books 1989)

CHAPTER 1

9   Phillip Hermann *Better Settlements through Leverage* (New York: Lawyers Coop 1965) 125-36

CHAPTER 3

18   Gerry Spence, *How to Argue and Win Every Time* (New York: St. Martins Press 1995) 67-74

20   Barry Tarshis, *How To Write Like A Pro* 18

23   Lawrence Smith & Loretta Malandro, *Courtroom Communication Skills* (New York: Kluwer 1985) 6-16

25   Gerry Spence, *How to Argue and Win Every Time* (New York: St. Martins Press 1995) 28-31

33   Schlesinger, Arthur, *The Cycles of American History* (Boston: Houghton Mifflin 1986) 1-48

CHAPTER 5

49   Bert Decker, *You've Got to be Believed to Be Heard* (New York: St. Martins Press 1992) 16

      Bart Kosko, *Fuzzy Logic* (New York: Hyperion 1994)

CHAPTER 6

59   Honorable Jerome Frank's *Courts on Trial* 14-26

60   Honorable Jerome Frank's *Courts on Trial* 19, quoting Leonard Moore's 1946 ABA handbook

61   Bart Kosko, *Fuzzy Logic* (New York: Hyperion 1994)

65-67 Phillip Hermann *Better Settlements through Leverage* (New York: Lawyers Coop 1965) 7-27, 110-31

CHAPTER 7

65   Ray Jackendoff, *Patterns in the Mind* (New York: Basic Books, 1994) 165-175

66   Id. 202

CHAPTER 8

80   Max Gunther, *The Luck Factor* (New York: Ballantine 1978) 125-195

CHAPTER 12

107   David Rogers, *Waging Business Warfare, Negotiating* (New York: Zebra 1987 reprint 1995) 74-78

119   Louis Nizer in *My Life in Court* (Cutchague, N.Y.: Buccaneer 1993) 7-14

CHAPTER 13

133   Louis Nizer in *My Life in Court* (Cutchague, N.Y.: Buccaneer 1993) 7-14

146   Robert Heinlein, *Stranger in a Strange Land*.

CHAPTER 14

148   Herb Cohen, *You can negotiate anything* (Secaucus: Lyle Stuart, Inc. 1980) 50, 51-113

149   Gerry Spence, *How to Argue and Win Every Time* (New York: St. Martins Press 1995) 32-33

149   Gerard I. Nierenberg, *The Art of Negotiating* (New York: Barnes & Noble Books, 1968 reprint 1995). See also, *The Complete Negotiator* (New York: Barnes & Noble Reprint 1996)

150   Daniel Kehrer, *Doing Business Boldly: The Art of Intelligent Risk-Taking* (New York: Random House -Times Books 1989) 168-70

152   Pat Zunin, *Contact: The First Four Minutes*, Ballantine Books, 1972

159   Max Gunther, *The Luck Factor* (New York: Ballantine 1978) 182-94

162   Milo Frank, *How to Get your Point Across in 30 Seconds* (New York: Pocket Books 1986)

165   John McDonald in *Strategy in Poker, Business and War*, (1950) (Reprint 1996)

      Phillip Hermann, *Better Settlements through Leverage* (New York: Lawyers Coop 1965) 1-7, 49-50

Charles Craver, *Effective Legal Negotiation and Settlement*, Minnesota CLE June 1996 pp35-40

CHAPTER 17

209   Cheryl Reimond, *How to Write a Million Dollar Memo* (Des Plaines: Dell Publishing 1988)

      Sol Stein, *Stein of Writing* (New York: St. Martin's Press 1992)(on fiction)

210   Louis Nizer in *My Life in Court* (Cutchague, N.Y.: Buccaneer 1993) 7-14

CHAPTER 18

225   Milton Fischer, *Intuition* (New York: Dutton and GreensFarms, CO: Wildcat Publishing Co., Inc 1981)

      Gerard I. Nierenberg, *The Complete Negotiator* (New York: Barnes & Noble Reprint 1996) 250-252

CHAPTER 20

258   Gerry Spence, *In How to Argue and Win Every Time* (New York: St. Martins Press 1996) 47-54, 63-64

INDEX

serving lawsuit to, 205–206
as witness for trial, 253, 261
Clarity, 46–47
Clients. *See also* Screening potential
     clients
   as audience, 21
   controlling expectations of value,
       105–107
   desire for trial, 246–247
   explaining importance of facts to,
       104–105
   giving early homework assignment,
       108
   importance of educating clients
       about values, 125
   initial interview with, 98
   intangible goals of, 158–161,
       235–236
   limiting commitment to, pre-suit,
       104
   personalities of, 21
   preparing for depositions, 216–220
   primary unknowns related to,
       67–68
Cohen, Herb, 150
Communication
   appellate judges, 39–40
   audience-centered communication,
       18–19
   with clients, 21
   with employers, 22–24
   everchanging audience in, 19–20
   with judges, 27–35
   with jury, 36–39
   with opposing counsel, 24–27
Compensatory damages, 27, 123-146,
       158, 177, 235, 247, 261, See also
       damages, 160

Complaint
   adopting point of view of defen-
       dant and, 122
   caption for, 117
   EEOC, 227, 278
   expanding fact base, 120–121
   individual or corporate only, 117
   number of counts, 117
   outlining, 116–119
   polishing, 119–122
   revision of, 123–124
   showing gaps to client, 120
   starting lawsuit and revising, 206
   thinking backwards to polish,
       121–122
   word choices, 123
Computer research, 112–113
Conceptualizers, 38
Conclusions, vs. facts, 58
Confidentiality
   negotiating, 181
   in settlement agreement, 193–194
   four types of, 181
Conlin, Roxanne, 251
Conservatism, 31
Counterbalances, 82, 171, 195, 242
Crap detector, 98
Craver, Charles, 162, 170

Damages
   compensatory, 30, 126-128, 141,
       160, 176, 238, 249, 265
   economic losses, 126–131, 234
   emotional injury, 53, 131–141,
       234–235
   facts of, 100–104
   hard, 126
   humiliation and embarrassment, 70
   intangible pain, 52

momentum, 49–55

punitive, 14, 107, 143–146, 160, 250–251

in relation to liability, 54–55

reputation damage, 141–143

retaliation effects on, 143

soft, 126

using uncertainty of, 52–53

Demand

changing near trial, 247–251

delay delivery, 163–166

deliver in person, 178

finalize written, 176–177

in mediation, 190–192

narrative form for, 165

prepare written demand, 163-166

preparing comparison data, 163–166

re-computing at mid-stream negotiation, 233–239

reducing demand, 180–181

trial value in, 176–177

uncertainty and, 66–67

withdrawal, 248

Demand letter, 11

as initial negotiation overture, 153

Demand value. *See also* Settlement value

advance notice of later increases in, 166

bottom line and, 175

determining market value, 5–7

education of client, 125

excessive, 160

summary of principles, 147

Depositions

getting jump on defendants, 210–211

human factor, 213

maneuvering, 214–215

preparing client, 216–220

prioritize sequence, 212–213

recency of memory, 214

script in planning, 213–214

using fuzzy logic to prepare, 215–216

Depression, cases on, 45, 63, 67, 110-112, 129-133, 220-221, 218-219

Discovery, 209–226

first strike advantage, 210–211

interrogate live witnesses, 212–216

limit early interrogatories to hard data, 211

organizing around elements, 209, 212

plan some discovery for jury, 212

prioritizing your, 210–212

protecting your client, 216–222

using admissions, 220–221

using depositions for surprise factor, 211

using opponent's interrogatories to your advantage, 220

Discrimination claims, 24, 58, 63, 71, 99, 105, 144, 155, 158, 170, 178, 196-199, 200-202, 204, 219-224, 228, 234, 247, 262

filing claims with EEOC, 201

immediate right to sue, 118-119

statistical evidence, 63

waiting on investigation, 201–202

Doty, Hon. David S., 245, 259

Draft complaint

as initial negotiation overture, 153–154

reversing inertia and, 46

specificity of facts in, 156

Drucker, Peter, 71

Duddleston, David, 158

Economic losses, 126–131
  adjusting for mid-stream settle-
    ment, 234
  back pay, 126
  front pay, 127, 144, 172, 230
  growth factors, 129–131
  loss of income, 102
  lost earning capacity, 127–129
  reputation evidence, 130–131
  true career damages, 130–131
EEOC
  filing charges with, 118, 194–195,
    201
  immediate right to sue, 118-119
  help on retaliation, 208
  no probable cause, 202
  subpoena power of, 119
  waiting on investigation, 201–202
Either-or thinking, 62–63
Emotional injury, 53, 131–141
  adjusting for mid-stream
    settlement, 234–235
  causation and symptoms/diagnosis,
    133–135
  diagnosis, 132–133
  exams by adverse psychiatrists,
    221–222
  factors that decrease value,
    140–141
  factors that increase value, 138–139
  gathering facts on, 103–104
  medical records, 131
  obtaining expert evaluation,
    133–134
  pre-existing condition, 135, 139
  questions to ask, 132
  separating from humiliation and

  embarrassment, 136–137
  sources for translating into dollars,
    133–141
  symptom checklist, 131
  thin skull concept, 139
  as unknown, 69
Emotional stamina of lawyers, 77–78
Employers. *See also* CEO
  aggressive jerks, 23
  blind, but educable, 22
  cost-conscious, 22
  image-conscious, 23
  philosophies of, 24
  serving lawsuit to, 205–206
Experiencers, 37

Facts, 57–64
  anticipating worst facts and creat-
    ing context, 162–163
  basic, 100
  blocking tactics for, 162
  compromise, 57–58
  credibility, 60–61
  damages, 100–104
  evidence to hold back, 162
  evidence to share, 161
  explaining importance of, to client,
    104–105
  extracting subtle facts, 101–102
  fuzzy thinking vs. either-or
    thinking, 62–63
  as guesses, 59–60
  hard, 114–115
  identifying initial, 97–99
  identifying key facts, 115–116
  inferences and conclusions, 58
  instability of, 63–64
  liability, 100
  linchpin, 100